Joe Nuxhall
THE OLD LEFTHANDER & ME

My Conversations with Joe Nuxhall
About the Reds, Baseball & Broadcasting

BY JOHN KIESEWETTER

John Kiesewetter

Joe Nuxhall:
The Old Lefthander & Me

ISBN: 978-1-7359194-1-6

For information, contact the author:
John Kiesewetter
Fairfield, Ohio
tvkiese@gmail.com
www.tvkiese.com

Published by:

Chilidog Press LLC
pbronson@chilidogpress.com

Chilidog Press
Loveland, Ohio
www.chilidogpress.com

Cover illustration by Jim Borgman
Cover and interior design by Craig Ramsdell, Ramsdell Design

Contents

Foreword by Marty Brennaman v

1 The Old Lefthander and Me. 1

2 Tell Us About the Old Days 9

3 The Inside Pitch 27

4 My First Win on the Mic! 51

5 A Wild Pitch! Here Comes Foster! 65

6 Little Buddy. 75

7 Marty & Joe. 85

8 Pranks for the Memories 115

9 If You Swing the Bat, You're Dangerous!. 139

10 The Marge and Pete Show 155

11 The Nux Hall of Fame 169

12 Toss Me the Salad. 187

13 Batting Practice 199

14 Should We Keep Nuxhall? 209

15 The Next Nuxhall. 229

16 Star of the Game .239

17 A Very Honorable Legacy. 257

18 Heading for Home. 271

Joe Nuxhall Pitching and Batting Statistics. . . .282

Sources and Credits 285

Acknowledgments .289

About the Author. .291

Foreword by Marty Brennaman

Of all the great things that happened in my career—and I've had a lot of great things— they all pale by comparison to Joe Nuxhall and me sitting together, side by side, for 31 years broadcasting Reds games. We had some great times. My 31 years with Joe equals the longest tenure of any Major League Baseball broadcast team, along with Vin Scully and Jerry Doggett of the Los Angeles Dodgers. That's the thing I'm most proud of, along with being one of five announcers with 40-plus years working with the same ballclub.

I'll never forget the day I met Joe. The Reds announced my hiring in January 1974, and I came to town on Feb. 1. That first day I was up in Dayton, as part of the Reds caravan. Before the event I had to go to a photography studio in Dayton and have publicity pictures taken with Joe. We shook hands, and the first thing I said to him was, "I have your baseball card." I was very familiar with Joe, being a baseball card collector. And that was the beginning of a very special and unique relationship. We genuinely loved each other.

Once we got to spring training in 1974, I was just a little puppy following him around when no one knew me. I questioned whether I was good enough to be there. Everywhere I went in Cincinnati people were saying, "Boy you've got big shoes to fill! To fill Al Michaels' shoes!" And I'm thinking: What the hell did I take this job for?

Joe welcomed me with open arms. I knew he was very close with Al during their three years together before Al left for the San Francisco Giants job. Joe was in a position to make my life difficult, if he wanted to. But Joe, without missing a step, made it clear to everyone that, "Marty is my partner now. He's going to be good, and he's going to be the beneficiary of whatever I can do to help him make the transition to a big league broadcasting job." He was something, I tell you.

Joe, Sparky, Bench, Rose and Perez bent over backwards to make it easy for me. But Joe was the most important of that group because I spent the most time with him. He's the biggest professional influence I've had since I came to Cincinnati. I learned more baseball from being around him. He showed me the ropes. Joe couldn't have been better to me, and I never forgot that. I always felt indebted to him.

The longer we were together the closer we became. We were so close—as I've said a million times—that I could stop a sentence in the middle and he could finish it. I loved him like he was my own blood.

People talk about icons in Cincinnati. They talk about Pete Rose and Oscar Robertson. But Joe Nuxhall was the most iconic sports figure in the history of this town—from any walk of life—who was born and raised here, or spent the majority of their lives here. Nobody can hold a candle to Joe and I'll tell you why: I never heard anyone ever say one negative thing about him. I never saw him be rude to fans. He's one of the most beloved people who ever came from this area. And as long as people have memories of Joe, and what he did, and the impact that he had on the Cincinnati area, he'll always be No. 1 in my book.

Joe was one of the best storytellers of all time. He knew everyone in baseball and had a story about each one of them. In this book, my old friend John Kiesewetter has collected Joe's favorite baseball stories that he told to groups and organizations for years throughout Reds Country. I loved hearing Joe's stories. I know you'll enjoy reading them.

— *Marty Brennaman*
Hall of Fame Cincinnati Reds broadcaster

1

The Old Lefthander and Me

My sons David and Joseph Kiesewetter met Joe Nuxhall as he arrived for his "Rounding Third" book signing at Hamilton's Lane Library in 2004.
JOHN KIESEWETTER PHOTO

My favorite baseball player was lefty Joe Nuxhall when I was a young lefthander growing up in Middletown, Ohio, just up the road from Hamilton. I became a huge Cincinnati Reds fan in 1961, at age 8, when they won the National League pennant—and then got slaughtered in the World Series by Mickey Mantle, Roger Maris, Whitey Ford and the powerful New York Yankees dynasty.

"Hamilton Joe" was called up from San Diego in July 1962 when my National League champion Reds were mired in fourth place, 10 games behind the Dodgers. Nuxhall's debut was impressive against the Mets, relieving Jim Maloney in the fourth inning at Crosley Field on July 22. He pitched 3 shutout innings and hit a two-out, two-run double in the sixth inning to give the Reds a 7-4 lead. As Joe would say often on the radio, *"If you swing the bat, you're dangerous!"*

Only being 9, I thought Nuxhall was some young stud pitcher who percolated up through the Reds farm system like Maloney and Jim O'Toole. My dad set me straight. He told me about Nuxhall's historic debut at age 15 for the Reds in 1944, the youngest player in Major League Baseball. Dad told me how Nuxhall returned to the Reds in 1952—after seven years in the minors—to become a star pitcher. He won 83 games for the club in the 1950s, going 12-5 in 1954 and 17-12 in 1955. He led the National League with five shutouts in 1955 and made the All-Star teams in 1955 and 1956.

1

In 1962, at age 34, Nuxhall pitched like a young phenom. He appeared in 12 games, going 5-0 with one save and a 2.45 earned run average. He also hit .269, with a home run and a double. The next year he was 15-8 with two shutouts and two saves. The Cincinnati Chapter of the Baseball Writers of America presented Nuxhall its "Comeback Of The Year Award" for 1963. I had found my baseball hero. I put his Topps baseball card in a picture frame on my dresser. It's still there.

So began my 45-year devotion to the Old Lefthander until his death in 2007. When he retired to the Reds Radio booth at 38 in 1967, Nuxhall became the soundtrack of my summers. In 43 years on the radio with Al Michaels, Claude Sullivan, Jim McIntyre and mostly with another lefty named Marty Brennaman, my favorite player evolved into the most beloved person in Reds history. As a devoted Reds fan, I continued to listen to broadcasts after Joe died, at 79, and smiled whenever Brennaman would quote the Old Lefthander while calling games with Jeff Brantley, Tommy Thrall, Jim Day, Doug Flynn or Jim Kelch. Marty kept Joe's spirit in the air for 12 years after his death, telling Nuxhall stories through his own final week on the air. Marty's retirement on Sept. 26, 2019, after 46 seasons, was a very sad day. The Marty and Joe era was over, ending Nuxhall's 75-year presence which started in 1944 and spanned half of the team's 150 years when that anniversary was celebrated throughout the 2019 season.

As *The Cincinnati Enquirer*'s TV/radio columnist for 30 years, I was fortunate to interview Nuxhall and Brennaman many times. The paper would send me to Los Angeles twice a year to attend TV show tapings and interview celebrities at the Television Critics Association's summer and winter press tours. But my favorite trips were to the Reds Radio booth at Riverfront Stadium or Great American Ball Park to watch Marty and Joe. I'd always bring along my tape recorder and transcribe our conversations.

For the first time, in this book you'll read Joe's comments on players, managers, owners and on all of the fun he had on and off the air. I was surprised to learn, years after Nuxhall's death, how lucky Reds fans were to have them on radio together for a record-tying 31 years—considering the schemes by Reds executive Dick Wagner to cut short their partnership, and numerous attempts by other clubs to lure Brennaman away from Cincinnati. Stay tuned, as they say.

I interviewed Joe and his wife Donzetta twice in their Fairfield home. Joe gave me a private tour of the framed photos, plaques and memorabilia in the basement which I called the "Nux Hall of Fame" in my *Real Mr. Red* profile on May 16, 1996. But nothing compared to sitting in the radio booth, to witness the magic of Marty and Joe. I loved watching these two best friends playfully ripping on each other. Invariably the exchange ended with Joe's explosive laugh, which filled the booth and the WLW-AM airwaves reaching 38 states. As with his pitching, Joe put his whole body into the hearty howl. Donzetta described it to me this way: "He laughed from his toes up. He laughed so hard, it seemed like it came from his toes. You could hear him all over, laughing."

My wife, Sue, and I built a home in Fairfield, a couple miles from Joe and Donzetta, soon after I was named TV critic at *The Enquirer* in 1985. I would see Nux around town signing autographs at a store opening, attending Fairfield High School basketball games, eating breakfast with his son Kim and pals at Bob Evans, or holding court with his buddies at the Joe Nuxhall Driving Range in Hamilton's Joyce Park. When Santa arrived at the Fairfield Municipal Building to light the city Christmas tree in the 1990s, Nux would be there, too. He'd follow Santa into council chambers, sit down next to him and pass out candy canes to kids. One year when I took my sons to see Santa I teased Nux by asking, "Joe, can I get you a Budweiser?" He frowned and said, "No, I don't think I should be drinking in front of the kids." Nux thought I was serious. He really wanted a beer.

After Nuxhall's full-time radio career ended in 2004, and his health began to fail, I'd arrange my interviews through Kim. He'd say, "Meet us at Bob Evans" on Dixie Highway. Joe would be sitting at the counter on a chair that was marked by a bronze plaque in his honor until the restaurant closed in 2018. We talked about his many charitable projects, his lasting legacy in Butler County. We had a long conversation in 2006, a year before he died, comparing Reds greats he played with (Maloney, Johnny Bench, Frank Robinson, Ted Kluszewski, Pete Rose, Tony Perez,

Gus Bell) with the stars he watched from the booth (Eric Davis, Barry Larkin, Joe Morgan, George Foster, Adam Dunn, Sean Casey).

My neighbor Dave Briede once invited me to hear Nuxhall speak to the Knights of Columbus Council 8115 at Sacred Heart Catholic Church in Fairfield. After Nux provided the obligatory overview of the Reds' prospects for the upcoming season, he told hilarious stories about his playing days, some ending in a meltdown from his infamous temper tantrums. Nuxhall seldom told these stories on the radio, even though Marty calls Joe one of the greatest storytellers of all time. And he didn't tell many of his best stories in his 2004 book, *Joe: Rounding Third and Heading for Home,* with Greg Hoard. Maybe Joe thought what was said in the clubhouse should stay in the clubhouse—or in the banquet room. Anyway, these stories haven't been heard since Nuxy died in 2007. They needed to be preserved, prized and passed on to generations of Reds fans to keep Joe's memory alive. That's why $1 from the sale of every copy of this book benefits the Joe Nuxhall Scholarship Fund, which has awarded more than $900,000 to Butler County high school seniors since 1985.

Over his 64 seasons with the Reds, Nuxhall grew in stature from a popular player into an icon. In my first extended interview with Brennaman in 1986—a year after player-manager Pete Rose shattered Ty Cobb's all-time hit record—Marty said the Old Lefthander was far more revered than Rose.

"Joe is the No. 1 sports institution in this town. Pete Rose is not even in the same league with him. Not even close," Brennaman said three years before Rose was banned from baseball.

Unlike Brennaman, Nuxhall was never honored with the National Baseball Hall of Fame Ford C. Frick Award for broadcasters, despite repeated fan efforts before and after his death. Nuxhall's achievement as the youngest big league pitcher at age 15, however, was on display at the Baseball Hall of Fame—along with sportswriter Tom Swope's scorecard from Nuxhall's debut June 10, 1944—when I took my sons to Cooperstown for Barry Larkin's induction in 2012. By my count, Nuxhall played with or against 75 Hall of Famers active in the game during his 16 Major League seasons, from Mickey Mantle, Whitey Ford, Ted Williams and

Jackie Robinson to Sandy Koufax, Nolan Ryan, Stan Musial, Jim Bunning, Ernie Banks, Steve Carlton, Brooks Robinson, Frank Robinson, Johnny Bench and Tony Perez. The total jumps to more than 100 when you count games he broadcast involving Hall of Famers, and keeps growing with each induction class.

Nuxhall's association spanned nine decades of Reds' ownership, from industrialist/WLW owner Powel Crosley Jr., who bought the club in 1934, to Bob Castellini, owner since 2006. A few months before Nuxhall died, Castellini called Joe "the heart of the Cincinnati Reds franchise." When he wasn't at the ballpark, Nuxhall was speaking to numerous groups and organizations throughout Reds Country in his unique Old Lefthander's lexicon, littered with phrases like "without a doubt," "I'd guess you say," and "in all honesty." He was the Reds' Casey Stengel or Yogi Berra, a storyteller who spoke his own language, no question about it. Until his 60th birthday, Nuxhall threw batting practice, showered and ate in the clubhouse before going up to the radio booth. Players considered him a mentor, unofficial coach and teammate. Bench said Nuxy was "one of the guys. He was everybody's grandfather. He was Santa Claus. He was all those things rolled into one."

I think of Nuxhall as the Reds' Forrest Gump. Like the Tom Hanks movie character, the Old Lefthander was witness to a lot of history. His manager in 1944 was Bill McKechnie, the skipper of the Reds' 1939-40 World Series teams. Young Joe's teammates included 1939 MVP Bucky Walters and 1940 MVP Frank McCormick. Nuxhall broadcast all the regular season games for the Big Red Machine's 1970, 1972, 1975 and 1976 National League championships, and every game of the 1990 wire-to-wire season through the World Series sweep of the Oakland A's. When the team established the Reds Hall of Fame with inaugural members McCormick, Walters, Ernie Lombardi, Johnny Vander Meer, Paul Derringer and Ival Goodman on July 18, 1958, Nuxhall was in the dugout resting his arm after beating the Cubs the previous afternoon. He was there when the Reds Hall of Fame inducted 1869 team founders Harry and George Wright, and 1919 World Series centerfielder Edd Roush. Nux shared the Crosley Field clubhouse as a player with 30 of the 89 Reds Hall of Fame members, and broadcast games involving 41 Reds Hall of Famers.

When rookie Pete Rose hit his first Major League home run in 1963, Nuxhall was the winning pitcher. When Pete broke Ty Cobb's record at Riverfront Stadium in 1985, Joe was next to Marty in the Reds Radio booth. Nux also was at the mic when Pete Rose Jr. debuted in 1997.

Nuxhall broadcast every game of Barry Larkin's 19-year Hall of Fame career (1986-2004). When Larkin worked out for the Reds at Riverfront after graduating from Moeller High School in 1982, Nux was throwing batting practice. "Let this kid really get a feeling for the big leagues, and let him smack a few," said Nuxhall, recalling his first impression of Larkin years later.

When Tom Browning pitched his perfect game in 1988, and Tom Seaver threw his only no-hitter in 1978, Nux was on the mic. When Maloney threw 10 no-hit innings against the Mets in 1965, Nux was on the bench. When former Red Ken Johnson no-hit the Reds in 1964, Nux was on the mound in Houston's old Colt Stadium. More about that later, too.

When Eric Davis hit for the cycle against the San Diego Padres at Riverfront on June 2, 1989, Nuxhall called his single in the third, three-run homer in the fourth, and triple in the seventh. Thirty years earlier, Nuxhall was watching from the Crosley Field dugout in 1959 when Frank Robinson hit for the cycle with a single and triple off Dodgers starter Johnny Klippstein, a homer off Koufax and double off Carl Erskine.

Of course, Nux didn't see everything. He was in grade school when Vander Meer threw back-to-back no-hitters in 1938. He was pitching in the minors for the Charleston (West Virginia) Senators in 1949 when Walker Cooper drove in a Reds-record 10 runs against the Cubs. But Nux saw catcher Smoky Burgess almost tie the record. Burgess drove in nine runs against the Pirates in a Reds' 16-5 win on July 29, 1955, with three home runs and a single. You can bet Nux was screaming *"Get outta here! Get outta here!"* for each homer, since he was pitching that night at Crosley, going for his tenth win.

One night after broadcasting a road game, a bored Nuxhall pulled out his media guide and checked off names of guys he had played with or "was in contact with." He stopped at 1,000.

The Old Lefthander and me talked about a lot of Reds. No way did we talk about a thousand guys Nux knew. So I'm also telling some of my favorite Reds stories from over the years, and my encounters with Brennaman, Bench, Browning, Rose, Jim O'Toole, George Foster, Ron Oester, Ed Bailey and Marge Schott; entertainers George Clooney and Jonathan Winters; and former Reds broadcasters Al Michaels and Red Barber.

This is not intended to be a comprehensive history of the Reds. Most Reds fans in Cincinnati know all about Pete, Johnny, Barry, Sweet Lou, the Big Dog, Little Joe, the Big Red Machine and the wire-to-wire Reds. This is a collection of Joe Nuxhall's best baseball stories, and a few of my own.

Enjoy.

Tell Us About the Old Days

JOE NUXHALL VS. STAN MUSIAL
June 10, 1944

Nationally renowned C.F. Payne illustrated 15-year-old Joe Nuxhall pitching to Stan Musial at Crosley Field on June 10, 1944. KIM NUXHALL COLLECTION

Everyone knows Joe Nuxhall was the youngest player in Major League Baseball history. He pitched for the Reds at age 15 in 1944, when World War II depleted rosters. It wasn't pretty. He was torched by the first-place Cardinals at Crosley Field during an embarrassing 18-0 loss.

The young lefthander from Hamilton's Wilson Junior High gave up five runs on five walks, two hits and a wild pitch on Saturday, June 10, 1944, four days after the World War II D-Day invasion. Nuxhall started the ninth inning with a ground out, a walk and pop up to the shortstop. Then he realized where he was. A wild pitch and another walk, and he was facing future Hall of Famer Stan Musial, who was hitting .365. The 1943 National League MVP and batting champ hit a rocket to right. The wheels fell off. The next four batters reached on three walks and a hit.

9

Nuxhall didn't get his third out in Major League Baseball for eight years. He pitched seven seasons in the minors before rejoining the Reds in 1952, at 23, and becoming one of the club's most popular pitchers until he retired to the radio booth in 1967, at 38.

Everyone knows, right?

No. Not the Reds executive vice president who was second in command of the club for the 1990 World Championship season. His name? Stephen Schott, cousin to owner Marge Schott's late husband. The Cincinnati native was a senior vice president at Shearson Lehman Hutton/American Express on Wall Street before Marge hired him in 1988. At a Reds Caravan stop in Lexington, Steve tried to make small talk with Joe and Gordy Coleman, the Reds speakers bureau director and Nux's 1960's teammate, as they took a smoke break outside Shriners Hospital for Children.

"We're standing under this canopy, with a light rain falling, and Steve says, 'Gordy, you were a first baseman, weren't you?' And Gordy said, 'Yeah.' And Steve said, 'How long did you play?' And Gordy said, 'Nine years.' And then Steve asked me, 'Joe, what position did you play?'"

What position did you play???

Years later, when Nux recalled the story again, he was still fuming over it. "I said to myself, 'You've got to be kidding me! *What position did you play???*'" Marty Brennaman, who witnessed the conversation, still marveled years later at Steve's ignorance. "I'm standing there thinking: Man, you've got to be kidding me! He had no idea! No eye-de-a!"

⚾   ⚾   ⚾

Teen-aged Joe Nuxhall fell on his face when he made his Reds debut in 1944. And that was before taking the mound in the ninth. Nux tripped on the dugout steps after manager Bill McKechnie told him to warm up. I never tired of hearing Nuxhall talk about his disastrous debut. The Reds took a chance with Hamilton Joe while pitchers Johnny Vander Meer, Ewell Blackwell and Joe Beggs were fighting World War II. Over the years, I heard the story in various bits and pieces about how he gave up five runs for a 67.50 earned run average. My favorite account is from

WCET-TV's *Joe Nuxhall: My Life, Baseball and Beyond* series with sportscaster Dennis Janson in 2005:

"As I described it many times, I would go down to the ballpark on weekends. This particular weekend, we were playing the Cardinals. And as you recall, the St. Louis Cardinals and the St. Louis Browns wound up in the World Series that year, in 1944. So I'm sitting on the bench and watching the game, and I'm admiring the way the Cardinals are hitting the baseball, line drives everywhere. And this was really a treat to be sitting that close to all the action.

"It was the ninth inning, and all of the sudden I hear this voice say, 'Joe!' And I said, 'He can't be talking to me.' We had a couple of Joes on the ball club. And he (McKechnie) says 'Joe!' a little louder. And I looked, and he said, 'Go warm up!' ...

"There are three steps out of the dugout at Crosley Field, and now I'm nervous—but not near as bad as I'm going to be—and I made the first two steps and tripped over the third one. And it was a dusty day, and I landed flat on my face, as flat as you could. I got up and I'm dusty all over, and I'm cleaning myself off ... Anyway, I go down and warm up ... and I'm wilder than a March hare, as they say. About every other pitch, I missed the catcher ...

"Now I'm in the ballgame. And I'm nervous. Like I've said, probably two weeks prior to that I'm pitching to 12-, 13-, 14-year-old kids at Wilson Junior High School, and now here are the St. Louis Cardinals, who will be world champions. So the first batter up, I went 3 and 2 on him, and he grounded to short. The second batter, I'm 0-2 and I ended up walking him. The next batter, I'm 3 and 2, and he ends up popping up to shortstop.

"Now I've got two outs and a man on first. And the fourth batter, I'm 0 and 2 on him, and then I realize exactly where in the world I am. This is the St. Louis Cardinals and Crosley Field, and from that point on I walk him, and then Stan (Musial) comes up, and I'll never forget it—let me see, it was 13 to nothing—and I'm throwing balls all over the place, and this is the ninth inning. So Musial—you know that (closed) stance he has—and you'd think he'd be worried about this kid.

'He might drill me! I'm going to get back out of the batter's box and get out of harm's way,' you might say. But the first pitch I threw, he hit a screaming meanie, as we used to say, to right field, an absolute bullet. And from that point I walked three more, gave up one more hit, and a wild pitch, and that was it …

"That was a Saturday. On Sunday, Mr. Giles, he was the boss man (general manager) then, he said, 'We're going to send you to Birmingham, Alabama.' And on Monday night I was on a train to Birmingham, Alabama. At that time, the Birmingham Barons were the Reds Double-A farm team in the Southern Association. And a new phase started, I guess you could say. I was going to be away (from home) for the summertime basically, and that part was tough to grasp …

"Now the day came for the game against the Little Rock Travelers, and there's a pretty good crowd at the stadium. I start the ballgame, and I think I walked the first guy. The next guy I struck out, I believe. But anyway, it was the same result, basically. I gave up five more runs (actually six), walked five more, threw a wild pitch, and gave up one base hit, and I got my first strikeout as a professional ballplayer. That was in two-thirds of an inning. After that I didn't pitch anymore."

In his first pro year, before he was even 16, Joe gave up 11 earned runs on three hits, 10 walks and two wild pitches in 1-1/3 innings. "I got homesick. I told a falsehood I'm still not proud of, but I was homesick and I wanted to go home. I told (the manager) my mother was ill and I needed to go home. I came home in the middle of August. There were two more weeks left in the season. So that's the story of my first year."

Many of my favorite memories of Nuxhall are from watching him speak to groups, service clubs or the Knights of Columbus at my Sacred Heart Church in Fairfield. It was Joe Unplugged, away from the Reds Radio microphone, telling stories about teammates Ted Kluszewski, Jim Maloney, Billy Martin and baseball greats from Rogers Hornsby to Gaylord Perry. Somebody would say, "Joe, tell us about the old days!" And he'd tell stories without any notes for more than an hour. He'd talk until the host would call for one last question. Or to say they had run out of beer. K of C members tell me that it wasn't unusual for Nuxy to stay past midnight playing cards with the guys.

Nuxhall loved to tell about falling on his butt trying to field bunts on wet Wrigley Field grass. He fell twice, when two consecutive batters bunted. (Nux always said "three straight bunts," but Lou Smith's *Cincinnati Enquirer* story and the box score from Monday, May 28, 1956, revealed only two bunted in the fifth.) Nuxhall had swung the bat dangerously in the third. His sacrifice fly scored shortstop Roy McMillan for a 1-0 lead over the last-place Cubs. In the first four innings, Nuxhall struck out seven and gave up only three hits "under threatening skies," Smith wrote. And then, as the *Enquirer* headline writer put it, "Nuxhall Pops Cork!"

Joe opened the fifth by walking pitcher Bob Rush. Then Eddie Miksis laid down a sacrifice bunt in front of the plate. Nuxhall rushed to the ball, but had trouble with his footing because the spikes on his cleats were shorter than most. (Nuxhall would file down his spikes whenever he got a new pair. If his cleats were normal length, they "would hit the ground and throw me out of kilter" during his delivery and follow-through.) When he tried to field Miksis's bunt, his cleats couldn't get a grip, and Nux was charged with an error. Cubs manager Stan Hack ordered the next batter, Gene Baker to bunt, too.

"The first guy bunts, and I slip and fall down. The next guy up bunts, and I slip and fall down again. I couldn't make a throw," Nuxhall said. "The grass was wet from the rain. And all of the bunts were to the right side of the mound. They were perfect. I braced to throw, and my right leg gave out. Had I stayed on my feet, I throw the guys out. But I go down—Bam! Bam! Bam! Three straight times!—and the bases are loaded. You put all three of them (bunts) together, they wouldn't reach third base."

Smith wrote that as Nuxhall "fielded his position like an old burlesque comedian … his blood pressure moved into the danger zone." After striking out Dee Fondy, Ernie Banks doubled in Rush and Miksis. Walt Moryn singled in Baker. Out came manager Birdie Tebbetts to bring in reliever Art Fowler.

"Oh, I was so mad! That's when I tore up my glove," Nuxhall said. Smith described it this way for *Enquirer* readers: "He drop-kicked a Reds' helmet into the dugout, scattered the bats, and fired his glove into the stands before taking off for the clubhouse to cool off under a shower."

Smith and the 1,202 in Wrigley couldn't see that his tantrum continued in the clubhouse. "I kicked the helmet box—It was right after we started wearing batting helmets—and I got my foot stuck through it. I had this great big, long box stuck to my foot, and I couldn't get it off. I was walking around with this big box on my foot! The clubhouse guys finally got it off of me. That was one of my more embarrassing moments. I tore up my glove, stuck my foot through the hat box, it was crazy. And that didn't help a damn thing."

Nuxhall popped his cork often in the 1950s. One day Mount Nuxhall erupted inside the Crosley Field clubhouse. He was fuming "big time," to use one of his favorite phrases. He ripped off his jersey and flung it. The next day nobody could find his uniform shirt. Several years later, the mystery was solved when an air-conditioning repairman inspected the overhead air ducts.

"I'll be damned, there's my jersey. When I threw it, that's where it landed," he said.

ⓧ   ⓧ   ⓧ

Nuxhall's favorite first baseman was Big Klu, the sleeveless slugger who led the National League in 1954 with 49 home runs, and was third in the NL with a 1.049 OPS (on-base plus slugging). Ted Kluszewski, a four-time All-Star, held the team's home run record (251) when he retired in 1961 with a .298 lifetime batting average. Then he fine-tuned the Big Red Machine, as Sparky Anderson's hitting coach in the 1970s.

Big Klu, at six-foot-two and 225 pounds, cut off the sleeves so his bulging biceps could swing the bat easier—and to intimidate pitchers. At speaking engagements, Nuxhall recalled the time Klu walked over to the mound when Joe was on the verge of walking in a run.

"I was mad. I had walked the bases loaded, and I was 2-0 on the batter, if I'm not mistaken," Nuxhall said. "Klu came in and said something like,

'Come on! Let's get them out!' And I snapped at him: 'Go back and play first base, and I'll do the pitching!'

"And he said, 'Yeah? When are you going to start?'"

(2) (2) (2)

Nuxhall's worst moment on the mound came in 1960, as he was struggling through a 1-8 season. He was pitching middle relief in Wrigley Field on July 25, with the Cubs leading 5-4. Future Hall of Famer Ron Santo flied out to right, Jerry Kindall singled to center, and Ed Bouchee struck out. Then speedy centerfielder George Altman hit a roller to first. Nuxhall sprinted to cover the bag. Umpire Ed Vargo called Altman safe in what the *Enquirer* called a "photo-finish play." Nuxhall exploded.

"I took off after Vargo, and got suspended for five days," Nuxhall said.

The *Enquirer* said Nuxhall shoved Vargo "a good six feet." When Vargo threw Nuxhall out of the game, Joe charged him again. Teammates Coleman and Billy Martin tackled Joe before he could make contact with the umpire a second time. Nuxhall later explained that Vargo didn't signal out or safe right away. The next day, NL President Warren Giles suspended Nuxhall for five games and fined him $250 after calling Joe at his Fairfield home. Son Kim, then 4, answered the phone.

Kim recalled, "The phone rings, and I hear, 'Hello, this is Mr. Giles from the National League office. Is your father there?' The phone was in the kitchen, and there are steps right outside the kitchen to go downstairs, so I sat on the steps and listened. Dad had to tell Mr. Giles what he said to the umpire, in words I can't even repeat today. It was bad."

(2) (2) (2)

Stories about Joe's temper always got big laughs. But they came with a price. Nuxhall told me his temper cost him lots of wins and the opportunity to pitch for the Reds in the 1961 World Series.

"People kept telling me, if I would have done what they said (about taming his temper), I might have won 200 games," said Nuxhall, who retired with a 135-117 record in spring 1967.

After his horrible 1-8 season in 1960, the Reds traded Joe to the Kansas

City Athletics at age 32 for right-handed pitchers John Tsitouris and John Briggs. "When I left, the fans were really on me, which I really deserved, because I was terrible," he said.

Nuxy was 5-8, mostly as a reliever, in Kansas City in 1961, while the Reds won the National League pennant for the first time since 1940. When the Reds were playing in St. Louis on September 5, Nuxhall drove from Kansas City on his off day to see his first-place buddies at Hotel Chase after Bob Purkey threw a six-hitter to win, 5-2, over future Hall of Famer Bob Gibson. Reds pitcher Jim Brosnan wrote in his *Pennant Race* book about the Reds' 1961 season that the Old Lefthander had wanted a change of scenery after losing his spot in the rotation during his 9-9 season in 1959, and his 1960 nightmare.

"Nuxhall had spent two years in the Cincinnati bullpen moaning about how nice it would be somewhere else, 'suckin' up a couple of Hudies,' a beer brewed in Cincinnati," wrote Brosnan, referring to Hudepohl 14K Beer, the Reds TV sponsor.

The 1961 season ended with the Reds playing the Yankees in the 1961 World Series. After splitting two games in New York, the series came to Crosley Field October 7. So did Nuxhall. He had flown from Kansas City to Hot Springs, Arkansas, and then to Memphis, where he sat in the airport until 4 a.m. to catch a flight to Indianapolis. He finally arrived in Cincinnati at noon.

"I went straight to the ballpark, I'll never forget it. I hadn't shaved. I started to go into the clubhouse, and they ran my butt out of there! They said, 'Uh-uh! You've got to have the proper credentials.'" So he watched his pals play in the World Series, sitting with 32,588 other fans packed into Crosley Field. The Yankees swept the Reds in Cincinnati to win the series four games to one.

⚾   ⚾   ⚾

The youngest player to play in the Major Leagues at age 15 also holds another record: Joe Nuxhall was the only person to win a Major League no-hitter he didn't pitch.

Nuxhall was on the mound in Houston on April 23, 1964, when Ken

Johnson became the first pitcher ever to lose a no-hitter. Two errors in the ninth doomed Johnson, including one of his own. I was listening to Waite Hoyt broadcast the game on radio with my Dad in our basement as Johnson breezed through the Cincinnati lineup, giving up only two walks, pitching for the old Colt .45s in Colt Stadium. (When the Astrodome opened in 1965, the 1962 expansion club was renamed the Astros.)

With one out in the ninth, Pete Rose bunted in front of the plate. Johnson threw wild to first, with Rose taking second. Chico Ruiz grounded out, with Charlie Hustle going to third. Then Vada Pinson grounded routinely to future Hall of Fame second baseman Nellie Fox, who made his second error of the night. Rose scored. Frank Robinson flied out to end the inning. One run, no hits, two errors, and one for the record books.

Nuxhall, 35, struck out two batters in the ninth to seal the 1-0 victory. It was his first win of the season, a complete game five-hitter. After the game, Fox tried to apologize to Johnson, according to the *Houston Chronicle*. But Johnson said: "It's my fault. I put the runner on, or we'd have been out of the inning. I knew Rose was fast, and I was going to have to throw quick, and I had three fingers wrapped around the ball, but no time to change the grip. A halfway decent throw and I had him."

Talking about the game more than 20 years later, Nuxhall disagreed with Johnson, who had pitched for the 1961 Reds before being drafted by the Houston expansion team. "I will always say it was a one-hitter. Pete put down a perfect bunt. Hell, he was nearly on first base when the throw went wild. It was the ninth inning, so they gave him an error. That makes sense, I guess."

Johnson grinned when he told writers: "I guess that will put me in baseball history. What a way to get into the (record) book."

Johnson probably wasn't smiling after the clubhouse attendant failed to get the ball from the final out. Nice guy Nux wouldn't surrender the souvenir. When Johnson sent a clubhouse guy to the Reds locker room, "I reached in the ball bag and looked around for one that looked like a 'gamer,' and I said, 'Here, take this one to him.' I've got the original at home," he told me in 1986.

Why not? That ball got Nuxhall into the record book.

Joe Nuxhall argues a pitch called by home plate umpire Mel Steiner (black coat) as manager Fred Hutchinson watches minutes before Nuxy was ejected in the Reds 6-2 win over the Phillies at Crosley Field on July 20, 1964.
RHODES/KLUMPE REDS HALL OF FAME COLLECTION

⚾   ⚾   ⚾

On a trip to Houston the next year, Nuxhall almost made history again. He came within four outs of throwing a no-hitter in the new Astrodome, which would have been Major League Baseball's first indoor no-hitter. The game on Saturday, July 24, 1965, was just the 50th played in the 'Dome, the Astros home through 1999.

In the top of the eighth, Rose broke a scoreless tie with a two-run triple. Nux took the mound in the eighth having faced only two batters more than the minimum. (He hit Jimmy Wynn in the first and walked rookie Joe Morgan in the sixth.) With one out, .216 hitting shortstop Bob Lillis lined a single up the middle. Nuxhall finished the one-hitter with 11 strikeouts and two walks to raise his record to 7-3.

"I'll never forget it, I can see the pitch right today," Nuxhall said more than two decades later. "Bob Lillis singled right over my head to center field. That was the only hit. If I would have been able to throw the no-hitter, that, of course, would have been the first one of my career—and it would have been the first one ever indoors—which would have been kind of a nice thing to have."

①   ①   ①

Toss out a name, and Joe Nuxhall told a story.

Why did the Reds trade Curt Flood, the seven-time Gold Glove outfielder winner, when he was just 18? Flood, who hit .293 over 12 seasons for the Cardinals, was traded after the 1957 season with outfielder Joe Taylor for pitchers Willard Schmidt, Ted Wieand and Marty Kutyna. Flood helped the Cardinals win three pennants (1964, '67, '68) before sitting out the 1970 season to protest baseball's controlling "reserve clause," paving the way for free agency.

Flood's potential was no secret. He hit .340 with 29 homers and 24 doubles as an 18-year-old for High Point-Thomasville in the Carolina League in 1956. Midway through that year, Reds manager Birdie Tebbetts bragged to *Sports Illustrated* about young Curtis Flood. "Three years! Three years at the outside, and then you'll see a real major leaguer," Tebbetts said in the July 16 story.

It took only two years for Flood to play regularly in St. Louis in 1958. He hit .322 in 1961, and won his first of six straight Gold Gloves in 1963. So why did the Reds trade him? Because the outfield was filled with Frank Robinson, Wally Post and Gus Bell, with 19-year old Pinson expected to be called up in 1958. Did the Reds have any clue Flood could be a superstar?

"I don't think anyone felt he would do the things he did. He had really good abilities, really good tools," Nuxhall said.

Someone once asked about former teammate Billy Martin, the combative second baseman who managed the Yankees, Oakland A's, Rangers, Tigers and Twins over 16 seasons. Martin played 103 games with Nuxhall on the 1960 Reds, a year before he retired as a player. He was in five World Series as a Yankee in the 1950s, then kicked around with Kansas City, Detroit and Cleveland before coming to Cincinnati. He's best known as the hard-drinking manager hired five times by Yankees owner George

Steinbrenner in the 1970s and '80s. His Yankees were swept by the Reds in the 1976 World Series, then won it all in 1977.

Nuxhall called Martin "a feisty little squirt" who liked to argue baseball strategy in bars after games. "He didn't have the greatest talents baseball-wise, but he used what he had," Nuxhall said.

On road trips to San Francisco in 1960, Martin invited Nuxhall and other teammates to his mother's house in nearby Berkeley for spaghetti dinners. Nux loved to tell how Martin's mom couldn't remember his name. She would ask Billy, "How's that Joe Nutsoff?"

Yeah, ol' Nutsy.

⚾   ⚾   ⚾

When I became *Cincinnati Enquirer* TV/radio columnist in October 1985, I was determined to cover sports broadcasters too. I loved sports, especially baseball. Reds games described by Hoyt, Nuxhall and Brennaman were the soundtrack of my summers. And this lefthander from Middletown was determined to meet Hamilton's famous lefty. When the TV season ended in May 1986, I persuaded Sunday magazine editor Bill Thompson (the *Enquirer* produced its own Sunday magazine back then) to do a Nuxhall cover profile called "The Old Lefthander," published July 13, 1986.

It was a flattering piece, although I mentioned that Nuxy had better command of a slider than the English language. I noted examples of his convoluted lexicon—"When you talk about (fill-in-the-blank), and that's certainly was one of them"—and penchant for saying "without a doubt," "certainly," "honestly," "basically" and "you know."

"Like I tell people, I'm no English major," he told me. "All I want you to do is understand it. It might sound a little different, but as long as you understand it, then that's what I'm concerned about."

Got that? I still can't believe I got this line into my Sunday magazine story:

"Joe Nuxhall interviewed Tony Perez on the *Star of the Game* show. Neither spoke English."

⚾ ⚾ ⚾

As a young kid, I would anxiously await getting a Reds yearbook maga-zine each year. I'd read all the players' profiles and the team statistics and study pictures from the previous season. Years later, when I pulled out old yearbooks I was amazed at the personal information printed in the players' bios. In addition to their height, weight and hair color, it listed hobbies, wedding anniversary, ancestry, children's names and winter street addresses. The 1953 Reds yearbook said Nuxhall lived at 630 Fairview Ave., Hamilton. Three years and a second baby boy later, the 1956 yearbook listed Nuxhall at 3935 Arlington Ave., Hamilton. It was a different time.

One of my favorite pictures showed players in uniform walking through the stands on Fan Appreciation Night. "Before the game—I can't tell you for how many years—every player went to a section in Crosley Field, along with the manager and the coaches too, and you shook hands with the fans. When they blew a whistle, whoever you were shaking hands with, you took them down to the field and they were presented some kind of gift or something," he said.

Can you imagine the mob scene if the Reds did that when Brandon Phillips, Barry Larkin, Ken Griffey Jr., Eric Davis, Aroldis Chapman or Jay Bruce played?

In the 1960s, Reds players also took part in a skills competition on Norge-Zenith Nights, sponsored by the kitchen appliance and TV manu-facturer. Outfielders threw to home plate. Catchers threw to second. Pitchers tried to throw balls from the mound into the opening of a TV set frame. Whoever threw the most into the TV won a television.

Nux was allowed to participate in 1967, his first year as a broadcaster and Reds batting practice pitcher. In fact, he pitched to the TV twice. Maloney was scheduled to start against the Giants on Thursday August 31, 1967, so the Reds ace asked Joe to do the TV toss for him.

"I throw for myself, and I get three out of five into the TV set. So then I throw for Maloney, and I put four of the five in there—and he wins the damn TV set!"

⚾   ⚾   ⚾

Ask Nuxhall about Hall of Famer Rogers Hornsby, and he didn't talk about how Hornsby was one of the greatest hitters in baseball history, with a .358 lifetime average second to Ty Cobb (.366). He wouldn't tell you that "The Rajah" won seven batting titles, two MVP awards and a World Series ring in 23 years for the Cardinals, Giants, Braves, Cubs and old St. Louis Browns.

To Nuxy, Hornsby was a mean old man who finished his managerial career in 1952-53 with a 91-106 record for the Reds. He's one of many names on my list of Reds who "Washed Up On The Banks Of The Ohio," ending their careers in decline in Cincinnati. Nuxhall didn't say anything nice about Hornsby, even though Hornsby was badgered by *Cincinnati Post* baseball writer Earl Lawson into trying Nuxhall as a starter in 1952. Players disliked Hornsby for a lot of reasons. One was his habit of urinating in the clubhouse shower, said Reds historian Greg Rhodes.

"It was just the way he treated people. Hornsby expected everyone to be a .340 hitter," Nuxhall said. Nux particularly didn't like the way he handled pitchers. Hornsby refused to go to the mound when he brought in a reliever in the middle of an inning.

"Hornsby would just stand there at the top of the dugout step and yell, 'Hey you!' And then he'd point to the bullpen. And you'd stand out there on the mound like an idiot with the ball until someone came out of the bullpen. Oh, the jolly Rajah," Nuxhall said sarcastically.

Back then, players took infield and outfield practice before every game. Hornsby loved to hit the fungoes, tossing the ball in the air and swatting it to the outfielders. "He gets done one day, and he throws the fungo bat toward the dugout. But he throws it too hard, and it hits (star outfielder) Jim Greengrass, who was standing in the dugout with one foot up on the steps. It hit him in the shin. Greengrass takes the bat, and breaks it all to hell. He just obliterates it. And then he threw it back to Hornsby and said, 'Here, you old bastard. Throw it again!'"

⚾   ⚾   ⚾

Never check a good story. My friend Mike Precker had a Columbia University journalism professor who jokingly told students never to check a good story because sometimes facts don't support the tale.

Which brings me to Bob Gorbous. I think. Or Bob Borkowski. Maybe it's Glen Gourbous. Or Bob Marquis. I don't know, in all honesty. One of the problems with talking to Nuxy late in life was that he tended to tell stories in shorthand, since he had repeated them so often. Sometimes he'd mix up names and years. According to Nuxhall, Bob Gorbous was a center fielder when Hornsby managed the Reds. But nobody named Bob Gorbous ever played Major League Baseball. However, in 1955, Glen Gorbous played for the Reds under Tebbetts. He played five games in left field in April before being part of the trade to get Smoky Burgess from Philadelphia.

Hornsby used two Reds named "Bob" in centerfield. Bob Borkowski played 67 games in center, but more often was a corner outfielder. Bob Marquis, mostly a pinch-hitter, played eight games in center in 1953 before being sold in July to Portland in the Pacific Coast League. These are the facts, which I won't let stand in the way of a good story by Joe:

> "Bob Gorbous, he was there when Hornsby was there. I tell the story all the time. He was adequate for an outfielder, you know, but for a center fielder he wasn't good. I remember when he ran up the terrace at Crosley Field for a high fly ball, and he ran too far back. He had to come back down the terrace, and he fell down. Face first! And the ball drops.
>
> "I can always remember Hornsby getting on him. Hornsby said, 'You practice all the time going up and down the terrace, what the hell happened?' And Gorbous said, 'You taught me how to go up it. You didn't teach me how to go down it!' I'll never forget that as long as I live."

Never check a good story, I'd guess you'd say. That's for dang sure.

⚾   ⚾   ⚾

Of all of Joe's stories, I heard this one the most. Nuxhall told it at every speaking appearance I attended. It was his favorite story, and mine, too.

Yet he didn't tell this one in his own book. It's a classic, about a pitching duel at Candlestick Park in 1966, his last season as a player. Maloney (16-8) was pitching against Gaylord Perry for the Giants.

Maloney was one of the hardest-throwers in Reds history. They didn't have radar guns then, but Nux estimated that Maloney's fastball was 95 mph. Maloney threw two no-hitters for the Reds and set the club season strikeout record (later broken by Mario Soto). Perry, the future Hall of Famer known for illegally doctoring the ball, was in fine form that day, tossing spitballs or greaseballs that broke 12 inches. Reds batters and manager Dave Bristol were getting frustrated. Bristol knew Maloney could throw a spitter, and urged him to retaliate with it.

"Jim didn't throw it regularly, because he didn't really think he could control it. And he threw so damn hard, you never knew where it was going, basically. It could take off and hit someone in the coconut," Nuxhall said.

Maloney kept putting Bristol off. Finally, Maloney told him: "If Gaylord throws one to me, I'll start throwing mine." The next time up, Perry struck out Maloney with a spitter.

"The war was on. And all hell breaks loose as Maloney starts throwing his. Herman Franks is the Giants manager, and he's yelling from the dugout, *'He's throwing a spitter! What was that!?!? What was that!?!?'* Every time Maloney threw one, Franks screamed from the dugout at the home plate umpire: *"What was that!?!? What was that!?!?"*

Late in the game, Maloney threw a spitter to Willie Mays that dropped off the table. Willie nearly came out of his shoes in the batter's box. Franks exploded again: *"What was that!?!? What was that!?!?"*

The ump took off his mask, turned to the Giants dugout and said: "I don't know what it was—but it's the best one I've ever seen!"

Nuxhall's Debut on June 10, 1944

With St. Louis leading 13-0 in the top of the ninth at Crosley Field, Joe Nuxhall came in to face the Cardinals' eighth, ninth and first batters.

George Fallon grounds out, shortstop to first.

Mort Cooper walks.

Augie Bergamo flies out to shortstop.

Wild pitch, Cooper to second base.

Debs Garms walks.

Stan Musial singles to right to load the bases.

Ray Sanders walks, Cooper scores.

Walker Cooper walks, Garms scores.

Danny Litwhiler walks, Musial scores.

Emil Verban singles to left, Litwhiler scores.

Nuxhall replaced by Jake Eisenhart.

George Gallon walks to load bases.

Mort Cooper pop foul to first base.

Nuxhall faced nine batters in 2/3 of an inning, giving up five runs on two hits, five walks and a wild pitch. The Reds lost 18-0.

Joe Nuxhall: The Old Lefthander & Me · John Kiesewetter

3

The Inside Pitch

***The Cincinnati Post's Jack Klumpe photographed Joe during 1958
spring training in Tampa.*** RHODES/KLUMPE REDS HALL OF FAME COLLECTION

Joe Nuxhall told hilarious stories about his playing days and his explosive
temper, sometimes making fans forget his accomplishments in a Reds
uniform. He was no joke as a player. The Old Lefthander was a very
good pitcher—without a doubt, in all honesty, to use a couple of his
favorite phrases.

In 16 seasons, Nuxhall won 135, lost 117 and struck out 1,372 for the
Reds, Kansas City Athletics and Los Angeles Angels. He was 130-109 for
the Reds, with a 3.80 earned run average, 20 shutouts, 18 saves and 1,289
strikeouts. Nuxhall also hit 15 home runs, and drove in 78. As he loved
to say on the radio, "If you swing the bat, you're dangerous!"

His 135 victories included wins against future Hall of Famers Sandy
Koufax, Bob Gibson, Jim Bunning, Fergie Jenkins and Juan Marichal,

and many top pitchers of his era: Cy Young winner Vern Law, Lew Burdette, Carl Erskine, Bob Friend, Johnny Podres, Ray Sadecki and Curt Simmons.

Nuxhall set a franchise record for pitching 15 seasons, unbroken for more than 50 years through the 2021 season. When he retired in spring 1967, Nuxhall was the club's all-time leader in games pitched (484) and strikeouts (1,289). He also ranked sixth in innings (2,169.1) and eighth in wins (130)—as well as fourth in issuing walks (708) and fifth in giving up hits (2,168). He had two spectacular seasons for the Reds, eight years apart, after being released by a second-year expansion team. You can't say that about many Major League pitchers.

At age 26 in 1955—more than a decade after his disastrous debut—he was 17-12 with 14 complete games and a 3.47 ERA, and pitched in the All-Star Game. He led the National League with five shutouts and tied future Hall of Famer Warren Spahn for most victories (17) by a NL lefty. Nuxhall also was second in the league to future Hall of Famer Robin Roberts for innings pitched (257). Fast-forward eight years, after another stint in the minors, and Nuxhall in 1963 put together arguably his best season, 15-8 with a 3.03 ERA, and earned the Cincinnati baseball writers' Comeback Of The Year Award at 35.

Nuxhall was durable and versatile, dependable and volatile. In addition to leading the 1955 Reds with wins (17), complete games (14) and starts (33), he also earned three saves, tying him for second on the club with reliever Joe Black. His dominance actually started in the second half of 1954, when he was 9-3 after July 19, for a 26-13 record over one-and-a-half seasons.

In 1956, Nuxhall returned to the All-Star Game despite a lackluster 6-8 record and 4.06 ERA at the break. He went 7-3 in the second half for a 13-11 record with 10 complete games, two shutouts and three saves. In a three-year span (1954-56), he was 41-25 with 29 complete games, seven shutouts and six saves. The late 1950s were another story. His wins, starts and innings dropped, bottoming out in 1960 with a 1-8 record. He pitched only 112 innings in 1960, mostly in middle relief. The Reds dealt him to the Kansas City Athletics in January 1961 for pitchers John Tsitouris, who played seven years for the Reds, and John Briggs, who never pitched in the big leagues again.

For Kansas City, Nuxhall was 5-8 in 37 games, mostly in relief. It got worse. He was released in December. Baltimore signed him, and he went to camp with future Hall of Famers Brooks Robinson, Whitey Herzog, Hoyt Wilhelm and Roberts. Two days before Opening Day, the Orioles sold him to the expansion Los Angeles Angels before their second season. The Angels released him in May after five games.

His career was resurrected at the Reds' Triple-A franchise, the San Diego Padres in the Pacific Coast League. An older and tamer lefthander returned to the Reds in 1962, at 33, to go 5-0. After his 15-8 season in 1963, his record evened out in 1964 at 9-8, but his four shutouts ranked sixth in the NL behind the likes of future Hall of Famers Koufax (7), Bunning and Don Drysdale (5 each). In the first four years of his Reds comeback (1962-65), Nuxhall was 40-20 with 27 complete games, seven shutouts and seven saves—similar to his stats a decade earlier (41-25 with 29 complete games).

Pete Rose called Nuxhall "the most competitive SOB I ever played with." And not just on the field. "No matter if it was ping-pong, he just was competitive," said his wife Donzetta.

It wasn't quick or easy for Nuxhall to return to the Major Leagues after his teen-age debut. He spent seven years in the minors before he pitched again for the Reds in 1952. Without that strong competitive streak, he might never have put on a Cincinnati uniform again, or returned in 1962.

After Ted Williams, Joe DiMaggio, Stan Musial, Hank Greenberg, Bill Dickey, Enos Slaughter, Johnny Vander Meer, Bob Feller and dozens of others traded their baseball jerseys for Army and Navy uniforms, baseball scouts looked for talent in weekend leagues and schoolyards. That's how they found Nuxhall and Carl Scheib.

Carl who? Scheib was the youngest pitcher in American League history. The Pennsylvania farm boy made his debut as a reliever for the Philadelphia Athletics on September 6, 1943, in an 11-4 loss to the Yankees. He was 16 years and 294 days old. Scheib pitched two-thirds of an inning, giving up a run on a triple and a single. He's the answer to this trivia question: Who was the youngest Major League Baseball player before Joe Nuxhall? Scheib held the record for nine months, until Nuxhall pitched on June 10, 1944. Joe was 15 years and 316 days old.

A Reds scout watching Joe's dad, Orville "Ox" Nuxhall, pitching in Hamilton's Sunday League was impressed with his young boy playing with men. When Joe's father turned down a Reds contract offer, the club went after his son. Joe so impressed scout Eddie Reese at a Reds tryout in summer of 1943, after pitching two no-hitters for his knothole team, that the Reds took the 15-year-old on a road trip to St. Louis, where he pitched batting practice. The Reds signed him February 18, 1944, and agreed he could finish his freshman year at Wilson Junior High School before joining the team.

Scheib, 15, was recommended to the A's by a part-time scout who saw him pitch for Gratz High School in 1942. Scheib dropped out of school in 1943 to pitch batting practice for the A's before his big-league debut. Unlike Nuxhall, Scheib stuck with the club. He pitched six games that September; 15 games in 1944; and four in 1945 before going into the Army. He returned in 1947, and had his best year in 1948 with a 14-8 record and 3.94 ERA at 21. He was 45-64 when traded to the Cardinals in 1954.

Two weeks later, the youngest players in baseball history sat in opposing dugouts in St. Louis on May 21, 1954. They didn't know their careers were headed in different directions. Nuxhall (2-0) pitched in relief Friday night, blowing a save in the 10th in an 8-7 loss. On Saturday, Scheib (0-1) pitched two scoreless innings, striking out three. It was a vast improvement over his first appearance for the Cards when Scheib gave up five runs in two innings.

Scheib, 27, pitched in relief two days later. He wild-pitched in a run, walked two, and gave up a homer to Cubs catcher Joe Garagiola in a 6-2 loss on May 24. It was his last game in the majors, although he pitched two more years in the minors. He retired at 30 in 1957 with a 45-65 record and a 4.88 ERA in 11 big league seasons. Nuxhall, 25, would play 12½ more years. He retired in 1967 at 37 with a 135-117 record and .390 ERA.

Scheib died in 2018 at age 91. If Nuxhall hadn't pitched for the Reds in 1944, Scheib would have been celebrated as the youngest Major League player for the last 75 years of his life.

⚾ ⚾ ⚾

Often Nuxhall's toughest competitor was Joe Nuxhall. His short fuse—as hits, walks and runs mounted—cost him dearly, especially during the 1950s with the Reds. It took him a long time to master his control. Control of his pitches, and his temper. When he did get control, Nux spent more time concentrating on the batter and less time pacing around the mound while shouting at the home plate umpire.

"He had a beautiful fastball and a beautiful curve ball, but he was wild as a March hare," said Don Briede of Fairfield, who caught Nuxhall for a 1946 Moose Lodge team. Briede told my buddy Howard Wilkinson for a 2002 *Cincinnati Enquirer* story that Joe "threw as hard back then as he did in the major leagues."

Nuxhall spent 1944 and '45 pitching for Birmingham, Syracuse and Lima, then sat out 1946 to regain his amateur status and play football and basketball for Hamilton High School. He returned to the Reds after high school in 1947, at 18, to pitch for Muncie in the Class D Ohio-Indiana League. He walked 145 batters in 100 innings while posting a 7-7 record and 3.78 ERA.

"I was about as wild a pitcher as you ever saw. I remember one game when I walked 14 men and fanned 13 and hadn't given up a hit, and the other team was leading 4-2. And it was only the seventh inning," Nuxhall said in 1973, the Muncie *Star Press* reported.

During his five years in the minors, before rejoining the Reds in 1952, Nuxhall walked more (609) than he struck out (524) pitching for Muncie; Tulsa, Oklahoma; Columbia, South Carolina; and Charleston, West Virginia. He returned to the big club at 23, despite a losing record in seven minor league seasons (50-65). For the '52 Reds he was 1-4 with a 3.23 ERA with 35 relief appearances, five starts and two complete games. Nux followed in 1953 with a 9-11 record, 4.32 ERA and eight hit batters (tied for third in the NL).

Nuxhall finally blossomed into a fine major leaguer in 1954, posting his first winning season (12-5) with 85 strikeouts, just 59 walks, and a 3.89 ERA. His only Opening Day win came in 1954, in relief of starter Bud Podbielan. He was summoned with one out and two on in the second, and pitched 6-1/3 innings in the Reds 9-8 win over the Milwaukee Braves. Nuxhall was a footnote in baseball history that day. Henry Aaron, in his debut, was hitless in five at-bats. Nuxhall got him three times—on a ground out to third, a pop out to second and fly to right.

With his maturity in 1954, Nux became a Reds workhorse, often late in the season when the pitching staff was worn out. Manager Birdie Tebbetts could count on "Big Joe" to start, pitch a couple innings of middle relief, or close. It was not unusual for him to pitch three or four times in one week. Twice in a five-day span in August 1954, Nuxhall pitched really long relief again behind Podbielan. Nux essentially threw a complete game on August 3 in a 7-2 win in Forbes Field when Podbielan faced only one batter. On August 7, when Podbielan got only four outs against the Dodgers, Nuxhall pitched 7-1/3 innings to get the win, increasing his record to 6-3.

In 1955, Nuxhall was 17-12, with 14 complete games. He came home from the All-Star Game to pitch 14 times in 35 days, going 6-2 with two saves. From July 29 to September 1, three of his eight starts were complete games. But in two starts he failed to pitch past the first inning. He also came out of the bullpen six times, pitching 22-1/3 innings in relief. He won his 12th game on August 7, despite giving up a three-run homer to Willie Mays at Crosley. It was Mays' 35th homer of the year, and the 100th of his career, on his way to his first NL home run title (51). The future Hall of Famer and 19-time All-Star hit 10 homers off Nuxhall. To be fair, Mays lit up everyone. Mays hit his most home runs off Braves Hall of Famer Spahn (15), the Pirates' Bob Friend (13) and Dodgers Hall of Famer Don Drysdale (11).

Nuxhall's and Mays' careers basically were parallel. Mays came up to the Giants in 1951, at 19, and won Rookie of the Year by hitting 20 homers, 22 doubles and five triples. When Mays hit his last home run—No. 660 in Shea Stadium on August 17, 1973—Nuxhall was there, too, at the Reds

Radio microphone to call his bomb to right-center field in the fourth inning off Don Gullett.

⚾   ⚾   ⚾

Fifteen future Hall of Famers played in the 1955 All-Star Game in Milwaukee, and Nuxhall nearly stole the show. He just missed being the most valuable player in a game featuring Aaron, Mays, Williams, Mickey Mantle, Stan Musial, Ernie Banks, Yogi Berra, Whitey Ford, Nellie Fox, Al Kaline, Eddie Mathews, Robin Roberts, Red Schoendienst, Duke Snider and Early Wynn.

With the bases loaded and two outs in the eighth, and the NL leading 5-2, Nuxhall relieved Cubs righty Sam Jones. He struck out Ford on three pitches. "Joe Nuxhall comes through in magnificent fashion, as he strikes out pitcher Whitey Ford," said announcer Earl Gillespie on the Mutual Radio Network. Sportswriter Harry Golden of the Madison, Wisconsin, *Capital Times* said that "Ford, batting against lefty Joe Nuxhall, looked as helpless as a 5-year-old against Bobby Feller in his prime."

Nux threw three more shutout innings. In the top of the ninth, he gave up a single and walk, then got Mantle to fly out to center and Berra to pop out to shortstop. He opened the 10th by walking Kaline, then struck out Mickey Vernon, Al Rosen and pitcher Frank Sullivan. Mantle singled with two outs in the 11th, but Nuxhall retired Berra on a grounder to second.

It could have been much better. With one out in the ninth, New York Giants Manager Leo Durocher let Nuxhall hit against Sullivan. Nuxy nearly ended the game with a walk-off home run. Kaline caught the drive at the right field wall. In the 12th, Durocher gave the ball to Braves pitcher Gene Conley. He was the winner when Musial hit a walk-off home run.

"Yeah, I almost hit one," Nuxhall told the *Hamilton Journal-News* in 1977. "If I'd a gotten it up in the air, it would've gone out."

Nearly a no doubter, I'd guess he'd say.

⚾   ⚾   ⚾

"He gives us the stopper we've searched for so long."

That's how Tebbetts described Nuxhall in his 1956 Reds yearbook profile after Joe's All-Star season. Since the All-Star break in 1954, Nuxhall was 26-13. "I think Joe Nuxhall proved to be the outstanding left-handed pitcher in the National League in 1955," Tebbetts said in the yearbook.

Sports Illustrated noticed Nux, too. In its April baseball preview, *SI* listed Nuxhall as one of the Reds' five "mainstays," along with Ted Kluszewski, shortstop Roy McMillan and outfielders Gus Bell and Wally Post. Among the "newcomers to watch" were rookie outfielder Frank Robinson ("tremendous prospect") and pitcher Brooks Lawrence ("big man, throws hard, looked good in spring training") obtained from St. Louis. *SI* wrote about Nuxhall: "Pitched briefly in majors at 15 in 1944 but departed then until 1952. Big, left-handed fast baIler, won 17 games last year, is stopper. His good fast ball may put him in 20-game class this season."

Nuxhall never won 20 games. He was barely over .500 in 1956 (13-11). Yet the Reds surprised *SI*, and the entire baseball world, by flirting with first place much of the season. For the first time since Nuxhall's 1944 debut, the Reds had a winning record. The team finished third (91-63), three games behind the Brooklyn Dodgers, powered by a NL record-tying 221 home runs, including two by Nuxhall. Robinson hit 38 homers and won Rookie of the Year.

In his only Opening Day start, Joe held the Cardinals in 1956 to two runs over eight innings. He lost the game when Red Schoendienst singled off Nuxhall's glove with two outs in the ninth. "I closed my glove on the ball too soon, and it bounced away for the silliest sort of error (though scored a hit). Then Stan (Musial) hit a fastball into the seats, and we lost it, 4-2," Nuxhall told Ritter Collett, the Dayton *Journal-Herald* sports editor who received the Baseball Hall of Fame's J.G. Taylor Spink Award in 1991. But Reds fans had a reason to smile on the way home. Robinson, 20, got on base three times with two singles and a walk.

On the first of June, after a loss to the Giants at Crosley, Nuxhall was 1-5. But Tebbetts had found his stopper. Lawrence, from Springfield, Ohio, was 13-0 before losing to the Pirates on July 21. Nuxhall turned things around in June, going 12-6 the remaining four months. Nux made *Enquirer* headlines on June 19—"Nuxhall Puts Reds Second—Blanks

Giants In Nightcap After Locals Drop Opener 7-6"—after tossing a two-hitter against the Giants in a Polo Grounds doubleheader. Lawrence and Nuxhall made the 1956 All-Star team, but neither pitched in the NL's 7-3 win. Lawrence ended the season 19-11, with 11 complete games, one shutout, 96 strikeouts and a 3.99 ERA in 218 innings. Nuxhall finished 13-11 with 10 complete games, three saves and a 3.72 ERA in 200 innings. Nux also led the staff with 120 strikeouts and two shutouts. Not bad for a couple of guys from blue-collar Ohio towns, when you think about it.

Nuxhall never developed into Tebbetts' ace. He didn't win 13 games or more until 1963, after he returned from exile in the American League. He continued to be plagued by inconsistency, which drove managers and pitching coaches crazy.

At Connie Mack Stadium on June 20, 1954, the Reds scored nine runs in the first, and two more in the second, for Nuxhall. But Joe was gone with one out in the second, after giving the Phillies four runs on six hits and a walk.

Twice in August 1956 he was knocked out in the first inning. After his second straight early shower, two days later he threw a complete game · against the Giants on August 28. In 1957, he made three starts in five days—lasting only 2/3 of an inning each on August 31 and September 1, then pitching a complete game September 4 in Wrigley Field to beat the Cubs. From 1957 to 1960, he was 10-10, 12-11, 9-9 and 1-8.

On a windy Thursday afternoon in San Francisco's old Seal Stadium on June 18, 1959, Nuxhall got the hook from Manager Mayo Smith in the sixth after giving up six runs on 13 hits and four errors, three by second baseman Johnny Temple and one by shortstop Eddie Kasko. Nuxhall's record dropped to 3-5. This is how Reds reliever Jim Brosnan described the game in *The Long Season,* his 1959 book:

> Nuxhall stood helplessly on the mound, muttering to himself as Giants base hits fell safely all over the ballpark. Of the 13 Giants hits, nine had been bloops, squibs or Texas League singles. The wind, blowing

in erratic gusts, had dropped two pop fly balls into right field instead of in Robinson's first-base glove. Temple, the second baseman, had booted three ground balls to add to Nuxhall's frustration.

"Tomorrow's paper will say Nuxhall was blasted for 13 hits. Watch and see," I said [Brosnan quoted himself].

"Joe's had this kind of luck all year long. I never saw anything like it," said Brooks Lawrence.

Then came Nux's 1-8 season in 1960. His only victory was June 9 in San Francisco. He was 1-5 when he was suspended for five days for shoving umpire Ed Vargo July 25. Ernie Banks ruined his chance for a second victory with a walk-off homer in Wrigley on August 30. Despite his record, Nuxhall didn't pitch that poorly in 1960. He kept the ball in the park, giving up just eight home runs in 112 innings, and walking only 27. Joe's bad luck carried into 1961. General Manager Bill DeWitt Sr. traded Nuxhall to Kansas City on January 25, unaware that Nux had just finalized a new contract with Business Manager John Murdough, wrote Greg Hoard in *Joe: Rounding Third And Heading For Home*. That's contrary to the widely held belief that Nuxhall requested the trade.

"When I left, the fans were really on me, which I deserved. I was terrible," Nux told me in 1986.

⚾   ⚾   ⚾

Two months shy of his 34th birthday, baseball lifer Nuxhall was out of the game for the first time on May 15, 1962. After the Angels bought him from Baltimore in April, Nuxhall was lousy in La La Land—giving up six runs in five games on seven hits and five walks, with a 10.13 ERA in 5-1/3 innings.

"Five innings in five weeks with the Angels. How in the heck did they know whether I could pitch or not?" he told Collett.

Nuxhall started calling clubs. Reds farm director Phil Seghi was interested. "To be honest with you, the Reds were the last place I thought I'd come back to. That really surprised me. Phil Seghi said, 'We'll send you to (Triple A) San Diego. I want you to go there to get back to the major leagues.' They were very good to me. I went down there and started, and was called back up," Nuxhall said.

He signed with the Reds on May 19. The sunny Southern California climate improved his disposition on the mound. Or perhaps it was knowing this could be his last shot at returning to the majors.

"My temperament changed. I didn't let things bother me anymore," Nuxhall explained in 1996. "There's no one that got any madder out there than I did, and it didn't help a damn thing. Everybody preached to me about (my temper). When I finally realized it, I became a decent pitcher. If I had the same outlook 15 years prior to that, I know I would have won a whole bunch more games. I know that. The temper cost me, and it cost the ball club, because it's just stupid to get mad at yourself if you walk someone or whatever."

He also shortened his windup, stopped trying to overpower hitters, and started pitching to spots. "I found I had my eye constantly on target for the first time in my life," he told *Dayton Daily News* sports editor Si Burick. The new Nux was spectacular. For San Diego, he was 9-2 in 11 starts with seven complete games, three shutouts and a 3.21 ERA—in only two months. He struck out 72 in 84 innings, and walked only 22.

"He just made up his mind that he was going to show them he could still pitch. Some people just give up when they're sent down," Donzetta said. It was the pivotal moment in his career. Nuxhall could have packed up his cleats and headed to Hamilton after being released by the lowly Athletics and Angels. Instead he transformed himself at an age when many would quit the game.

Nuxhall was recalled by the defending NL champs and back on the Crosley Field mound July 22.

He wore No. 41, since lefty Ted Wills was wearing his No. 39 from the 1950s. (Joe wore No. 43 when he debuted in 1944, as depicted on his Crosley Terrace statue.) Nuxhall was nervous when Paul Sommerkamp announced his name as he walked from the bullpen to relieve Jim Maloney. Fans had booed the last time they saw him.

"I'm scared to death, because I remember the receptions I got when I went to the mound in 1960, and this concerned me. But my friend Waite Hoyt had set things up for me," Nuxhall said.

The Reds radio voice was one of Nuxhall's biggest boosters in 1962, along with *Hamilton Journal-News* sports editor Bill Moeller. "Waite Hoyt was really selling him to the public. And everything good Joe did, Bill put in the paper. Bill wouldn't say anything bad about anybody," Donzetta said. Nuxy was relieved to hear the Sunday doubleheader crowd cheer for him. "There was a change (in his attitude), and they loved him," she said.

Nuxhall pitched 3-1/3 shutout innings, striking out three Mets. He also drove in two runs with a double to center in the sixth. After almost a two-year absence, Nuxhall rounded third and headed for home with a win, two RBIs and a .500 batting average.

"I very well could have been out of baseball in 1962. So it's really a real pleasant feeling to know that you're still wanted, and in fact are still able to pitch yet," he told a radio interviewer in 1966.

⚾   ⚾   ⚾

When I asked Nux to describe himself on the mound, he said: "I was basically a fastball and slider pitcher." Pitching coach Tom Ferrick taught Nuxhall the slider during 1954, "and it has been a tremendous asset," said Nuxhall's 1956 Reds yearbook profile.

Catcher Ed Bailey told me he kept Nuxhall's temperament in line by "staying away from him during a ball game. I left him alone. He knew what we were going to do before we went out there. Managers and coaches go over the hitters, you know. It was kind of hard for him to throw a sinker to a right-hander, but he had a good slider. Joe was a good pitcher. He had good stuff," Bailey said before a 2003 Fairfield Community Foundation dinner honoring Nuxhall.

At Kansas City, manager Joe Gordon "got me throwing a change-up, a slip pitch" to augment his fastball, Nux said. Jim Turner, the former Yankees pitching coach hired by manager Fred Hutchinson before the 1961 pennant-winning season, "really helped me. He had me throwing a very good curveball" after being recalled from San Diego in 1962.

Mastering the breaking ball was elusive throughout his career. "If I could have gotten that pitch over consistently, things would have been a lot different. Even when I was having good years, I had only a few good days with the curve," he told a Dayton sportswriter in 1963. "It's how you throw a curveball. There are guys working on a curveball today," he told me in 1996, "and they've been pitching 10 years in the big league." The change of pace, he told me in that conversation, was "probably the most difficult to get a grasp on, to get comfortable throwing it, with the right release and grip. That's why the 'circle change,' as they call it, has been a big help to a lot of pitchers. For some reason, it's easy to grip, and find the comfort zone of getting a grip on it."

Catcher Johnny Edwards was impressed with Nuxhall's stuff in 1966. "Nuxhall's come up with some real fine control since he's rejoined our ballclub. I think that he can throw the ball where he wants to almost every time. He's got a fastball, a curve, a slider and a change-up. Of the first three, he can control them real well," Edwards said in a radio interview.

Johnny Bench, the Reds 1965 draft pick, caught and hit off Nuxhall during spring training in 1966 and '67. "He was what we called 'a crafty lefthander,' because he knew how to turn it over. He knew how to throw a little slider. But he couldn't overpower anybody at that point," Bench said.

⚾   ⚾   ⚾

Did Nuxhall ever throw a spitter? I had to ask, since Nuxhall loved to tell the story about the spitball duel between Maloney and Gaylord Perry.

"Yeah," he replied instantly. Like many pitchers looking for a competitive edge to extend their careers, Nuxhall experimented with it after returning to the Reds in 1962. He had been taught the pitch in the 1950s by teammate Art Fowler, who "did a pretty good job with 'the wet one,' we'll call it." Fowler showed him how to wet his fingers, grab the ball off the seams, and throw it slightly slower than a fastball to make it tumble. Nuxhall developed enough confidence in the spitter to throw one to Willie Mays in San Francisco. He had Willie at no balls and two strikes when he loaded one up.

"I wind up and I throw that rascal and it comes in a little bit below belt high, and Willie starts to swing at it. The ball gets right out in front of the plate, and the bottom falls out of it. And Willie swings down on it, and fouled it off," Nuxhall told WCET-TV in 2005. Mays stepped out and yelled: "Joe! What the hell was that?" Nuxhall covered his face so Mays couldn't see him laughing.

Nuxhall threw his last spitball to Dodgers outfielder Lou Johnson at Crosley Field. Nuxy was running out of gas in the sixth inning. With the bases loaded, Nuxhall was sure he could get Johnson to ground into a double play with his spitter.

"I load that sucker up, and he hit it off the scoreboard in left-center field and cleared the bases. I'll never forget it," Nuxhall told me in 1996. "Usually a spitter will do something (move in some way), but I could never control it. It's like a knuckleball. If a knuckleball doesn't knuckle (flutter unpredictably), then it knuckles way out there."

Most longtime Reds fans remember 1963 for Pete Rose's Rookie of the Year season, and 23-year-old Maloney emerging as a dominating power pitcher. Maloney was 23-7 with 265 strikeouts, 88 walks, 13 complete games and a 2.77 ERA. Overlooked is Nuxhall, at 35, going 15-8 with 169 strikeouts, only 39 walks, 14 complete games and a 2.61 ERA.

In terms of wins, Nuxhall's 1955 season (17-12) was his best. But when you take a deep dive into Nuxhall's career, it's clear 1963 was the pinnacle of Joe's career. His 2.61 ERA ranked sixth in the NL; while Maloney didn't make the top 10. Nuxy's strikeouts/walks ratio was third in the NL (4.33) behind future Hall of Famers Koufax (5.27) and Drysdale (4.40). Maloney was eighth (3.01). Nuxy's Wins Above Replacement (WAR), a sabermetric calculation that represents the number of wins a player added to the team above what a replacement player from the minors would add, was 4.8. Maloney's WAR was 5.0.

Nuxy also had a fine 2.38 FIP (Fielding Independent Pitching), an ERA predictor based on strikeouts, walks, home runs and batters hit by a pitch (items a pitcher controls). He was second on the team by a hair to Maloney's 2.37. Maloney threw more innings with more strikeouts, but Joe walked 49 fewer hitters and had a slightly lower ERA. Maloney had 12 games with six or more runs support, while Nuxhall had only six games with six-plus run support. That was the difference in their win-loss records that year.

Starting 1963 in the bullpen, Nuxhall didn't win his first game until May 3. It was the first of five straight complete-game victories. Nux's sixth complete game, on June 29, was his 100th career win, which one writer noted took him 20 years to accomplish. He finished 1963 with five more consecutive complete games, ending the season with two wins over the Cardinals as Stan "The Man" Musial was retiring.

My Dad made sure his little lefty saw Musial, the greatest left-handed hitter, play his final game at Crosley Field on September 22, 1963. Gene Wilkinson in Dayton, Ohio, and Cliff Radel of Cincinnati's West Side wanted their southpaw sons at Crosley Field that day, too. It wasn't until about 30 years later that I realized two of my *Enquirer* colleagues, Howard Wilkinson and Cliff Radel, were among the 25,706 that Sunday afternoon to see Musial's Cincinnati finale.

Nuxhall struck him out in the first. With the Reds up 3-0 in the fourth, Musial flied to right. In the bottom of the fourth, Mike Shannon, a future Cardinals broadcaster, replaced Musial. Unlike the first time Nuxhall faced the future Hall of Famer, as a shaky teen, Joe was at the top of his game. He struck out 10, including whiffing first baseman Bill White, the future National League president, three times. I went home happy. I saw The Man play his last game in Cincinnati, and I saw my man pitch a winner, 5-2.

The two teams met in St. Louis to end the season the following weekend. In Musial's final game September 29, he singled twice off Maloney. Musial ended the day with a career total of 3,630 hits, the National League record until Rose, playing second base that day, broke it in 1981. The previous day, Musial faced Nuxhall for the last time. Joe threw a three-hitter to win his 15th. Nuxhall continued his mastery over Musial, who grounded to Rose in the first and to Nux in the fourth. How would history be different if Musial had bounced out to the mound in 1944 instead of lining a laser to right, which shattered Joe's confidence? What if Nuxhall hadn't walked two Cardinals to bring Musial to the plate?

"Lord knows what might have happened if I would have retired the first three hitters I faced. I might have been there (with the Reds) from that day on. That's something we'll never know," Nuxhall told an interviewer in 1966.

It haunted him all of his life. Nuxhall would talk about his debut while relaxing in the clubhouse with clubhouse director Rick Stowe, son of Joe's closest friend, Bernie Stowe, the team's longtime equipment manager. Everywhere Nuxhall went, people asked about his big league debut. Former Reds publicity assistant Joe Kelley recalled riding the elevator at San Diego's Jack Murphy Stadium in the early 1990s with Joe when the elevator operator recognized the name on Nuxhall's credential.

Weren't you the youngest player in Major League history?

"Yes, I am," Nuxhall said.

Did they score any runs off you?

"As many as they wanted that day," Nuxhall said with a hearty laugh. "As many as they wanted."

When the Cincinnati Chapter of the Baseball Writers of America presented Nuxhall the 1963 Comeback Of The Year Award for his unbelievable turnaround, Nuxy brought down the house at the banquet by saying, "I hope I never win this again."

Without his transformation in San Diego, Nuxhall would not have returned to pitch for Cincinnati. Without his 20-5 comeback in 1962-63, he probably wouldn't have had a shot at the Reds Hall of Fame or the radio booth. I consider it the greatest comeback in Reds history.

⚾ ⚾ ⚾

Nuxhall nearly fulfilled a lifelong World Series dream in 1964. Going into the final week, the Reds were in first place, after the Phillies' collapse, behind strong starting pitching by Jim O'Toole (17-7), Maloney (15-10), Bob Purkey (11-9), Joey Jay (11-11) and Nux (9-8).

The club had a special incentive. Fred Hutchinson, their beloved skipper, was dying of cancer before their eyes. The Reds were 22-22 the first two months, falling to sixth when Milwaukee beat Maloney June 2. From that point, the Reds went 71-49 chasing the Phillies. Hutch was hospitalized for two weeks in July and turned the team over to coach Dick Sisler immediately after Hutch's 45th birthday celebration on August 12. The Reds rallied for Hutch, going 29-18, and taking first place on Sunday, September 27, with five games left.

Nuxhall started out strong in '64 with four complete games. His first victory was Ken Johnson's no-hitter on April 23, when the Houston righty became the first pitcher to lose without surrendering a hit. On May 27, Nuxhall out-dueled Koufax, 1-0, at Crosley Field. Koufax scattered three hits over seven innings, struck out seven and walked five. Nuxhall gave up six hits, and struck out six, with no walks. And Nux stole a base—the second and last of his career—with a head-first slide into second.

"Koufax wasn't paying the slightest attention to me. If I make it, and Pete (Rose) gets a hit, we're up two runs. If I'm out, what's the difference? We've got the top of the order leading off the next inning. And it's a lot easier to pitch with a two-run lead than it is with one," he said after the game.

When the Reds rolled into Philadelphia on September 21, the Phillies (90-60) were in first by 6½ games. They had been atop the NL since July 15. Their luck changed. The Reds' 1-0 win started the Phillies' 10-game losing streak. To this day Phillies fans blame Reds infielder Chico Ruiz for the collapse. Ruiz scored the lone run by stealing home with clean-up hitter Frank Robinson at the plate in the sixth. Pitcher Art Mahaffey was so shocked he threw a wild pitch past catcher Clay Dalrymple.

"The count was no balls and two strikes, I'll never forget it," Nuxhall said. "Art Mahaffey was pitching. He threw a curveball—he had a good curveball—and we look up and here comes Ruiz! All of us ducked. We could just see Robby getting one in here (belt high) and hitting a rocket, and taking Chico's damn head off. But it was a curveball way outside, and Ruiz got in there really easy."

The Reds won seven in a row to take first place, then dropped two to the Pirates. Nuxhall, in relief of Purkey, beat Pittsburgh on Thursday, October 1, to pull within a half-game of the first-place Cardinals.

It turned out to be the Reds' last win. On Friday, Deron Johnson hit into a triple play with Robinson and Vada Pinson on base in the fourth. The Reds were up 3-0 in the seventh when pitcher Chris Short hit shortstop Leo Cardenas. Little Leo charged the mound. That shook the Phils from their September slumber. The next inning, the Phillies erupted for four runs to win, 4-3. Jim Bunning, the Hall of Famer from Fort Thomas, beat the Reds 10-0 on Sunday, while Bob Gibson pitched four innings of relief against the Mets to win his 19th and clinch the pennant for St. Louis. Hutchinson died on November 12.

"Hutch was sick. We all knew what our goal was, because of Hutch, but it didn't work out," Nuxhall said. "The Phillies came to town, and they just beat us. We had that incident with Chris Short and Leo Cardenas, which lit them up. Short hit Leo with a pitch in the left thigh and that started a big ruckus. From that point on, the Phillies kicked our butts. Jim Bunning shut us out on Sunday. And then we had to sit in the club-house and wait on the end of the Cardinals-Mets game. But we had it. The Phillies had blown a seven-game lead. That year we had it."

⚾   ⚾   ⚾

Nuxhall was back in the bullpen again in 1965, and it wasn't easy for him at age 36.

"I just can't pitch relief ball in the way they operate out of the bullpen today," Nuxhall once explained to Dayton's Collett. "I tried it at Kansas City, but my arm tightens up between times I pitch, and I'm simply not able to get loose and work two, three or four days in a row. When I warm up to pitch, I gotta go in. I can't sit back down and start up again a couple minutes later."

Half of Nuxhall's 32 appearances were out of the 'pen for the staff led by Sammy Ellis (22-10) and Maloney (20-9), who held the Mets hitless 10 innings June 14 and won a 10-inning no hitter, 1-0, over the Cubs Aug. 19. Nuxhall didn't win his first game until May 22. After moving into the rotation in June, he compiled an 11-4 record, his last winning season, which included a 9-1 streak during a summer surge into first over the Dodgers. He caught the attention of Associated Press national

Joe chats with legendary Reds radio voice Waite Hoyt at Crosley Field a few months before Hoyt retired in 1965. RHODES/KLUMPE REDS HALL OF FAME COLLECTION

baseball writer Murray Chass after beating the Phillies on July 15 for his fifth straight win, improving to 6-2.

"Put Sandy Koufax and Don Drysdale together, and they barely come out ahead of Joe Nuxhall. Nuxhall has the Cincinnati Reds in first place in the National League, and the best Koufax and Drysdale can do for the Los Angeles Dodgers is second. Nuxhall kept the Reds three percentage points ahead of the Dodgers Thursday night, stopping Philadelphia 8-1 on eight hits," Chass wrote. "The triumph for Nuxhall was his fifth straight, all having come in Cincinnati's last eight victories since June 29. In the same period, Drysdale (14-8) and Koufax (15-3) ... have combined for six of the Dodgers eight victories." The story inspired this headline in the *Iowa City Citizen-Press*: "Ancient Joe Nuxhall Keeps Reds In Front Of Dodgers."

Nine days later, the Old Lefthander nearly no-hit Houston in the new Astrodome. Bob Lillis singled with one out in the eighth for the only hit. Nux struck out 11 and walked two to keep the Reds one game behind the Dodgers.

"I'd be lying if I said I didn't care about pitching a no-hitter," Nuxhall told writers after the 2-0 victory. "But winning is what this game is about. If a no-hitter should come my way, I'd just have to consider it a bonus. I knew what was going on out there tonight though, and I was trying for the no-hitter. I was a little tired, but in a game like that there's no time to relax." After the game, Reds manager Dick Sisler said Nux "has done a heck of a job just when we needed help. You have to respect a guy like that. He's almost 37 years old and he fought his way back from the minors to win a job on our staff" in 1962.

Nux had a shot at a 13-3 record going into the last week, after missing three weeks with a sore elbow. But reliever Billy McCool blew a save after Joe held the Astros to one run in eight innings on September 26, and Nuxhall in his final start served up a walk-off homer to the Giants' Orlando Cepeda. The Reds finished third (89-73), seven games behind the Dodgers, despite having two 20-game winners.

In 1966, at 37, Nuxhall definitely was ancient on a staff comprised of Maloney (26), Ellis (25), Gerry Arrigo (25), McCool (21) and World Series veterans Jay (30) and O'Toole (29). There were also a couple of new faces in the clubhouse after DeWitt made the worst trade in Reds history: Frank Robinson to Baltimore for starter Milt Pappas (27), reliever Jack Baldschun (29) and outfielder Dick Simpson (22).

New manager Don Heffner used Nuxhall mostly in relief after he rehabbed another sore elbow in May. When Heffner was fired at the All-Star break, Nuxhall was 1-2, with a 6.16 ERA in 30-2/3 innings. Coach Dave Bristol, just 33, replaced Heffner and put Nux to work, using him in relief four times in five days. Unable to crack the starting rotation, Nuxhall began contemplating life after baseball. A week before his 38th birthday, Nuxhall confirmed talk in Hamilton about running for Butler County Sheriff. He didn't give it serious consideration.

"I don't think it would be fair to the people up there," Nuxhall told

Jim Ferguson of the *Dayton Daily News*. "What do I know about being sheriff? It would be like playing me in center field. What do I know about that? I'm a pitcher."

Nuxhall beat Fergie Jenkins in relief in an 18-inning marathon in Wrigley on July 19. Three days later, Bristol gave Nuxy the ball when Pappas was scratched. Joe responded by pitching seven innings to beat the Braves at Crosley on July 22. He made 12 more starts for Bristol, and seven relief appearances, throwing almost 100 innings. He pitched his first complete game on August 24 in San Francisco, beating Perry (20-3) on three days' rest. On August 29, Nuxhall threw his only shutout, to push his record to 6-4. The *Enquirer's* Lou Smith called Nuxhall "fabulous" for moving the ball around the strike zone "with almost infallible skill." It was the pinnacle of his season—his last career win, shutout and complete game.

Nux lost his last four decisions to finish 6-8 with a 4.50 ERA. In a 7-2 defeat by the Cubs at Wrigley Field on September 22, Nuxhall got the last of his 152 hits, a single off rookie Dave Dowling. The Astros beat him 3-2 at Crosley in his final start on September 29. He gave up three runs on seven hits in eight innings. On October 2, Nux took the mound for the last time. He threw one-third inning in relief for the final game of the season, getting Braves' rookie George Kopacz to fly out to center.

Over the winter, Nuxhall broadcast his fourth season of Miami University basketball games on Hamilton's WMOH-AM. Executives at the Geo. Wiedemann Brewing Co. had been talking to Nux since summer of 1966 about retiring to the booth. "We accepted the job, but we weren't going to announce it until spring training," Nuxhall said.

O'Toole wasn't surprised that folksy Nuxy transitioned to broadcasting. "Nuxhall did his homework before he decided to retire. At a certain age, you know it's time to retire. He was doing Miami basketball games, and he was ready to go when the time came," O'Toole told me in 2003.

⚾ ⚾ ⚾

When Nuxhall arrived in Tampa in February 1967, he was greeted with an *Enquirer* headline calling him "The Old Warrior." Nuxhall did full workouts along with two talented 19-year-olds, Gary Nolan and Bench. Nolan, a first-round draft pick in 1966, was so impressive he made Bristol's rotation. Nolan struck out eight Astros in his April 15 debut in a 7-3 win. Bench was called up August 28, and won Rookie of the Year in 1968.

"We basically knew that I was going to do it (retire)," Nuxhall said. "I had gone all through spring training and was really ready to pitch in the season. Our only experienced left-handed pitcher, Ted Davidson, was shot in a bar by his ex-wife (in Tampa). So I went to Dave Bristol and said, 'Gee, we can call this thing off, since you don't have any (lefthanders).'" Nuxhall and Bristol went to see Bob Howsam, the general manager just hired by the new ownership group led by *Enquirer* publisher Frank Dale. Howsam had another idea. He told them Philadelphia and Detroit were interested in him, Nuxhall said. Joe decided to make his own trade— pitching for broadcasting.

"When he said that, I said, 'No way! Uh-uh! I'll stay retired. That's final," Nuxhall said. So on April 1, a day after pitching against the Astros, Nuxhall tearfully announced his retirement to Reds beat writers. "I certainly feel real bad about retiring from baseball, but in the long run I'm sure it will be the best for me and my family."

Thirty-five years later, when he announced he would retire from the Reds Radio Network after the 2004 season, Nuxhall reflected on transitioning to radio.

"This opportunity was presented to me, and I said I'd have to look at it very strongly," he told reporters on November 1, 2002, at Riverfront Stadium, eight weeks before it was imploded to make way for Great American Ball Park. "I was 38 years old. It was a good decision, without a doubt."

It was great for Reds fans. In all certainty, no question about it.

"I could have played another two to four years. Physically I felt that way," he told me in 1986.

Actually, he pitched another 20 years. After rounding third and heading for radio, Nuxhall threw batting practice the very next day, and the day after that, and through the Big Red Machine era and well past Rose's return as player-manager in 1984.

Error on the Reds Hall of Fame

Looking up the box score from the night of Joe Nuxhall's Reds Hall of Fame induction in 1968, I made a startling discovery. His plaque is wrong.

It says: *"Joseph Henry Nuxhall. LHP—Inducted July 4, 1968."* But the Reds were playing Houston in the Astrodome that week. Explained Chris Eckes, Hall of Fame operations manager and chief curator: "From newspaper coverage, it appears the date on the plaque references the date he was announced as having been voted into the Hall—July 4, 1968. The ceremony honoring him for being inducted (not an induction ceremony) was held before the Reds-Giants game at Crosley on July 12, 1968."

Nuxhall was inducted with "Wahoo Sam" Crawford, the MLB triples leader (309) who played for the Reds (1899-1902) and Tigers (1903-1917). Crawford, who had been enshrined in Cooperstown in 1957, died June 15, a month before the Reds' honored him. Nuxhall, in his second year on radio, easily won the fan mail vote (7,935) over former teammates Roy McMillan (2,648) and Bob Purkey (1,759).

"The whole thing is stranger still since the plaque of Sam Crawford, Nuxhall's fellow inductee, includes no reference to an induction date at all," Eckes said. "We need to dig some more to find out if the dates on other plaques are tied to announcement dates or ceremony dates. Like you, we have always assumed the latter, as that has been the case for many years."

4

My First Win on the Mic!

Joe held an old Wiedemann Beer poster stashed in his basement when I interviewed him at his Fairfield home in 1996.

CINCINNATI ENQUIRER PHOTO

The jitters were gone. Marty Brennaman's first game as the voice of Reds Radio was in the books. Brennaman, 31, made his debut with Joe Nuxhall on Saturday, March 9, 1974, when the Reds opened Grapefruit League play against the Pirates in Bradenton. Five weeks earlier, the team had hired Brennaman, who had called games for the Mets' Triple-A Tidewater Tides and Julius Erving's Virginia Squires in the old American Basketball Association.

"I'd been around for a month, and then I go to Tampa the last week in February," Brennaman said. "I was scared of my own shadow. I questioned whether I was good enough to be here, because people in Cincinnati were saying, 'You've got big shoes to fill! To fill Al Michaels' shoes!'"

He felt much better on the ride back to the Reds' Tampa complex. He had a bounce in his step. He felt he had passed a major test.

On Sunday, Marty and Joe sat in front of the microphones to call the spring home opener at the Reds' Al Lopez Field in Tampa. The engineer cued Marty.

BRENNAMAN: Good afternoon everyone, and welcome to Reds baseball from Al Michaels Field in Tampa, Florida!

"I knew immediately what I had said. I was humiliated. I was completely devastated. As loose as I was that first day, that's how tight I was the opening home game. Then I drop Al Michaels' name rather than Al Lopez, and Joe damn near fell out of his chair. I had to live that down. It was an interesting beginning."

At the commercial break Joe said to Marty, "I can't believe it. We haven't got to the regular season yet, and I've already got material for the banquet circuit next fall!"

Nuxhall in 1974 was starting his eighth season on radio. During 1967 spring training he had joined Claude Sullivan and Jim McIntyre 18 months after the retirement of legendary announcer Waite Hoyt. The Geo. Wiedemann Brewing Co., which replaced Burger Beer as the main radio sponsor in 1966, wanted a player's perspective. That had been missing since Hoyt, a Hall of Fame pitcher who played with Babe Ruth's Yankees, left when Burger lost the rights. Wiedemann folks knew that Nux had also worked for Burger.

"You had to work in the offseason. Ninety percent of us did, and most of us worked for Burger Beer. I worked for Burger for two years. We would go around with salesmen and visit accounts in the three-state area, and we'd talk about the Reds," he told me in 2006.

Wiedemann had another concern. Sullivan, the University of Kentucky basketball and football announcer added to help Hoyt in 1964, was having health problems. He missed five weeks in 1966 after cancer surgery at the Mayo Clinic in Minnesota. Sullivan, 42, broadcast Jim Maloney's 6-1 Opening Day victory over the Dodgers in 1967, then skipped a West Coast trip. At midseason he gave up baseball to strengthen his voice for UK football—despite pressure from Wiedemann, wrote his son Alan Sullivan and Joe Cox in their *Voice of the Wildcats* book in 2014. Sullivan broadcast his last UK football game on November 25, a 17-7 loss to Tennessee. He died during surgery on December 6, 1967.

"Claude Sullivan was one of the nicest people that I've ever met in my life. He was a class act, without a doubt," Nuxhall said.

⚾ ⚾ ⚾

When Nuxhall rounded third for the radio booth he stepped into a storied tradition of baseball broadcasting in Cincinnati, where Reds fans have enjoyed an impressive lineup of voices honored in Cooperstown, from Red Barber to Waite Hoyt, Al Michaels and Marty Brennaman.

The first Reds game was heard in 1924 on WMH-AM (now WKRC-AM), which had become the city's first radio station in 1921. By 1930, games were broadcast by three announcers: Harry Hartman, who did both radio and the stadium public address announcing; Sidney Ten-Eyck; and Bob Burdette. Ten-Eyck said he and Burdette did about a dozen games in 1930 on Crosley's WSAI-AM from front-row box seats. The schedule was unpredictable.

"They'd come to us and say, 'We were going to do the game next Friday.' Sometimes we'd have to break away in the middle of a game for a half hour. We'd say, 'We'll be right back after our regularly scheduled program,'" Ten-Eyck told me in 1988. He quickly discovered baseball's magical bond with the radio audience. "My mother-in-law wouldn't allow anyone to talk in the house when the game was on radio."

Players loved radio, too.

"We had on (Cardinals) Dizzy Dean and Leo Durocher. They'd crouch down in front of the box seats on the field. It wasn't any problem getting players on the broadcast. The problem was getting them off," Ten-Eyck said.

The game changed in 1934, when Powel Crosley, Jr. bought the struggling Reds on February 4, two months before Opening Day. Crosley, who manufactured radios and owned WLW and WSAI, decided to broadcast Reds games to promote radio sales. The station offered the baseball job to a young Florida sportscaster, Walter Lanier "Red" Barber, whose career would take him from Crosley Field to New York City and the Hall of Fame in Cooperstown. Barber accepted the job for $25 a week, when WLW stood for "World's Lowest Wages," he liked to say. He reported for spring training in Tampa to the Reds' young publicist, James Reston, who would later become a *New York Times* editor and a nationally syndicated columnist.

Barber, 26, had never seen a professional baseball game until Opening Day 1934. His bosses didn't take any chances with the rookie redhead screwing up the owner's pet project. Before the first pitch, Barber noticed Peter Grant, WLW-AM's star announcer, in the back of the booth.

"About the middle of the ballgame, about the fourth or fifth inning, Grant left. And so that told me I was doing all right," Barber told me in 1992 before being inducted into the Greater Cincinnati Broadcast Hall of Fame. "The big surprise was I almost had a no-hitter. Lon Warneke of the Cubs had one man out in the ninth inning before (outfielder) Adam Comorosky got a single right between his feet. That was the only hit for the Reds. The Reds lost Opening Day, and they never came out of eighth (last) place all year."

During his five years with the Reds (1934-38), Barber made some historic broadcasts. He described the first Major League Baseball night game, a Reds 2-1 victory over the Phillies at Crosley Field on May 24, 1935; interviewed manager Bob O'Farrell in mid-air when the Reds were the first team to fly to a road game (Chicago) in June 1934; and called the first of Johnny Vander Meer's back-to-back no-hitters on June 11, 1938. He didn't call Vandy's second in Brooklyn because New York teams banned radio broadcasts in the 1930s, fearing they would hurt attendance. He also broadcast Ohio State football for WLW-AM.

Barber loved to say he was watching games from "the catbird seat," a phrase he picked up in a Cincinnati poker game. Hyde Park resident Frank Koch told me in 1988 how he raked in winnings while boasting he had been "in the catbird seat" with an ace in the hole. "Inasmuch as I paid for the expression, I began to use it," Barber said.

Barber made it to the World Series before the Reds. WLW agreed in 1935 to become a founding member of the Mutual Radio Network—with New York's WOR, Chicago's WGN and Detroit's WXYZ—if young Barber could call the 1935 World Series. He left Cincinnati after the 1938 season for New York, where he would work for the Dodgers, Yankees and CBS Sports. When I asked if he regretted missing the Reds' 1939-40 NL championships, Barber replied indignantly: "No! I wanted to go to New York City. I wanted to go to a bigger job, of course. That's all."

It worked out OK, without a doubt. Barber and former Yankees radio colleague Mel Allen were the first broadcasters to receive the Baseball Hall of Fame's Frick Award in 1978.

⚾ ⚾ ⚾

I remember lying in bed as a kid in Middletown in the early 1960s, listening to Hoyt on a glowing tube radio. Reds owner Bob Castellini did the same thing as a kid.

Hoyt was hired by Burger in 1942 after winning 237 games in 21 years for the Yankees, Giants, Red Sox, Tigers, Athletics, Pirates and Dodgers. Hoyt, inducted into the Hall of Fame in 1969, did Reds games on WKRC-AM, WSAI-AM, WCKY-AM and old WCPO-AM. An alcoholic, he retired at 66 instead of working for another brand because Burger had stuck with Hoyt in 1945 when he missed 10 weeks of Reds broadcasts "due to amnesia." After Hoyt checked himself into Good Samaritan Hospital, Babe Ruth sent that famous telegram: "Read about your case of Amnesia. Must be a new brand."

The son of a vaudeville performer born on September 9, 1899—or 9/9/99, he liked to say—Hoyt entertained Reds fans during rain delays with stories about the Yankees, especially "the big fella" Ruth. The stories were so popular that Burger released two record albums, *The Best of Waite Hoyt In The Rain (Vol. I* and *Vol. II)* in the 1960s on Personality Records. Nuxhall and his teammates also tuned in to Waite out rain delays. "There'd be a group of us who would sit around the table in the middle of the clubhouse and listen to him expound about the Yankees. It was interesting," Nuxhall said.

At his press conference after buying the club in 2006, Castellini told how his passion for the Reds was ignited by hearing Hoyt on a clunky old portable radio.

"They called it a 'portable radio,' but it was twenty times bigger than today's portables. I'd hide it under the covers at night when I was six or seven years old," he said. "Some of you may remember, those old radios had vacuum tubes, and they really got hot. One night, I dozed off and that radio got so hot it set my covers on fire. My parents were pretty hot, too. It was a while before I could listen to Waite Hoyt and the Reds again."

⚾ ⚾ ⚾

Among the many awards given to Nuxhall was a lifetime membership in the Miami University Alumni Association. Nux never attended classes there, but "that's where I got started in radio," he said.

In fall of 1963, after his 15-8 Comeback Of The Year season with the Reds, Nuxhall started doing Miami basketball games on Hamilton's WMOH-AM, with sports director Ray Motley. He broadcast four seasons, calling games played by future Redhawks coach Charlie Coles at old Withrow Court. He would tape pregame interviews with coach Dick Shrider using a reel-to-reel tape recorder as big as a suitcase. He would "lug that big box recorder up to the office, and then he'd play back the interview and realize he had it on the wrong settings, and have to tape another," said Darrel Hedric, who was Shrider's assistant before taking over the team in 1970.

Joe was at the mic once when Miami had the ball, with the score tied and time running out. Nuxhall yelled, *Shoot the damn thing!* The player threw up a shot, it went in, and Miami won.

"I'll never forget that. I was embarrassed," Nuxhall said.

Donzetta said Joe's decision to go into radio came as a shock. "I just couldn't imagine him on the radio. English was never his good subject."

⚾ ⚾ ⚾

It wasn't very long into his first year before the Old Lefthander was "rounding third and heading for home" on the radio. Reds coach Whitey Wietelmann, a former infielder-pitcher for the Boston Bees (later Braves), told Joe he needed a catch phrase. He suggested: "This is the Old Lefthander rounding third and heading for home."

Joe thought the expression was too corny, in all honesty. He told me his initial response: "Jesus Christ, Whitey!" Wietelmann persisted and Nux agreed to give it a spin. "I tried it for about 10 days and I said, 'Shit, that's terrible! I'm not using it anymore.' So I stopped using it for a week or so. And then I started getting mail saying, 'Hey, you stopped using the Old Lefthander!' It was really neat. I guess they liked it," he said.

They loved it, without a doubt. It was immortalized in lights when Great American Ball Park opened in 2003.

To promote their new radio star, Wiedemann's delivered three-foot by two-foot cardboard cut-outs of Nuxhall to bars and convenience stores. Nux was pictured sitting behind a Reds on Radio microphone, wearing a red pinstriped baseball uniform with Wiedemann's Fine Beer logos on his chest and hat.

"NOW! Joe Nuxhall pitches for Wiedemann Fine Beer," the sign said.

Perhaps you've seen one in the Reds Hall of Fame. I first saw the poster in 1996, when Nuxhall gave me a tour of his photos, plaques, awards, autographed baseballs and other memorabilia displayed in his Fairfield home basement. Nuxhall took me into his workshop and pulled the old Wiedemann's poster from behind the door. Photographer Gary Landers asked him to pose with it. Nux liked the idea.

"It hides my belly," he said.

Nuxhall had a rocky rookie year for Wiedemann with McIntyre and Sullivan. "I was nervous. I was scared to death, and I thought I had to say something every pitch. I wore those guys out—and me too," he said. When Nuxhall announced in 2002 that he would retire at the end of the 2004 season, he said that McIntyre, Sullivan, Michaels and Brennaman "helped me an awful lot, because I was pretty bad. And it hasn't improved a whole lot," Nuxhall said with a laugh.

⚾ ⚾ ⚾

One of Nuxhall's most famous calls came just five weeks on the job. Nux went nuts calling a walk-off win in the 10th inning at Crosley Field on Monday, May 15, 1967. The audio clip has appeared in numerous Nuxhall retrospectives. It's also played when the Hamilton Joes, a college-age, wooden-bat league team in Nuxhall's hometown, win at Hamilton's Foundation Field.

It happened when Tony Perez doubled to center with two outs and Pete Rose on first. Rose raced around the bases to beat the Pirates, 8-7, after the Reds had clawed back from deficits of 4-0 and 7-5.

NUXHALL: There's a long drive into centerfield. That ball can't be caught! It might be out of here! It's off the boards. Rose around second! Now he's around third! And he's going to score easily! And we win! We have won the ball game! Yes sir, my first win on the mic! I'm happy! I'm happy! I'm happy!

I didn't hear Nuxhall on radio that night because I was at the game. I went with Greg Hume and Robby Brandenburg, two classmates at St. Mary's School in Middletown. Mr. Brandenburg took us as an early eighth-grade graduation celebration for us.

It was a great game. Perez was 4-for 5, scored three times and drove in two. Lee May was 3-for-4 with four RBI. Rose scored three times. Future Hall of Famer Roberto Clemente hit three home runs for the first time in his career. Clemente, the 1966 NL MVP, was 4-for-5 for the Pirates with seven RBI, raising his batting average to .390 on the way to his fourth batting title. He smashed the third homer with two out in the ninth, a solo shot off Gerry Arrigo, to go up 7-5. May tied it in the ninth with a homer after Perez singled.

Nuxy had every right to be as excited as a giddy teen-ager when the Reds won despite Clemente's heroics—because we were, too ... without a doubt.

⚾   ⚾   ⚾

Midway through the 1968 season, Joe Nuxhall made a very important announcement during a Reds game. To me, at least. Nuxhall told WCKY-AM listeners that the Kiesewetter family from Middletown was at the Reds-Astros game in the Houston Astrodome on Monday night, July 1. We heard about it when we got home.

On the way to the 1968 World's Fair in San Antonio, my parents took us to the new Eighth Wonder of the World—the Houston Astrodome. Every summer we'd take a vacation. If there was a World's Fair in the United States, that was the destination for Mom and Dad. As teen-agers during the Great Depression, Dad went to the 1933 Chicago's World's Fair, and Mom went to the New York World's Fair (1939-40). My parents took us to World's Fairs in Seattle (1962), New York (1964), Montreal (1967) and San Antonio (1968).

We arrived at the Astrodome early to tour the indoor facility. We ate supper at tables behind the right field wall, watching batting practice through screened windows. While we went to our $2.50 reserved seats on the mezzanine level, Dad must have slipped a note to the broadcast booth on the press box level. I've since seen it done over the years, baseball fans getting as close as possible to the press box and handing a note to the guard.

In the 'Dome, we saw a great game. The Reds won 3-2 in 11 innings. My 25-cent scorecard shows me that Perez opened the 11th with a walk, stole second, took third on the catcher's throwing error, and scored on Tommy Helms' sacrifice fly. Maloney gave up two earned runs on nine hits and striking out eight in eight innings. I love looking at my old scorecards for the hidden gems they reveal:

- Big Bob Watson, feared slugger for the Astros, Yankees Red Sox and Braves, hit lead-off for the Astros as a 22-year-old in his first full season. Watson, remembered as a first baseman, was in left field while 22-year-old Rusty Staub played first. After retiring in 1984, Watson was general manager for the Astros and Yankees, and a Major League Baseball vice president.

- May, the Reds "Big Bopper," also played outfield that night. He moved from first to right in the ninth, with Rose moving from right to center when pinch-hitter Don Pavletich stayed in the game to play first. A stat check showed, to my surprise, that May played 88 games in left or right in 1967-69, before becoming full-time first baseman in 1970. (How many remember Joey Votto playing outfield when he came up in 2007, because Adam Dunn and Josh Hamilton were injured?)

- Rose entered the game hitting .345. Left fielder Alex Johnson was hitting .314, second on the team. Johnson, 25, was acquired from the Cardinals in the offseason for Dick Simpson, 24, the outfielder from the Frank Robinson trade before the '66 season. Johnson was a nice surprise at the plate, finishing fourth in the National League in batting (.312) and hits (188); seventh in doubles (32); and eighth in triples (6).

⚾ ⚾ ⚾

For the second straight year, manager Dave Bristol's Reds in 1968 finished fourth (83-79), buried 20 games behind the Cardinals. But it wasn't hopeless. "I saw the Big Red Machine being built. Some of us were teammates: Pete Rose, Tommy Helms, Johnny Bench and Tony Perez," Nuxhall said.

Bench, 20, gave the club its third Rookie of the Year in six years, following Rose (1963) and Helms (1966). Rose won the first of his three batting titles, and finished second for NL Most Valuable Player. The last weekend of the season, Rose went 5-for-5 off Perry in a Saturday home loss to the Giants, 10-4, to raise his average to .335. Pirates outfielder Matty Alou went 4-for-4 to head into the last day of the season at .334.

"Gaylord pitched that day, and I got 5-for-5 off him," said Rose at a 1991 press conference I attended. "Matty was playing in Chicago, and he got 4-for-4. And I remember after I got my fourth hit—I hit one down the left field line—Gaylord looked over at me and said, 'You got enough yet?' And I said, 'Not if I get another at-bat.' And lo and behold, I needed that next hit. Gaylord Perry threw me 15 spitballs one night. And he'd say, 'Hit the dry side, you son of a bitch.' He was a great competitor."

On Sunday, Giants lefty Ray Sadecki held Rose to a first-inning double to finish .335. Alou went hitless, dropping to .332.

Nuxhall, after retiring to radio rather than be traded, watched Howsam transform the club in the late 1960s. Howsam added Sparky Anderson, outfielder Bobby Tolan, shortstop David Concepcion, left-handed starter Jim Merritt and relievers Clay Carroll and Wayne Granger to the young core who played with Nuxhall. Gone were Bristol, Maloney, Cardenas, Pappas, Arrigo, Pinson, Sammy Ellis and Ted Davidson.

⚾ ⚾ ⚾

In 1970, Nuxhall said goodbye to an old friend. Nuxhall and McIntyre broadcast the last Crosley Field Opening Day, a 5-1 win over the Montreal

Expos behind Merritt. Nux had only missed two Crosley Field openers in 19 years—playing with Kansas City in 1961 and with the Angels in 1962.

For the first time in years, the Opening Day excitement lasted all season. Merritt blossomed into an ace, winning 20 and losing 12. Sparky's Big Red Machine tore up the National League, winning 70 of their first 100. The Reds said farewell to Crosley with a come-from-behind 5-4 victory over the Giants on June 24, on back-to-back homers by May and Bench in the eighth off pitcher Juan Marichal. After the game, home plate was flown by helicopter to Riverfront Stadium. The Reds opened Riverfront Stadium on June 30 with a 52-22 record (.703) and a 9½-game lead in the Western Division over the Dodgers. Cincinnati hosted the All-Star Game two weeks later, on July 14, which turned out to be a dress rehearsal for the World Series. It was a magical year, with a marvelous new 51,000-seat multipurpose stadium on the river, plenty of parking and easy access for fans throughout Reds Country.

Baseball had been played in Cincinnati's West End since 1884. More than three decades after Crosley Field had closed—and after Riverfront Stadium had come and gone—Nuxhall reminisced about the intimacy of the 29,603-seat ballpark at Findlay Street and Western Avenue. When I asked what he missed about Crosley, he said, "the friendliness of it. The way we had to get out onto the field was by walking through the stands."

Players walked across the main concourse under the third base-side seats to get from the clubhouse to a tunnel leading to the field. The design of Crosley's grandstand was similar to Wrigley Field from foul pole to foul pole. Crosley had two decks with wooden seats. Metal columns supporting the upper deck and roof blocked the view for some folks. I love taking my sons to Wrigley and telling them how it reminds me of Crosley. Until a recent renovation, the Cubs clubhouse was tucked under the second deck stands, as was the original Reds clubhouse.

"In the 1940s, the clubhouse was up on the second floor," Nuxhall said in 2006, three years after Great American Ball Park opened. "You had to walk down these iron steps in your spikes, and then you had to walk a couple hundred feet through the fans to get to a tunnel to get onto the field. We'd go right by the concession stand. Later on, they built the tunnel to left field beyond third base. But you still had to walk down through the fans to get out on the field."

Phil and Kim Nuxhall knew the place inside and out from coming to Crosley early with their dad in the late 1950s and '60s. Often Reds TV analyst Frank McCormick would carpool with them from Fairfield.

"We'd get down there super early for batting practice," Phil said, "and Kim would get on the field and toss with the players, and I would go and sit right behind the organ and wait for Ronnie Dale to start playing. Ronnie Dale was my idol. He's the reason I took organ lessons."

"Talk about a dream life for a kid who loved baseball," Kim said. "I was shagging fly balls at seven years old in the outfield with Robinson, Pinson, Bell and Wally Post."

⚾   ⚾   ⚾

"Get outta here! Get outta here!"

That's my favorite Nuxy phrase. It sums up his unbridled enthusiasm for the Reds, and life, and why Reds fans loved him so much. For years I'd use it when co-workers stayed late working on a story at the *Enquirer*, well past their scheduled shift. I could tell they were dragging. Someone needed to tell them to go home. So I'd walk by their desk and say:

"Like the Old Lefthander says: Get outta here! Get outta here!"

Reds fans associate Joe's cheering with working with Marty. You'd hear him yelling in the background as Brennaman called a home run. But it wasn't a Marty and Joe thing. If you listen to highlights record albums from 1970 with Nuxhall and McIntyre (*The Big Red Machine*), or from 1972 with Michaels (*The New Red Machine*), you'll hear Nuxy wildly cheering balls out of the ballpark. It's a carryover from his playing days, rooting for a blast to clear the cozy Crosley confines. He always felt he was part of the team, especially since he started every day in the clubhouse putting on a Reds uniform to pitch batting practice. He was unapologetic. Hamilton Joe was a Reds fan his entire life. He didn't get upset when people criticized him for rooting for the Reds.

Once I asked if he considered his radio role as an analyst, commentator or fan. "I'm what you say more the analyst-fan, than the commentator.

I've been questioned about it many times. Look, we have 100,000 people listening to a broadcast, and 85 percent of them are Reds fans. So who do you satisfy? The 15 percent or the 85 percent? That's my theory on it. I'll get some fan mail on it. But right away you know they are a Cubs fan or a Cardinals fan. You read it right like that. It doesn't bother me."

Translation: Cubs and Cardinals fan can just *get outta here, get outta here.*

Meet the Beatles

When the Beatles played Crosley Field on Sunday, August 21, 1966, Phil Nuxhall hatched a plot to meet the Beatles. Phil had been a huge fan of the Fab Four since seeing their TV debut on the *Ed Sullivan Show* in February 1964 with his brother, mother and father. "Dad just laughed and kept on shaking his head. I think he was just stupefied," Phil said.

Seated in the grandstand with his Fairfield Junior High School friends, Phil told them he knew the band must be in the Reds clubhouse where his dad had a locker for pitching batting practice.

"It was so off-the-beaten path, nobody else knew. They followed me as we ran frantically to the clubhouse. There was a steep, two-level ramp off the main concourse going up to the clubhouse door. And as soon as we get there, the door bursts open and one by one the Beatles came down the ramp. They were three inches from us! And of course, the girls were screaming at the top of their lungs. That was a thrill. They had their instruments over their shoulders. I remember them wearing their 'Beatle suits' with red pinstripes."

Entertainment reporter Dale Stevens wrote that Paul McCartney "showed me his red belt, and said it was our team colors, meaning the Redlegs," in the clubhouse before the concert.

Here's a trivia question that will stump most Reds fans: Who is the only guy to play in Crosley Field, Riverfront Stadium and Great American Ball Park?

Paul McCartney.

5

A Wild Pitch! Here Comes Foster!

Al Michaels was only 26 when he debuted with Nuxhall on Reds flagship station WLW-AM in 1971. CINCINNATI ENQUIRER PHOTO

Journalists are trained not to use the word "we," but it's appropriate here. We take great pride in the Reds being the big league launching pad for Al Michaels. When we've seen him on NBC's *Sunday Night Football*, and before that on ABC's *Monday Night Football*, the Olympics, or calling the "Miracle On Ice" hockey game, we boast that Michaels started with Joe Nuxhall on the Reds Radio Network.

We felt a sense of affirmation when Michaels was inducted into the Television Academy Hall of Fame, honored with a Sports Emmy Lifetime Achievement Award, received a star on the Hollywood Walk of Fame, selected for Cooperstown's 2021 Ford C. Frick Award or presented the Pro Football Hall of Fame's Pete Rozelle Radio & Television Award, the equivalent of baseball's Frick Award. We knew he was something special. But before we break an arm patting ourselves on the back in Cincinnati, there's something you need to know: Michaels wasn't the Reds' first choice. The club made a run at someone with Major League broadcasting experience before hiring Michaels from the Triple-A Hawaiian Islanders in the Pacific Coast League.

Tops on the list for Nuxhall's new partner was Houston Astros' announcer Harry Kalas, says John Soller, the Reds' first director of broadcasting in fall of 1970. Soller, the longtime general manager of WKRC-AM in the 1980s, oversaw Reds broadcasting operations until 1973, before Jim Winters. Kalas, 35, debuted in 1965 with the Astrodome opening. After six seasons he wanted out of the shadow of veteran Houston voice Gene Elston. Kalas also wanted to do both TV and radio. So Kalas instead went to Philadelphia in 1971, where he did Phillies games for 38 years. Kalas would have been a fine pick. He received the Frick Award in 2002, two years after Brennaman.

A change in radio beer sponsors after the 1970 World Series, from Wiedemann to Detroit-based Stroh's, brought the change in play-by-play voices. Jim McIntrye "withdrew" as a candidate for the job he had done for four years on November 17, exactly one week before the Reds announced hiring 26-year-old Michaels. Like Brennaman and Barber, Michaels had never broadcast a Major League Baseball game. Michaels and Nuxhall called the first Opening Day at Riverfront Stadium on April 5, 1971; no-hitters by the Cubs' Ken Holtzman and Phillies' Rick Wise in 1971; and the 1972 National League Championship Series against the Pirates. After three years, Michaels took the San Francisco Giants radio job to be closer to Los Angeles.

Michaels left with a large debt of gratitude to Nuxy. Joe "couldn't have been more gracious, introducing me around town and making sure people knew I had his stamp of approval. In Cincinnati, where the Reds are almost like a public trust, his support made a huge difference," he wrote in his 2014 autobiography, *You Can't Make This Stuff Up: Miracles, Memories and the Perfect Marriage of Sports and Television.*

In a video played during Nuxhall's retirement ceremony at Great

American Ball Park on September 18, 2004, Michaels told Joe: "I'll never forget the way you took me under your wing when I came to Cincinnati, and people were saying 'Who's that guy?' and 'He's too young to be announcing!' You made it easier for me, something I'll never forget." Michaels thanked Nuxhall for teaching the ins and outs of traveling with a big league team. And the "inns" and outs.

"I can't thank you enough for getting me up for the two o'clock feeding most nights. Of course, that feeding was normally a Stroh's Light."

Michaels witnessed Nuxhall's unparalleled popularity when he carpooled with him to Greater Cincinnati Airport before a Reds road trip. "We have about 10 minutes to catch the plane. You explain the plight to the cop out on the curb. He said, 'No problem, Joe. Just leave it right here.' But we'll be gone for 10 days! The guy said, 'No problem, Joe.' And we got back 10 days later, and there was the car—completely washed."

Michaels almost turned down the Reds, too. He had second thoughts about coming to a city that "had two dominant colors on that November day, gray and brown … with the streets looking like Warsaw at rush hour," he wrote in his memoir. Reds Speakers Bureau Director Gordy Coleman drove Michaels around Greater Cincinnati and Northern Kentucky neighborhoods before the club offered him the job. That got Michaels thinking. "I had grown up in Brooklyn, and then moved to Los Angeles. Now I am living in Hawaii. How could I possibly tell my family and friends: We've just moved to Kentucky!"

Brennaman was dumbfounded reading Michaels' 2014 account of cruising neighborhoods with Coleman, a former first baseman who played with Nuxhall. The same thing happened to Marty. "I couldn't believe it. Gordy Coleman took Al around, Gordy Coleman took me around to all these different areas of the city. It never, ever occurred in my mind that they were offering me the job."

There was another similarity. Dick Wagner, Howsam's top assistant, warned each of them to not get too close to Pete Rose, the club's star player, or Bob Hertzel, the *Cincinnati Enquirer's* brash young baseball writer. It was Wagner's way of trying to control the narrative Reds fans heard on the radio.

Reds executives "wanted you to not like the people covering the Reds. They hated Hertzel. They thought Hertzel was a guy who would break confidences," and not keep information off the record and out of the paper. "After a year or two, I realized all that was not true, that Bob was the consummate baseball beat writer … and he'd never break your confidence. I talked to Hertzel about it one day, and he said, 'Al told me the same thing.' They didn't want me to like Bob. They didn't want me to like Pete. The longer I worked for them, the less inclined I was to be intimidated by them," Brennaman said.

Michaels' first year in Cincinnati was Sparky's worst (79-83), his only Reds losing season. The defending 1970 National League champs fell to fourth, 11 games out. Howsam knew the club needed more speed on the Riverfront Stadium artificial surface. One of his targets was Astros second baseman Joe Morgan.

In the final weeks of the '71 season, Howsam talked to Anderson, his coaches and scouts on how to improve the team, according to Anderson's 1978 book, *The Main Spark,* with Si Burick. They discussed the possibility of trading former Rookie of the Year Tommy Helms and/or first baseman Lee May; moving Tony Perez from third to first; and acquiring an infielder and a starting pitcher. While in Pittsburgh for the 1971 Pirates-Orioles World Series, Anderson and scout Ray Shore told Howsam they heard the Astros were talking to the Dodgers about trading Morgan for first baseman Wes Parker. Howsam tracked down Astros general manager Spec Richardson, who promised not to "do anything about a Morgan trade until he heard from Cincinnati," Anderson wrote. The Monday after Thanksgiving, Howsam announced the deal for the final pieces of the Big Red Machine: May, Helms and utility infielder Jimmy Stewart for Morgan, right-hander Jack Billingham, shortstop Denis Menke and outfielders Cesar Geronimo and Ed Armbrister.

How different would the NL West have been if Morgan had joined

Dodgers infielders Steve Garvey, Bill Russell and Ron Cey to create a Big Blue Machine?

"Are you kidding me? Getting Morgan was the single greatest trade this franchise has ever made, when you consider what it meant to the team. Howsam knew people were going to raise hell because of trading Lee May and Tommy Helms," Brennaman said.

Howsam was right. Reds fans were furious—until the Reds returned to the World Series in 1972, and won the 1975-76 World Series. "Little Joe" Morgan was a big cog in the Machine, leading the National League in runs, walks and on-base percentage (.417) in '72, and winning the NL MVP in 1975 and '76. He also won five straight Gold Gloves (1973-77) and was an All-Star all eight seasons with the Reds.

Ⓧ   Ⓧ   Ⓧ

By his own account, Michaels was young and naïve when he first sat next to Nuxhall in the radio booth. But the networks quickly noticed his work. After his Reds debut season in 1971, NBC Sports offered him his first NFL games. Then he was asked to be one of the eight NBC announcers for the 1972 Winter Olympics in Sapporo, Japan. Yes, only eight announcers did NBC's Winter Olympics back then.

Michaels did one hockey game, the 1972 gold medal match between the Czechs and Soviet Union. That experience earned him the ABC Sports' hockey assignment for the 1980 Winter Games. Everyone remembers him calling the United States upset of the Soviet Union at Lake Placid, New York. His exuberant *Do you believe in miracles? Yes!* was heard 'round the world on February 22, 1980. Two days later, the USA team completed the miracle on ice, winning gold against Finland.

In 1972, with Morgan hitting second behind Rose, the Big Red Machine rolled to its second pennant in three years. Michaels was at the mic on October 11 when Johnny Bench homered to right in the ninth to tie the Pirates 3-3 in Game Five of the NLCS at Riverfront Stadium. For a generation of Reds fans, it was Michaels' most memorable moment, even after the '80 Olympics.

MICHAELS: The wind. And the pitch to Bench. Change. Hit in the air to deep right field. Back goes Clemente! At the fence! SHE'S GONE! Johnny Bench, who hits most home runs to left, homers to right and the game is tied!

Perez singled, and was replaced by pinch runner George Foster. With two outs and Foster on third, reliever Bob Moose threw the most famous wild pitch in Reds history.

MICHAELS: In the dirt! It's a wild pitch! Here comes Foster! The Reds win the pennant!

NBC again invited Michaels to work with Curt Gowdy on NBC's World Series TV and radio team. The Oakland Athletics won in seven games. "That was a hell of a year for me," Michaels said.

Without a doubt.

When we talked in 2014 about his book, I told Michaels I still get chills when I hear his 1972 Bench home run call and Moose's wild pitch. Forty years later, Michaels had vivid memories, too.

"Oh, I can see every part of that in my mind, believe me. And I can feel the way the crowd responded. It was fantastic. I find that the really memorable calls made by broadcasters through the years for the most part come from the heart, not from the brain. Clearly, I'm seeing that with my eyes, but I'm also seeing that with my heart, as the announcer for the Reds. And in 1980, it's the Olympics, and if there's anything you could ever do on national television where you know you have an audience that's 99 percent going one way (supporting a team), that would be it. It's not that I said those words in Lake Placid because of that. I look back retrospectively now, of course, and it works because everyone is thinking the same thing in this country. But to me, it was spontaneity. You see something and you let it go. And all you can do is hope that the right words come out, because you have to live with it."

Michaels marveled at how times had changed since his Cincinnati days.

"Forty years ago, when you're making a call of an event, you're not thinking about how it plays in posterity. You've got hand-held tape recorders and cassette machines back then. It's not like it is now. No matter what you say—if you say something to somebody at dinner—there's a recording device there, and that lives on forever. It winds up on YouTube. It's *NOT* going to go away."

⚾   ⚾   ⚾

After the Reds lost the 1973 National League Championship Series to the Mets, Michaels accepted an offer to be the radio voice for the San Francisco Giants, who were tripling his salary. He told me he signed with the Giants because the rights holder also controlled UCLA basketball rights. From the West Coast he did regional NFL games for NBC, which led to ABC's *Monday Night Baseball* and *Monday Night Football,* and back to NBC for *Sunday Night Football* with John Madden and later Cris Collinsworth. The Giants also wanted him to do TV, the same reason Kalas rejected the Reds. Four decades later, Michaels wondered what would have happened if things hadn't fallen his way.

"I had very high hopes and aspirations, and probably had enough confidence at the time—but it was born out of naivete more than anything else," he said before a 2012 NBC telecast from Paul Brown Stadium. "There was a part of me that kind of felt things were going to work out really well. I got that great break at a very young age to wind up with a team that has just won a National League pennant in 1970."

Leaving Cincinnati was the right move, of course. NBC Sports claims Michaels has been seen on prime-time TV more than anyone in history. He's the only person to call the Super Bowl, World Series, NBA Finals, NHL Stanley Cup Finals and Winter and Summer Olympics on network TV.

"It's worked out great. But I look back now, and I go 'Whoa! Boy!' I'm glad I didn't know how many pitfalls there were, how many crazy things can happen, how much luck you need, how you have to be in the right place at the right time. I had great fortune all the way through."

What if the Giants job wasn't open in 1974? What if NBC didn't give Michaels a shot on NFL games or the 1972 Olympics? What if Michaels settled in next to Nuxhall and stayed longer? Maybe Brennaman would have ended up somewhere else?

Do you believe in miracles?

⚾ ⚾ ⚾

Good ol' Joe. He got along with everyone. The nicest guy on earth. Michaels couldn't have asked for a better teacher. Ditto for Brennaman.

"I know Joe and Michaels had a great relationship. But Joe bent over backwards for me in 1974. I didn't know anything about anything. He showed me the routines. He was in a position to make my life difficult, but he didn't," said Brennaman, who was hired from the Triple-A Tidewater Tides. Brennaman remembered Joe's kindness when Jim Kelch was promoted from the club's Triple-A Louisville Bats to the Reds Radio team (2010-17). "Many of the same things Joe did with me, I shared with Kelch."

Nuxy was one of a kind.

"I've never met anyone who was so completely, and solidly, and totally devoid of an ego," Brennaman has said often. "Honest to God, I've never known a person with a measure of celebrity who had zero ego like he did. I mean, we're in a business that breeds egomaniacs. I was blessed that I've been associated with him all those years. He taught me a hell of a lot about humility, because I've got a pretty good ego."

Once I asked Nuxhall how he gets along with everybody.

"Heck, it's not difficult," he said. Nuxhall explained his philosophy as only he could: "It's always been a good relationship (with radio partners). That's been very important. Whoever we work with, we've always got along with. That's important in any business, so to speak. Your partners, you get along good, and things turn out good. If you start to bicker, and accusing one another of different things, then problems crop up. With all these guys, there's never been a problem with any of them."

When Brennaman accepted his Frick Award in Cooperstown on July 23, 2000, Marty thanked the Old Lefthander before he mentioned his own family.

"It's awfully nice to work with a living legend, and that's what I've done since 1974. Whatever success I've had, I willingly and gratefully share it with the Old Lefthander, Joe Nuxhall," Brennaman said as Reds fans cheered Nuxy's name. "I can never begin to repay what he has meant to me. He's been a mentor, and he's also been a very, very wonderful friend.

Thank you, Joe, for so much of the things you've taught me since that first year together. "

Nuxhall, however, wasn't the first one Brennaman mentioned.

"There's one person I want to thank right out of the chute, and that's … Al Michaels. Had Al not left after the '73 season to go to the San Francisco Giants, I wouldn't be here today. So Al, wherever you are, thank you very much!"

Little Buddy

When Marty met Joe: This publicity photo was shot in Dayton during the Reds Caravan on Feb. 1, 1974, Marty Brennaman's first day on the club payroll.
CINCINNATI REDS PHOTO

On his way to a Reds Caravan appearance at Suttmiller's restaurant in Dayton on February 1, 1974, Joe Nuxhall stopped by a Dayton photography studio. The Reds needed publicity photos of Joe with the Reds' newest employee, 31-year-old native of Virginia Marty Brennaman. They shook hands.

"I've got your baseball card," Brennaman said.

Nuxhall, six-foot-three and 234 pounds, had met his new Little Buddy. "That was the beginning of a very special and very unique relationship," said Brennaman, who is five-foot-eight. "I can't imagine anybody had a better relationship than we had for each other. We genuinely loved each other."

Marty didn't know much about "Hamilton Joe" that day, his first on the club payroll. "I had his baseball card back in the 1950s, when I was 12, 13 or 14 years old. I knew what most people know, that he made his debut back in 1944 at age 15," he said. There's no way Brennaman or Nuxhall could have dreamed in 1974 that they would become an iconic part of Cincinnati Reds history, known simply by their first names like the team stars they broadcast: Sparky, Pete, Johnny, Tony and Barry.

Brennaman was called up from the Triple-A Tidewater Tides radio booth from 221 candidates. Reds Vice President Dick Wagner made the hiring for President Bob Howsam, after a group of employees reviewed their audio tapes. Until that day in Dayton, Nuxhall had only heard Brennaman's voice on tape.

"I always remember Marty walking through the door," Nuxhall recalled with a laugh in 2002. "I heard this voice on tape, and I thought, 'This must be a big ol' boy!' Then he walks through the door!"

⚾ ⚾ ⚾

Brennaman had heard Nuxhall once on the radio before they met. He tuned in WLW-AM while driving home from a Tides night game and caught Nuxhall and Michaels doing a Reds games.

As a young baseball fan in Norfolk, Franchester Martin Brennaman did what I did as a kid in Middletown. He scanned the radio dial at night to tune in baseball games from distant cities. I listened to the Detroit Tigers' Ernie Harwell; the St. Louis Cardinals' Harry Caray and Jack Buck; the Atlanta Braves' Milo Hamilton; and if the weather cooperated, the Astros' Gene Elston from WWL-AM in New Orleans. Brennaman, born July 28, 1942, in Portsmouth, Virginia, dialed in Milo Hamilton; Chuck Thompson of the Baltimore Orioles; Arch McDonald of the Washington Senators; and Nat Albright of the Brooklyn Dodgers. He also listened to Bill Currie do University of North Carolina basketball.

Albright lived outside of Washington, D.C., and re-created games—broadcasting them from a studio and embellishing telegraph information with sound effects—for 113 stations from Cleveland to Miami Beach, according to Curt Smith's *Voices of the Game*. Young Marty didn't realize Albright was nowhere near Brooklyn.

"That's how good they were. It was my first introduction to baseball on the radio. I had no idea this guy was sitting in a radio studio in Arlington, Virginia, broadcasting Dodgers baseball from a ticker tape. He had all the ambiance—vendors, the crack of the bat, the crowd noise—and I was just enthralled by his work. I was not a Brooklyn Dodgers fan, but I was just drawn to him. I think listening to him subconsciously planted the decision in my brain as a 12- or 13-year-old that this is what I want to do for a living," he said.

⚾ ⚾ ⚾

Before baseball, books were Brennaman's passion. Marty spent most of his childhood reading in his bedroom. His father, Chet, "was worried about me. I just read books. Then I discovered baseball."

Brennaman grew up in southeastern Virginia, four hours away from the woeful Washington Senators. He didn't see his first Major League game until he was about 12, when his parents surprised Marty and brother Tom during a trip to Washington, D.C. by taking them to two Senators-Yankees games at Griffith Stadium. During a 2017 Reds' road trip to the Washington Nationals, Brennaman told radio listeners about his memories—Yankees great Mickey Mantle going 5-for-5, Yogi Berra hitting a home run, and manager Casey Stengel batting pitcher Tommy Byrne eighth ahead of light-hitting shortstop Billy Hunter. Marty cheerfully pointed out that Stengel hit the pitcher eighth 50 years before Cardinals manager Tony LaRussa was thought by some to have invented the move. The Yankees beat the last-place Senators 6-0 and 4-0.

"We drove up to Washington, and drove past Griffith Stadium. We didn't know it, but they already had tickets," Brennaman said. He'll never forget walking into the old ballpark, built in 1911, to see "the greenest grass I'd ever seen. It's one of the most vivid memories that I have."

The lush green grass is also one of my most vivid memories of Crosley Field, and my first impression of Detroit's Tiger Stadium when Sparky Anderson managed there in 1980. That's what makes baseball unique.

People just don't talk about their vivid memories of going to their first NFL or NBA game. But they remember their first Major League Baseball game.

Brennaman could recall details of his first games—but not the year or scores. My reporter's instincts kicked in, and I searched Baseball-Reference.com for Yankees-Senators box scores in Washington, during Byrne's four seasons in pinstripes (1954-57), and for a 5-for-5 game by Mantle in which Berra homered. I found them: July 8-9, 1955. Byrne was enjoying his best season at age 35, en route to a 16-5 record. A career .238 hitter, Byrne was 1-for-2 in the eighth spot. Hunter (.211) was hitless batting ninth. Taking the loss was 21-year-old Camilo Pascual, a future five-time All-Star who would "Wash Up On The Banks Of The Ohio" with the Reds in 1969.

The next day's box score confirmed Marty's memory. Mantle, 23, hit four singles and a double, scoring three times. Berra, 30, went 3-for-4 and drove in all four runs. Brennaman remembered Berra's homer in the third—but not his triple to center in the first, or double to right in the ninth. Yogi was a single shy of the cycle! I would have loved seeing Yogi legging out a triple. Or hearing Marty describe it on the radio, without a doubt.

⊗   ⊗   ⊗

For a while, Brennaman considered becoming a different kind of entertainer, a professional actor. He enjoyed being in plays at Woodrow Wilson High School in Portsmouth, and performed in summer stock productions after his freshman year at Randolph-Macon College, a private all-male liberal arts college near Richmond, Virginia. Then he met a couple of off-Broadway actors who were practically starving.

"And I realized, no pun in intended, that I didn't have the stomach for it," he said.

As someone who made a living broadcasting baseball and basketball, Brennaman made a rather startling comparison between professional actors and athletes. Actors "are the most talented people in the world. They talk about baseball players, or football or basketball players, but they can't hold a candle to those people on Broadway who sing, and dance, and emote and act. I get goose bumps thinking about it," he said.

His father, a Pet Dairy manager, and mother Lillian, a longtime employee of the Chesapeake & Potomac Telephone Company, didn't push Marty or Tom down any career paths—although "if my mother had her druthers, I would be an attorney," Marty said. With his acting ambitions benched, Brennaman decided a radio play-by-play career was "the next best thing. I didn't want to be a guy who did the six and 11 o'clock (TV) sports. I wanted to be in the field, and broadcasting ball games." During his junior year, he transferred to the University of North Carolina, where he earned a bachelor's degree in communications at UNC in 1965.

Brennaman, who for years denigrated television as "the dark side" when partner Jeff Brantley missed radio games to do two dozen Fox Sports Ohio telecasts, actually started his career on TV. At 22, fresh out of UNC, Brennaman spent six months as a 7-8 a.m. news co-anchor with Aquilla Thacker on WGHP-TV in High Point, North Carolina, because he couldn't find a radio job. Before summer ended, Brennaman was hired by WSTP-AM in Salisbury, North Carolina, to do play-by-play for Catawba College football and basketball, high school sports, American Legion baseball and the local Soap Box Derby. After the ABA Washington Caps moved to Roanoke in 1970, Norfolk's WTAR-AM wanted someone with a local tie to call the games. Chet Brennaman suggested his son to a WTAR salesman. So Marty came home to do the new American Basketball Association Virginia Squires in 1970, and added Tides baseball and William and Mary College and Virginia Tech football.

Brennaman's theater training wasn't for naught. His skills at using voice inflection and pauses heightened the drama as he described important plays on the diamond. He conveyed the excitement by elevating his voice as he punctuated his delivery with short bursts of description.

"Swung on! Fly ball! Deep left-center field! And it's GONE! A home run!"

The style endeared him to Reds fans for 46 years and earned him a place in Cooperstown.

⚾ ⚾ ⚾

At the 1973 Major League Baseball winter meetings in Houston, Dick Wagner mentioned to Tidewater general manager Dave Rosenfield that he needed a play-by play announcer to replace Al Michaels. Rosenfield said the Reds should check out Brennaman. Wagner asked Rosenfield to have Marty send him a tape. He did. So did 220 others.

Of all of those applicants, Brennaman probably was the least interested in being Nuxhall's partner. He was having the time of his life traveling the country doing ABA games. The Squires in 1971 had drafted Julius Erving from the University of Massachusetts, and the acrobatic "Dr. J" led the Squires (45-39) under coach Al Bianchi to the ABA finals, losing to the New York Nets. The Squires added George Gervin in 1972, and lost in the playoffs to Louisville's Kentucky Colonels.

"I didn't care about the Reds job, one way or the other," Brennaman told the Reds Hall of Fame's Joe Nuxhall Chapter in Hamilton in 2018. "I loved basketball. Had I stayed with basketball I would have gone to the NBA when the merger came (in 1976). I had no idea Al had left. I only did it out of courtesy to Dave. Had it not been for a chance meeting between Dick Wagner and Dave Rosenfield, I would have never come to Cincinnati because I really was enamored with pro basketball."

Reds executives truly were conducting a national search. "We were wide open. No one had a favorite candidate to fill the job," said Roger Ruhl, the Reds publicity director in the early 1970s who later oversaw marketing for the Greater Cincinnati Chamber of Commerce. At least three candidates, Ruhl said, had Major League Baseball experience. Monte Moore was the main voice of the Oakland A's; Jim Woods had been the secondary man for the Pirates, Cardinals and A's (and would be hired by the Red Sox in 1974); and future Hall of Famer Dave Niehaus was the third guy in the Angels booth behind Dick Enberg and Don Drysdale. Niehaus would leave LA in 1977 to take the Seattle Mariners job and win the Frick Award in 2008.

Niehaus was born in Reds Country—in Princeton, Indiana, north of Evansville—but was considered a West Coast talent because of his work with the Angels, Los Angeles Rams and UCLA football and basketball. The Reds were wary of West Coast guys. Michaels and publicity director Tom Seeberg didn't stay long in Cincinnati. So the Reds passed on three men with big league experience to hire a second straight announcer without any. "I tell people I got the job because I was cheaper than them. I know I made less money than they did," Brennaman said.

But it wasn't a slam dunk for the voice of the Virginia Squires.

⚾   ⚾   ⚾

There was a problem with Brennaman's audition tape. The sound quality was very poor when Brennaman called a Tides game at the Rochester Red Wings in noisy old Silver Stadium.

Broadcasting director Jim Winters winnowed down the 221 tapes to about 30. Then he called a Saturday listening session in Wagner's Riverfront Stadium office for Ruhl; Publicity Director Jim Ferguson; Assistant Publicity Director Bob Rathgeber; Speakers Bureau Director Coleman; and Wagner. "At some point, someone went out and got a case of beer, so listening to the tapes became a lot more enjoyable," Ruhl said.

Despite the inferior sound, Brennaman's tape made the cut. Wagner was concerned about the "tinny sound of the broadcast. Wagner said it sounded like he didn't have any balls," Ruhl said. Ironically, Wagner would learn over the next decade that Brennaman had plenty of guts, particularly when pushing back against Wagner's complaints about Marty's critical style.

The group decided Winters should call Brennaman in Virginia to request a second tape. As he was explaining the quality issue to Brennaman, Winters started laughing. Why? Because Wagner "was grabbing his crotch, like he doesn't have any balls," Ruhl said. Ruhl felt sorry for Brennaman. The young broadcaster was getting a call about a big league job, and was being told his tape wasn't very good, then heard laughter on the other end of the phone. Brennaman agreed to send another tape. Wagner also asked Ruhl to call his old friend, Virginia Tech Sports Information Director Wendy Weisend, for a character reference on Marty, who was also the Hokies' play-by-play voice.

About a month later, *Norfolk Pilot* sportswriter George McClellan had news for Brennaman after covering the old Virginia Wings hockey team playing the Cincinnati Swords at Cincinnati Gardens. McClellan learned Brennaman was one of the Reds' 10 finalists.

"At that point, I decided that maybe I should have an interest in this (Reds) job," Brennaman said. As he was preparing for a Squires trip to play at the Indianapolis Pacers on a Saturday, Winters called and asked Brennaman to come to Cincinnati on his way to Indiana. They took him to dinner at the five-star Maisonette restaurant. The next day Coleman gave him an area tour, and he met Howsam. Before leaving town, the Reds offered him the job. Marty wouldn't give them an answer until he returned home from Indiana and talked with his wife. On Sunday afternoon, he accepted the job.

"It was a three-year deal, with the club's option after the first year," Brennaman said. "They could have canned me after the first season. But after the first season they opted to pick up my contract for the next three years, and I was home free."

On Monday, January 21, 1974, the Reds announced that Brennaman, 31, the top sportscaster in Virginia for the past three years, was the Reds' new voice.

"We think Marty Brennaman is one of the bright, young announcers in the country, and we feel sure that his voice and enthusiasm will quickly become popular with our great fans," Howsam said in the release

"I feel very privileged to be the choice as the voice of the Reds. An announcer in the minor leagues dreams of this opportunity ... If somebody could hand-pick the situation he wanted, I can't think of a better one than in Cincinnati. It's a contending team every season and should be for years to come," Brennaman said in the release. It concluded by saying that "as a play-by-play man, Brennaman will be working with Joe Nuxhall, longtime color man on the Reds' vast six-state radio network."

⚾ ⚾ ⚾

Once he had established himself in Cincinnati, Brennaman was lured back to basketball.

He did basketball television play-by-play for the NBA Pacers (1982-84), Atlantic Coast Conference (1984-86), University of Kentucky (1987-88) and Southeastern Conference (1989). He also broadcast 15 NCAA college basketball regionals and 11 NCAA Final Fours on radio. The University of Cincinnati wanted Brennaman to do Bearcats basketball in 1980, but the Reds denied permission.

He was at the CBS Radio mic in March 1992 for the NCAA East Regional final in Philadelphia when Duke's Christian Laettner hit a buzzer-beater for the defending national champs to knock off Kentucky in overtime, 104-103. Grant Hill threw an inbounds pass nearly the length of the court to Laettner, who dribbled once and fired a jump shot as time expired. *Sports Illustrated* called it the greatest college basketball game of all time in 2004; *USA TODAY* called it the greatest NCAA tournament game in 2002.

"It's the best college basketball game I've ever seen, and a lot of people who were there said it was the best one they had ever seen," Brennaman told me in August of 1992, six months after Laettner bombed the Big Blue. "I've had some great NCAA games, and great games make you better than you really are. When I do the NCAA every year, that's one of the highlights of my year, doing college basketball on the radio."

Brennaman was at peace with his career reversal, doing basketball in his offseason from baseball, instead of the other way around. Doing Reds games with Nuxhall in Cincinnati was such a perfect fit for Brennaman that he turned down more than a half-dozen overtures from other Major League Baseball teams. More about that later.

"I've never had a problem working with anybody," Brennaman told me in 1986, as he tried to explain the magic of Marty and Joe. "The chemistry between us, though, is unique. It's really amazing. From the first day we've always seemed to convey that, one, we were having a good time, and two, that we were having a good time because we genuinely enjoy being with each other."

Nuxhall put it this way back then: "We just get along. When we're on the road we'll go out to dinner together. We get along real good. We're able to make fun of each other, and we understand it and go with it. That's part of it."

Brennaman often said he was born to do radio. Although he did the Reds and basketball on TV, his first love was radio. The pictures are better on radio, especially when they are provided by a wordsmith like Brennaman.

"I love radio. I was born and raised on radio. I think doing baseball on the radio is the biggest challenge for a play-by-play announcer. I don't care what sport it is—I've done them all—this is the hardest one to do," he said. Basketball and football are so fast-paced that the announcer merely describes the action. A baseball announcer must fill time between the action with stories for three hours. "Anybody can do TV. Radio is so much more fun. I don't think there's anything like baseball on the radio."

Marty wasn't just born to do radio. He was born to do baseball with the Old Lefthander. Without a doubt.

7

Marty & Joe

Joe tosses a baseball to a fan in the green Plaza Level seats beneath the WLW-AM booth at Riverfront Stadium as Marty Brennaman and Bill "Seg" Dennision watch in 1999.

JOHN KIESEWETTER PHOTO

Just four batters. That's how long it took on Opening Day 1974 for the Reds new radio team of Joe Nuxhall and Marty Brennaman to record history on April 4, 1974.

Atlanta Braves outfielder Hank Aaron had waited all winter to tie Babe Ruth's seemingly unbreakable record of 714 home runs. Aaron being on the doorstep of baseball history was the talk of the town. I remember it well.

On April 3, tornadoes ripped through Cincinnati's Sayler Park neighborhood, damaging some buildings on Galbraith Road just east of Interstate 75, and obliterating most of Xenia, Ohio, about 55 miles northeast of Cincinnati and 15 miles east of Dayton. The powerful F5 tornados killed 33 people, injured more than 1,300 and damaged 1,200 homes in Xenia. It was one of a "super outbreak" of 148 twisters in a 24-hour period in the Midwest and South.

I was a junior journalism major at Ohio University in Athens at the time. I remember Columbus TV reports about personal papers and checks from Xenia raining down on Columbus—60 miles away—after being sucked up by the tornado. After sundown, news wire machines at *The Post*, OU's independent daily student newspaper, began reporting damage in Cincinnati and Xenia. The Ohio Highway Patrol sealed off Xenia, so fellow *Post* reporter Dale Keiger and I decided to drive overnight to do a story about the Sayler Park damage. While driving to Cincinnati, I was struck by two things: How bright the full moon was, as if blushing in embarrassment to illuminate Mother Nature's wrath; and how WLW-AM newscasts reminded listeners of the Opening Day broadcast just hours away, with Aaron poised to make history.

Hammerin' Hank didn't disappoint. Neither did Brennaman. Reds pitcher Jack Billingham walked lead-off hitter Ralph Garr, gave up a single to Mike Lum and got Darrell Evans to fly out before Aaron came up.

BRENNAMAN: Outfield shaded around toward left for Aaron. Billingham with the pause. The 3-1 pitch. Swung on! Long shot into deep left field! Rose is back, and that ball is gone! A home run!

NUXHALL: Unbelievable!

BRENNAMAN: Henry Aaron has just tied Babe Ruth's home run record of 714 with a clout over the 375 marker in left. The Braves are piling out of the dugout. The crowd is on its feet en masse here at Riverfront Stadium as Hank Aaron has just hammered a 3-1 pitch from Jack Billingham over the left-field wall, and the Braves are out in front 3-0.

The game stopped for a presentation at home plate by Major League Baseball Commissioner Bowie Kuhn and Vice President Gerald Ford. But the sell-out crowd went home with a win. The Reds rallied late, when Tony Perez hit a three-run homer in the eighth off knuckleballer Phil Niekro, and 1973 Most Valuable Player and batting champ Pete Rose doubled in George Foster in the ninth to tie the game. The Reds won 7-6 in the 11th when Rose doubled with two outs and scored from second on Buzz Capra's wild pitch.

When they went to the commercial break after the top of the first, Joe asked Marty, "What the hell are you going to do for an encore?"

Marty said, "I don't know. That's a pretty good way to start."

⚾ ⚾ ⚾

Sometime in his first month at Riverfront Stadium—Brennaman doesn't remember exactly when—the words just blurted out of Marty's mouth after a dramatic win: *"And this one belongs to the Reds!"*

"About three weeks into the first year, Davey Concepcion got a hit—it was the bottom of the ninth, or the bottom of an extra inning here at home—to win a game. And I just said it," Brennaman recalled. Instantly he knew he had something special—an iconic phrase for a Reds win, a line even Nuxhall loved to exclaim after an extra-inning victory.

My research of 1974 box scores indicates Marty probably first uttered his signature saying in his 16th game on Wednesday afternoon, April 24 against the Cubs. Starters Billingham and Bill Bonham were locked in a scoreless duel going into the ninth. Billingham had allowed five hits. Bonham, who would pitch for the Reds in 1978-80, had given up only three when Concepcion led off the ninth with a double. Bonham intentionally walked Cesar Geronimo. Terry Crowley tried to bunt the runners over, but Bonham threw out Concepcion at third. After Rose popped out to shortstop, Joe Morgan legged out an infield single with the runners holding. With the bases loaded, Bonham walked Foster—a walk-off walk—for a 1-0 Reds win. *And this one belongs to the Reds!"*

"I started thinking: Damn! This isn't too bad! I may just use this every time they win," Brennaman said. "And it's the best thing that ever happened to me."

Without a doubt.

⚾   ⚾   ⚾

It took 99 games for Brennaman to feel he'd been accepted as Nuxhall's partner and had finally vanquished the ghost of Al Michaels. After the All-Star Game the Reds resumed play on July 25 by sweeping the Giants in a twi-night doubleheader at Riverfront.

In the first game, the Giants scored 12 runs in seven innings off Clay Kirby, Pedro Borbon, Dick Baney, Will McEnaney, Clay Carroll and Tom Hall. Reds catcher Johnny Bench slammed a two-run homer to close the gap to 12-9 in the eighth. Billingham, in his only relief appearance that year, promptly served up a homer to Bobby Bonds in the ninth.

Then the Reds answered. Danny Driessen singled with one out in the ninth off closer Randy Moffitt. Merv Rettenmund walked. Rose singled in Driessen. Rettenmund scored on Morgan's grounder to first. Then

Bench reached on an infield hit that scored a run because Moffitt failed to cover first on a grounder to first baseman Dave Kingman. "Had he left the mound, Bench is out and the game is over. It gave Tony Perez a chance, and Tony took the ball to straight-away centerfield. The Giants were stunned. And I went crazy," Brennaman said.

BRENNAMAN: Moffitt mopping his brow. Quickly two strikes out in front of Perez. Has his sign. The pitch. Fly ball to center field! IT'S ALL OVER! IT'S ALL OVER! THE REDS WIN IT! THE REDS WIN IT! THE REDS WIN IT! A home run to center field by Tony Perez! THE REDS WIN IT! THE REDS WIN IT! 14-13! Perez with a home run to centerfield! The Reds have scored five times in the ninth inning and the Reds win on a Tony Perez home run to centerfield! OH MY GOLLY! HOLY COW! WHAT A FINISH!

WLW-AM listeners requested Marty's electrifying call throughout the night.

"That game made me feel like I had finally arrived as a broadcaster here, as far as a replacement for Al Michaels was concerned," he said.

And this guy belongs to the Reds—next to Nuxy!

⚾   ⚾   ⚾

Nuxhall and Brennaman called 98 wins and 64 losses their first year together. Bench led Sparky's 1974 club with 33 home runs and 129 RBI, followed by first baseman Perez with 28 homers and 101 RBI. The Reds finished second to the Dodgers, whose 102-60 record matched the Big Red Machine's 1970 and 1976 records.

By contrast, Michaels started his Reds career in 1971 by calling Anderson's only losing season in Cincinnati (79-83). After the 1970 World Series, the Reds finished fourth, tied with Houston. The following two seasons, Michaels and Nuxhall called back-to-back Western Division championships. Brennaman arrived in 1974, when the Reds came from 10 games out on July 9 to nearly catch the Dodgers. The pennant race helped fans accept Marty as Joe's partner.

"In 1971, Al's first year, the Reds were beat up because of injuries. I was lucky because I came in to replace Al in a year in which the Reds were very good. They didn't win the division, but they were damn good. The 'This one belongs to the Reds!' caught on because they won so much. Had I developed that line in 1982, when they were the worst team in baseball, it would have never caught on."

⚾   ⚾   ⚾

Reds fans know all about the 1975 Big Red Machine. They won a club record 108 games with only 54 losses, which still stands today. That included a Major League record 64-17 at home.

The Reds won the World Series over the Red Sox in seven games. Morgan won the '75 MVP award by leading the Reds in average (.327), triples (6), walks (132) and steals (67). Rose, who moved from left field to third base May 3 to get Foster into the lineup, led the team with 210 hits. His .317 batting average was eighth in the National League, but he scorched Boston pitchers at a .370 clip (10-for-27) to win the World Series MVP. Bench and Perez provided a powerful one-two punch: Bench with 28 homers, 110 RBI and a .283 average; Perez with 20 homers, 109 RBI and a .282 average. Foster contributed 23 homers, 78 RBI and a .300 average in only 134 games.

Brennaman had a good year, too. In his second year in Cincinnati, Brennaman helped NBC broadcast the World Series instead of Nuxhall, who had just completed his ninth year on radio. Wagner chose Marty over Joe. Years later, Brennaman said Wagner picked the wrong man.

"Quite honestly, it wasn't fair to Joe in '75 and '76 that he wasn't allowed to represent the club. By all rights, Joe should have been the guy to be there, not me. That was a Dick Wagner call. I think that really bothered him. And if it were me, it would have bothered me, too. But he never let it affect what we did as a team."

NBC, which held the World Series television and radio rights, used one home-team announcer from each participating club with Curt Gowdy, Joe Garagiola and Tony Kubek. Just 33, Brennaman was on national TV for Games Three, Four and Five from Riverfront Stadium, and on radio from Fenway Park. Nuxhall, 47, the Reds' most experienced broadcaster, was left sitting in the stands.

The NBC TV booth was frosty, but not from the early October chill. Gowdy, NBC's Saturday baseball *Game of the Week* announcer, and analyst Garagiola, weren't getting along. Executives at Chrysler, a major sponsor, insisted that their TV spokesman Garagiola—the former Cardinals catcher and *Today* show personality—be added to the '75 World Series TV team. Both "were battling to be No. 1, and Garagiola had the Chrysler contract in his back pocket. To their credit, they both treated me well, but it was a little icy. Gowdy treated me royally, because I was scared to death," Marty said.

It was the last NBC World Series for Gowdy, who continued to call NFL games for NBC, and later NFL and college football for CBS and ABC. It was also Brennaman's only World Series on TV, because NBC stopped using participating team announcers. In 1976, Brennaman was invited to join Brent Musburger and Win Elliott to call the World Series on CBS Radio. Joe sat in the stands again. Another change years later allowed Marty and Joe to do the 1990 World Series for the Reds Radio Network.

They call Game Six of the Reds vs. Boston Red Sox 1975 World Series the greatest game ever played. Boston, down three games to two on their home field, won in 12 innings on Carlton Fisk's walk-off home run.

Former Red Bernie Carbo had tied it 6-6 in the eighth with a two-out, three-run homer off Rawly Eastwick. After the Red Sox loaded the bases with no outs in the ninth, Fred Lynn lifted a fly ball down the left field line to George Foster, who gunned down Denny Doyle at the plate for a double play. In the 11th, Joe Morgan drilled one to deep right with Griffey on first. Dwight Evans jumped to make the catch at the wall and then doubled up Griffey. Sparky sent rookie starter Pat Darcy (11-5) to the mound in the 12th. With a 1-0 count, Fisk hit a towering shot down the left field line. He stood at the plate, waving his hands above his head, motioning for the ball to stay fair. His body language became the enduring image of the '75 Series.

I never spoke to Nuxhall about the game, but Brennaman told me several times about his view of Fisk's walk-off shot.

"When the Reds took a 6-3 lead in the eighth, they said, 'Go downstairs to the clubhouse for the postgame celebration.' So I sat there on a folding chair in the Reds clubhouse watching a black-and-white TV. I saw Bernie Carbo hit the three-run home run to tie the game in the bottom of the eighth and never went back upstairs. When people ask me how exciting it was to be in the ballpark that night, I say, 'It was no more exciting than you sitting at home watching the game on TV.'"

(Game Six trivia from Brennaman: Before the Carbo homer, writers voted to give the MVP award to Eastwick, who had two wins and a save. "The Carbo home run changed everything," Brennaman said.)

After the game, Rose was more confident than his manager. Sparky could see his chance of winning an elusive world championship slipping away for the third time in six years. When I talked to Pete in 2013 for the 50th anniversary of his Reds debut, he said: "After Fisk hit that home run, Sparky said, 'Big Red Machine? When are you going to win something! Big Red Machine my ass!' And I said, 'Spark, we've got them right where we want them. Relax. Take it easy.'"

It didn't look good in Game Seven when Boston scored three off 15-game winner Don Gullett in the third. Bill Lee (17-9) held the Reds scoreless until the sixth, when he tried to fool Perez with an "Eephus" blooper pitch, and Tony hit it out of the park. In the ninth, Griffey and Rose walked, and Morgan hit a two-out single to score Griffey for the 4-3 win. When the Reds won the title, Nuxhall "was just bawling like a baby," said Rick Stowe.

Years later, as Joey Votto and the Reds were heading into the 2012 postseason, I asked Brennaman to rank his favorite playoff moments. Game Six in 1975 topped his list. "In its entirety, that is arguably the greatest single baseball game ever played. There were so many great moments in the game: George Foster's catch in the ninth in left field, and throwing out Denny Doyle. And Dwight Evans made a great catch in right field in the 11th to rob Joe Morgan of a home run."

Ken Burns, the Emmy-winning PBS filmmaker—and a huge Red Sox fan—used Fisk's home run gyrations prominently in his 18.5-hour *Baseball* documentary in 1994. After Burns waxed poetically about Fisk's feat at the Television Critics Association press tour to promote *Baseball*, I had a couple of questions for him: Wasn't there one more game? Didn't the Reds win the seventh game, the Big Red Machine's first of back-to-back world championships?

Burns smiled sheepishly. "For me, it ended that way," he said.

Without a doubt, there was a seventh game. And this one belonged to the Reds.

⚾   ⚾   ⚾

What do you do for an encore after winning the greatest World Series ever? The Reds rolled through the NL with a 102-60 record the next year and swept the Yankees in the World Series. During the 1976 World Series, concluding Brennaman's third season with Nuxhall, retired Phillies announcer Byrum Saam asked Marty, "Young man, do you realize how lucky you are?"

Brennaman, never short on confidence, flippantly replied, "Yeah, I guess I do." Then he asked Saam what he meant. Saam explained: "You realize that you've been here three years and you have two World Championship rings? And I've been doing this since 1938, and I've yet to get one."

Saam, 62, had been waiting 40 years to call a champion. He became the first full-time radio voice for the American League Philadelphia Athletics in 1938, when Nuxhall was 9 years old. In 1939, Saam also added the National League Phillies, doing home games for both through 1949 (because radio announcers didn't travel back then). Each was a perennial second division dweller. Saam didn't call a winning season until 1947. When radio stations started doing road games in 1950, Saam stayed with the Athletics and missed the Phillies "Whiz Kids" NL championship. After the A's moved to Kansas City in 1955, Saam rejoined the Phillies—when Marty was 12, and Joe was heading to his first All-Star Game. Saam retired in 1975, but returned to help Harry Kalas call the Phils' game as they clinched the 1976 NL East pennant. The Reds swept the Phillies in the NLCS, and the Yankees in the World Series, and Brennaman got the ring again.

⚾ ⚾ ⚾

For more than three decades, Marty and Joe were the soundtrack for my summers. For many years only 47 games were broadcast by WLWT-TV and Reds television network, so fans tuned in Brennaman and Nuxhall from March to October in their dens, cars, kitchens and backyards. Nuxhall was the veteran broadcaster and beloved former player, but Brennaman got top billing because "Marty and Joe" rhymed with "on Reds Radio" for a nifty promotional jingle.

Brennaman also broadcast most of the game—the first, second, fifth, sixth, eighth and ninth—so the majority of the historic highlights came with Marty at the microphone. He called Pete Rose's hit No. 4,192; Ken Griffey Jr.'s 500th and 600th home runs; the final outs of Tom Browning's perfect game; Hall of Famer Tom Seaver's only no-hitter; both of Homer Bailey's no-hitters; the 1990 World Series; and Jay Bruce's NL Central-clinching home run in 2010.

"I've been lucky, because every time I've had a big moment, I don't feel like I screwed it up. Because it's going to be replayed ad nauseam for the rest of your life—and after you're gone," Brennaman said.

Nux only called three innings—the third, fourth and seventh—but he always had the final say on his *Star of the Game* show. (More on that later.) Doing only a third of the game limited his chances to call memorable moments, but I found some. In 1979, I thought Nuxy might leap out of the Riverfront radio booth when skinny Dave Concepcion muscled a home run into the top deck against the Montreal Expos. Concepcion's clout on June 9, 1979, was only the Reds' ninth "red seat homer" in 10 years—by a guy who hit only 101 homers in 19 years.

NUXHALL: Three and one. The wind. The pitch. Concepcion hits it deep to left field. (Warren) Cromartie looks up. And Davey got a whole bunch of—I don't believe it. I DO NOT believe it! I DON'T believe it! Dave Concepcion has just hit a ball in the red seats in left field! UNBELIEVABLE!

On April 18, 1981, he called Seaver's 3,000th strikeout.

NUXHALL: And the 1-2. Swung on and missed! He got him with

a high fastball! And that's No. 3,000 for Tom Seaver. And what a hitter he strikes out! Unbelievable! A standing ovation here for Tom Seaver here at Riverfront Stadium. His 3,000th strikeout, with the strikeout of Keith Hernandez!

When ESPN viewers showed pitcher Norm Charlton ignore third base coach Sam Perlozzo and try to score on *Sunday Night Baseball* June 24, 1990, radio listeners heard Nuxhall describe Charlton barreling into Dodgers catcher Mike Scioscia.

NUXHALL: Here comes Benzinger (home). Charlton's going to be held up at third base. But he's going to run through the stop sign! The throw to the plate! And I mean a real collision, and Charlton is safe!

Joe's call of catcher Jeff Reed's grand slam off the Padres' Andy Benes in 1991 was replayed in the postgame audio montage during the 1992 season: "*Reed swings and pulls it down the right field line! That might be outta here! IT IS! GRAND SLAM HOME RUN FOR JEFF REED!*"

On Johnny Bench Night—Bench's last game catching before retiring—Brennaman hosted the on-field pregame ceremony with Cincinnati TV personality Bob Braun on September 17, 1983. Inside my scorebook is a ticket stub for a $7 green plaza-level seat in Section 244 behind third base, my Johnny Bench Night "Certificate of Attendance" and a "We [Heart] Johnny Bench" bumper sticker.

Michaels, Nuxy's former partner, flew in from Los Angeles for the festivities. Michaels told the sold-out crowd: "When I first met Johnny, and he asked me to be the co-host of his *Johnny Bench* (nationally syndicated) television show in 1971, I heard him sing for the first time—and that's when I thought to myself, I hope this guy can catch." When Michaels visited Nuxhall and Brennaman in the booth for the second inning, Joe joked that Al was as tight with a dollar as Marty.

MICHAELS: I told Nux that I'd never spend more than he weighs!

NUXHALL: At the time I only weighed 230!

As Bench stepped to the plate in the third, the perpetually optimistic Nuxy told listeners he wanted "to see John let loose at bat, and hit his 12th home run of the year." He did. Nux went nuts.

NUXHALL: The 0-1. Swung on and hit well to left field! Get outta here baseball! IT'S GONE! Oh my God, can you believe it? Johnny Bench has tied it up! AMAZING! ABSOLUTELY AMAZING! He makes the tour, and I'll tell you what, you can't write anything like this! ABSOLUTELY AMAZING! I don't believe it! What more can you do to cap an evening? He is getting a hero's welcome ... The Astros, some of them are on their feet. And this is absolutely amazing! I mean a line drive! It's one of those no-doubters, if it's high enough, and it was high enough! And it's tied 2-2! And now John is out of the dugout, he's waving to the fans. My, oh my, oh my! Well, if anyone could write that script, it would be worth a multitude of dollars! ... AND HE DID IT! JOHNNY DID IT!

Bench told me his last Riverfront home run was extra special because Nuxhall was at the microphone. "He had tears in his eyes. It was just one of those special unbelievable moments for me, because of what it meant to Joe, and our friendship, and our respect for each other," Bench said.

Nuxhall and Bench did the postgame show on stools at home plate for all to see and hear. As he sometimes would, Joe opened with a statement instead of asking a question about Bench's 389th career home run, or about catching after playing most of the year at first or third base.

NUXHALL: Before we go any further—No. 389. There it is!

BENCH: I was nervous, I tell ya. I let a guy steal on me. I felt like a rank rookie over there to begin with when I walked out behind the plate. I couldn't have asked for anything better than to hit a home run, and this was for everybody here! It's just the greatest feeling, obviously, to my parents and myself. It was the greatest night of my life.

Nuxhall noted the banners around Riverfront Stadium. One read "BENCH: Baseball Excitement Near Cincinnati's Heart."

BENCH: When I circled the bases (with his index finger in the air), I've never done that in my career, so tonight was kind of special. And that's why I said it was for No. 1 Cincinnati. And that home run was for everyone here.

Six years later, Bench was inducted into the Baseball Hall of Fame on July 23, 1989. The *Cincinnati Enquirer* printed a 28-page commemorative section chronologically listing his career achievements. The *Enquirer* noted that after Johnny Bench Night, he homered in his final at-bats in Philadelphia and St. Louis. The next entry read:

"Sept. 30, 1983: Bench hits a home run with his last swing of the bat—off batting practice pitcher Joe Nuxhall."

Marty and Joe, Davey and Danny. That's what was left of the Big Red Machine in 1984—shortstop Concepcion and first baseman Driessen—after Bench retired, eight years after the '76 World Series. The rest of the Great Eight were gone, and so was the winning record. Perez was traded after the '76 series. Anderson was fired by Wagner in '78 after two straight second-place finishes. It didn't matter that Sparky was the Reds' best manager by victories (863-586) and winning percentage (.596).

The big purge came after the 1981 strike-shortened season, when the Reds had the best overall record (66-42) but didn't make the playoffs. Commissioner Bowie Kuhn split the season in half; the Reds finished second in each to the Dodgers and Astros. The Reds celebrated their "Best Record In Baseball" with a banner at the end of 1981, then fell from first to worst (61-101) after dumping George Foster, Ken Griffey Sr. and Ray Knight. The 1982 Opening Day lineup introduced catcher Alex Trevino (acquired from the Mets for Foster), rookie right fielder Paul Householder, center fielder Cesar Cedeno (from the Astros for Knight), future Pirates manager Clint Hurdle (from the Royals), Bench at third and Mario Soto on the mound. The Reds also moved up weeknight games from 8:05 to 7:35 p.m. so the final score would make the morning *Enquirer*, after Wagner met with *Enquirer* editors. The club also lowered the outfield walls, making it possible for Eric Davis to jump and steal a potential homer that Cesar Geronimo couldn't have reached.

All the losing made Nuxhall and Brennaman even more popular. Reds fans didn't tune in for the lousy games, they wanted to hear Marty and Joe. Vin Scully had told Brennaman in the late 1970s, while the Big

Red Machine was flattening opponents, that announcers improve their game when the team stinks.

Brennaman said, "I became a better broadcaster going through 1982, '83 and '84. You can't say: 'Well, if the Reds win tonight, the Reds will only be 19 games behind Atlanta because the Braves lost tonight.' Who cares? So you have to stay away from the pennant race, and take each game as a season unto itself."

Without a pennant race to talk about, Joe and Marty chatted about everything from pro wrestling, Elvis Presley, golf, gerbils, dog racing, wedding anniversaries (*"Ain't love grand!"*), to their tomato plants. Once when Marty promised to bring a photo of his ripe tomatoes to the game (years before iPhones or Instagram), Joe found that unacceptable. He wanted to inspect one, inside and out.

"I might want to take it down to the clubhouse and get Bernie (Stowe) to get me a saltshaker and go to work on it," Nuxy said. For years, Reds fans asked them about their tomato plants. "That's when you know people are listening. People loved that," said Dave "Yiddy" Armbruster, Reds Radio producer-engineer since 1987.

"We're not making something up for the sake of trying to endear ourselves to the people who listen to us, and make them erroneously think that we're one of them. I've got tomato plants. If people don't believe me, they can come to see them," Brennaman said in 1992. Later that summer, the *Cincinnati Post* sent a photographer to his home and printed a picture of Brennaman with his tomato plants for a story about the local tomato harvest.

There were times when the Marty and Joe show was more fun than baseball. When San Francisco 49ers All-Pro defensive back Deion Sanders was playing center field for the Reds in a 1995 spring training game in Plant City, Brennaman told listeners that the flashy two-sports star would be performing as a rap artist after the Reds-Tigers game. Marty speculated that Joe would join Sanders on stage.

BRENNAMAN: Deion will be performing tonight at the Club Atlanta, and rumor has it that Joe will be also rapping tonight with Deion to "She'll Be Coming 'Round the Mountain."

NUXHALL: No! No! There's a change.

BRENNAMAN: … You say they've changed the musical plans? It's not "She'll Be Coming 'Round The Mountain?"

NUXHALL: "Wabash Cannonball."

BRENNAMAN: You're going to rap to the "Wabash Cannonball?"

NUXHALL: Imitate Dizzy Dean. If there's a curtain call, we're going to throw in—uh—the one that I don't know.

BRENNAMAN: "After You're Gone?"

NUXHALL: "After You're Gone." Yes sir!

BRENNAMAN: That's good! … Have you picked out your attire for tonight yet?

NUXHALL: I've got it on.

BRENNAMAN: [LAUGHS HEARTILY] That will be big! I like that— [SEVERAL VOICES TALKING AT ONCE] If they'd outfit you in leather, you'd look like a couch.

NUXHALL: In those blue jeans, you'd look like an easy chair.

BRENNAMAN: I know it. But we'd both be comfortable! [BOTH LAUGH]

⚾   ⚾   ⚾

Marty was talking during a game about Elvis Presley, and out of the blue he declared 1996 "The Year of the King," 19 years after Presley died. Reds fans responded by sending Elvis memorabilia to decorate the Riverfront Stadium radio booth: velvet wall hangings; posters; photos; postcards; an "Elvis Presley Blvd." sign; a sketch of Elvis, Marty and Joe; concert tickets; a rare Elvis Barbie doll in its original box; an Elvis lamp; and a large Elvis bust which sat next to Marty in the window.

"It was just amazing the stuff that we got that the fans sent, that we displayed in the booth. That was one of those typical spur-of-the-moment things that came out of nowhere," Brennaman said. "Nothing was put on. It was all genuine. Everything was heartfelt. We never sat down and said, 'Why don't we do this because the fans will love it?' We never did that."

Reds Radio cashed in on Elvis the next year, with Brennaman reading a daily "Elvis Fun Fact" sponsored by Carlisle Equipment. Armbruster and WLW-AM producer Rich Walburg wrote the trivia bits, including this one from the last game in 1997:

BRENNAMAN: Years before becoming the King's manager, Col. Tom Parker worked as a carny, with a show called 'Col. Tom Parker and his Dancing Chickens.' The chickens danced because Parker covered a hotplate with sawdust, and then played music while they hopped up and down because of the heat. That's our all-time, classic Elvis Fun Fact!

The Kroger Company elevated their celebrity status by hiring them in 1984 to do TV, radio and print advertisements. Nuxhall and Brennaman were so popular that one year a preschool teacher named her classroom gerbils after them. Brennaman read her letter on the air saying that, much to the teacher's surprise, Marty and Joe had become proud parents to Barry, Griffey, Pokey and Casey, named for infielders Barry Larkin, Pokey Reese and Sean Casey and outfielder Ken Griffey Jr. She renamed the pair "Marty and Josephina."

Sometimes Marty mentioned topics knowing Joe had no clue, just to entertain listeners. When Ted Nugent played with a band named Damn Yankees in the 1980s, the rocker popped into the radio booth to plug their Cincinnati concert. Marty was talking to him about the Damn Yankees when Joe chimed in, "Oh yeah, I saw that on Broadway. What a show," referring to the 1950s musical. That was "a typical Joe response," Armbruster said. "That's why people loved Joe. We had so much fun in the booth. I laughed for three hours every night."

Some baseball announcers sound like every game is as serious as World War III. Not Nuxhall and Brennaman. They talked about their lives because "there are other things far more important than whether or not the Cincinnati Reds win," Brennaman explained in 2019. "We talked about our kids—We were self-deprecating—and about a lot of things that may not fly in other cities. All it did, I think, was draw us closer to the fans."

"Up in the booth, Marty and I will find something to say," Nuxhall explained in 1994. "Marty is never at a loss for words. I think he woke up talking."

⚾ ⚾ ⚾

When fans see replays of Pete Rose's hit No. 4,192 off Padres pitcher Eric Show, they hear Marty and Joe's call, even though they weren't doing TV that year. Their voices are the iconic call, replacing WLWT-TV audio by play-by-play man Ken Wilson on September 11, 1985. Few know that Nuxhall was embarrassed later about being too excited that night and stepping on his partner's shining moment.

> BRENNAMAN: He levels the bat a couple of times. Show kicks and he fires. Rose swings—
>
> NUXHALL: There it is! There it is! Get down! Get down! All right!
>
> BRENNAMAN: There it is! Hit number forty-one ninety-two! A line drive single in left-center field, a clean base hit, and it is pandemonium here at Riverfront Stadium. The fireworks exploding overhead. The Cincinnati dugout has emptied. The applause continues unabated. Rose completely encircled by his teammates at first base. Bobby Brown of the San Diego Padres coming all the way from the third-base dugout to personally congratulate Pete Rose. And the kind of outpouring of adulation that I don't think you'll ever see an athlete get any more of. Little Pete fighting his way through the crowd, and Pete being hoisted on the shoulders of a couple of his teammates.

More than 20 years after the Hit King's crowning achievement, Brennaman told me Nuxy apologized for ruining the big moment.

"That was the most embarrassed Joe ever was, because he knew he screwed it up. Every time he heard it—*'Get down! Get down!'*—It embarrassed him. In fact, he said something to me one day. He said, 'I'm sorry.' And I said, 'For what?' And he said, 'For talking over you when Pete got the hit.' I didn't give a shit, but Joe was legitimately embarrassed. It never bothered me—and it doesn't bother me today—because of the relationship we had. But it really bothered him."

100

⚾ ⚾ ⚾

"There it is! There it is! Get down! Get down!"

That was Joe being Joe. Marty knew it. And Marty knew that's why listeners loved the Old Lefthander. He was genuine. He was human. He made mistakes. He always pulled for the Reds, but he wasn't a total "homer." He could be critical at times, often couched in constructive criticism. He was honest and fair, even in evaluating himself.

"I would say I'm a homer, in a sense," Nuxhall said. "But basically I'm trying to make it as nice as I can for whatever happens on the field. And I think we've always given credit to the opposition. If they make good plays, and we're honest about it, and not say, 'What a lucky play!' or this or that or the other thing. That's always been my view."

Early in his career, Marty was a homer, too. He often used what he later considered "the foulest word in the English language" for a broadcaster: the word "We." A prickly scolding by Reds ace "Cactus Jack" Billingham cured him of using the plural pronoun.

"Boy, we really played well last night," Brennaman said to Billingham.

"How many hits did you get? How many people did you strike out?" Billingham replied. The light bulb went on: This one belonged to the players!

"Oh yeah, I was a homer. He was right. I'm not a part of what goes on down there on the field. That was one of the defining moments in my career. I don't use that word," Brennaman said.

⚾ ⚾ ⚾

On Opening Day in 1986, Reds ace Mario Soto outdueled future Hall of Famer Steve Carlton and the Phillies to win 7-4. The phones on Bob Trumpy's WLW-AM *Sports Talk* blew up that night.

But nobody wanted to talk about Soto winning a Reds record fourth consecutive Opening Day, or player-manager Rose winning his second straight Opening Day. Nobody wanted to talk about Eric Davis' three-run homer in the second. They didn't want to talk about Dave Parker going 3-for-4, with a homer, double and single. Or about rookie Tracy Jones going 1-for-3 with a stolen base.

No, callers complained about the break-up of Nuxhall and Brennaman. Executives at flagship WLWT-TV were boasting that they had added Marty and Joe to their Reds telecasts. Fans were not fooled. Channel 5 actually added Marty *OR* Joe. The popular radio duo was never together on TV or on radio. Each did TV with Channel 5 sports anchor Steve Physioc, and worked solo on radio.

"The magnitude of the outcry that night was a shock to us, but it was a compliment to us," Brennaman said a few months into the '86 season. WLW-AM afternoon host Gary Burbank seized on the controversy. He produced a comedy bit with Joe doing play-by-play with a duck, and Marty working with a monkey.

Poor Joe was stuck working alone for six innings on radio while Marty did most of the game on TV. "When you're used to having two people—and all of the sudden you're sitting there for six innings a game by yourself—you don't have the banter going back and forth," Nuxhall said in June 1986, three months into the TV arrangement.

For years, Brennaman had pitched the idea of doing both TV and radio, as his predecessor Al Michaels wanted to do and Dodgers voice Vin Scully had been recommending for years. Finally in 1986, Marty and Joe signed two-year deals to do both. The fans' negative reaction prompted owner Marge Schott to promise the Reds Radio situation would revert to normal in 1987. Brennaman objected. He told me during that season: "I've told her and her attorney that my contract, and Joe Nuxhall's contract, call for us to be on television in 1987, and that any change would result in a lawsuit."

The TV/radio arrangement did not change in 1987, but WLW-AM sports director Andy MacWilliams was added to the radio team to assist Nuxhall. Radio returned to normal in 1988, said Reds Vice President Don Breen, because "everybody wants Marty and Joe back (on radio) hands down—the advertisers, the station and the general public."

Everybody but Marty.

"I'm in one of those positions where I'm so good that it's going to cost me money," Brennaman told me after the TV deal ended. "I knew this was going to happen. I had wanted to do TV for a long time. Now, after two years, it's over. I don't have to be happy about it, and I choose not to be happy about it."

Marty mellowed eventually. He made it clear to me over the years he liked radio much more than TV, where the video delivers the action. Nuxhall agreed. "Radio I enjoy more because, in all honesty, I think we're entertaining people more on the radio, simply because people can't see it. We know we are entertaining those folks. It's really a nice feeling," Nuxy said.

⚾ ⚾ ⚾

They were a somewhat unlikely duo. Those aren't my words. That's how the Cincinnati Reds described Marty and Joe in the 1998 Reds Media Guide book in a two-page article honoring their 25th season together called "Marty & Joe 25 Reds Years of Excellence." The story described how "a somewhat unlikely duo" became "one of the most successful and entertaining tandems in all of sports broadcasting history."

They were The Odd Couple: Hamilton Joe, the folksy hometown hero, and Marty, the "Poofy-Haired Fancy Boy," as *Cincinnati Enquirer* columnist Tim Sullivan dubbed him. Joe cheered balls over the wall with *"Get outta here!, Get outta here!"* just as he did as a player from the dugout. Nuxhall was still part of the team as batting practice pitcher, and was often reluctant to criticize Reds players. If he was upset by poor fielding or a bonehead play, usually he'd lay the microphone on his scorebook rather than say something bad about a player, Armbruster said. Occasionally Joe couldn't refrain from complaining, like when Lenny Harris was caught stealing second against Dodgers ace Orel Hershiser in the late 1980s.

NUXHALL: There goes Harris, and they've got him! Boy, oh boy, oh boy! We're very tricky around here, I'm telling you. That's one way to get out of an inning. I thought you're supposed to win ball games.

Marty always told it like it was. He sounded like the college-educated professional sportscaster he was, leading the major leagues annually in using hyphenated phrases. Joe kept score in his scorebook with a ballpoint pen. Marty had a private stock of No. 1 lead pencils—not No. 2 pencils—which nobody was allowed to touch.

Cubs announcer Pat Hughes, in his 2006 *Marty Brennaman: Voice of the Reds* compact disc, praised Marty's descriptive phrases like "an opposite-field, game-tying, three-run homer." Hughes also marveled at Marty's call of Pete's 4,192: "With Joe and everyone else around him going wild, Marty somehow stayed in control the entire time. That's not easy for a broadcaster in a moment like that. And not many other baseball announcers would have even considered using words like 'unabated,' 'encircled,' 'outpouring of adulation' and 'hoisted.'"

Spoken like a true Hall of Famer, you would say.

Joe was the blue-collar common man at the mic. He delivered a straightforward narrative the best he could. He didn't pronounce every name right. Even Reds players. In 1993 he called new Reds outfielder Cecil Espy "EPP-see," prompting a fan in the Riverfront green seats below the booth to shout: "Joe! It's ESS-pee!" As he approached retirement in 2004, WLW-AM made fun of him in a promo saying that "nobody could call a fly ball to left-right-centerfield like the Old Lefthander." However, he was doing that at least 10 years earlier. I was surprised to see a reference to Joe "mixing up left-center field and right-center field" in a 1993 *Cincinnati Post* story. During a 2005 spring game against the Red Sox in Sarasota, Nuxy got confused again:

NUXHALL: Swung on and hit hard into right-center—LEFT-center field! —There we go again!—I just want to keep you all alert! [LAUGHS] Into second goes Pena. That was a hard one-bouncer by the shortstop into left-center and Wily Mo, with the good speed, is into second easily.

Brennaman will never forget the first time he heard Nux go crazy over a home run. A few weeks into the 1974 spring schedule, Joe leaped out of his seat screaming, *"Get outta here! Get outta here!"*

"I thought he'd fall out of the booth. It was an absolute shock," Brennaman said. "I was wise enough early on to realize that's part of his romance with the fans. They love it because they realize it's genuine. He just wants them to win. In his heart, he's still a player … I don't think there's anybody who has a deeper affection for the game than Joe. He might not articulate it as readily as someone else would, but I don't know anybody who has a greater love for the game."

⚾   ⚾   ⚾

Ask Brennaman about his favorite World Series—and favorite team—and he'll surprise you by saying the 1990 wire-to-wire World Champions. For two reasons: Lou Piniella's Reds came out of nowhere to dominate the National League and sweep the reigning champion Oakland A's. And just as important, the Old Lefthander and his Little Buddy shared the post-season experience together on the Reds Radio Network for their only time.

"While the Big Red Machine teams were the greatest teams I've ever been associated with, the 1990 club was the most special because nobody picked them to win anything when the season began. We did all the NLCS games against Pittsburgh, and the entire World Series. It was a fulfillment for Joe. It meant much more to him," Brennaman said.

After switching to radio in 1967, Nuxhall had remained involved with the team unlike any other player-turned-broadcaster. Nuxhall put on a Reds uniform and pitched batting practice before games for two decades, into the late 1980s. Until 1990, being in the radio booth and the clubhouse every day wasn't as satisfying for Nuxy as playing in a World Series.

"One of the dreams of any professional athlete—whether it be football, baseball or basketball—is to be the world champion, or to play on a world champion team, and I never had that experience," Nuxhall said. "They won a couple of World Series (in the 1970s), and that answered a lot of my dreams, because I threw BP all the time. So you have a feeling that you helped them in some way. I have a ring. But it would have been nice to have two wins and have that ring."

No question about it, basically, in all honesty.

For Reds fans, it was great hearing Nuxy at the mic when the Reds swept the A's. In Game Two, he called slugger Jose Canseco pounding a home run deep into the right-field seats. It didn't surprise me. I was among the media on the field for the A's batting practice, standing behind the batting cage, when Canseco launched one into the left-field top-deck red seats. I thought it was going out of the stadium. I never saw a ball travel that high and far.

Longtime Reds fans will never forget Joe calling Billy Bates scoring the winning run in the bottom of the 10th. Bates was the most improbable hero. The .125 lifetime batter, hitless in eight games for the Reds, singled on an 0-2 pitch from closer Dennis Eckersley. It was Bates' last big league at-bat, at age 26.

NUXHALL: Eckersley delivers. Swung on. A high chopper. Fielding Lansford. He can't handle it! That will be a base hit for Billy Bates. A high chopper, Lansford charging the ball, and couldn't come up with it, so an infield single for Bates with one out.

After Chris Sabo singled Bates to second, catcher Joe Oliver took a strike on the inside corner.

NUXHALL: I'm telling you, he does not throw anything over the middle of the plate. You might as well be ready. 0 and 1. Eckersley checks Bates. He delivers. Oliver swings and grounds it FAIR DOWN THE LEFT FIELD LINE! BILLY BATES WILL SCORE, AND THIS ONE BELONGS TO THE REDS! Well, how about that! Joe Oliver bounces one over the bag down the third base line, Billy Bates scores, and the Reds lead this World Series two games to none!

The Riverfront Stadium center field gate swung open, and in came a convertible carrying Nuxhall and Brennaman. It was "Marty & Joe Night" on September 3, 1993, celebrating 20 years of the radio team, and Nuxhall's 50th year with the Reds. The pregame ceremony was one of the few things for Reds fans to cheer in 1993, after Jim Bowden fired rookie manager Tony Perez (by phone!) after 44 games, and Davey Johnson's team was buried in fifth, 22 games behind the Giants.

"I can't remember the last time I was that nervous," Brennaman told

The Reds honored Marty and Joe in their 20th season together with this baseball card in the Kahn's Reds team set giveaway.

JOHN KIESEWETTER ARCHIVES

listeners during the game after coming through the outfield fence before 26,157 cheering fans. Nuxhall added: "I tell ya, when we came out of that gate out there, I don't care how calm you are! Forget it!"

Bowden announced Brennaman and Nuxhall had signed new three-year contracts. Kroger and WLW-AM released a *Best Of The Reds On Radio* audio cassette tape with highlights from Hoyt, Barber, Michaels, Nuxhall and Brennaman. Earlier in the season, the Reds included a "Marty & Joe" baseball card in the Kahn's Reds team set give-away to commemorate their 20th season (in lieu of a baseball card featuring Schottzie, owner Marge Schott's beloved St. Bernard, which was the Reds' mascot during Schott's tenure).

Bowden presented, "on behalf of Mrs. Schott and the Cincinnati Reds," special gifts to the broadcasters—an inscribed Rolex watch for Marty ("Rolex is a classic, and so is Marty Brennaman") and a new set of Ping Zing golf clubs for Joe. "Unfortunately Joe's golf game has never been as good as his broadcasting abilities. We want to do everything we can to cut down a few strokes and make him more competitive," Bowden said. The pregame ceremony included videos from Sparky, Scully and Piniella.

"I've been broadcasting Dodgers baseball since shortly after the invention of fire, so I understand what longevity means to those who are lucky enough to enjoy it," Scully said. "Joe Nuxhall, fifty years in baseball. Marty Brennaman, twenty years as the voice of the Reds. Cincinnati is so fortunate to have both of you. And you know what? You're lucky to have each other!"

Piniella pretended to be puzzled by the proceedings: "I've seen nights for managers. I've seen nights for players. I've never seen a special night for broadcasters. You guys do a heck of a job calling ball games. Unfortunately, it wasn't the same game I was watching during the three years I was there."

⚾ ⚾ ⚾

When the Reds were bad, Marty and Joe were the best. One of my favorite broadcasts was a 1995 spring training game when the Reds and other teams rounded up softball stars, college baseball players and all kinds of dreamers as "replacement players" during the Major League Baseball Players Association strike that canceled the 1994 World Series and continued into the next year.

The Reds started 0-4 with replacement players of varying skills. Nobody recognized their names, particularly the broadcasters, without a doubt. So Nuxhall and Brennaman found other things to talk about during inconsequential games with irrelevant players. When Joe started whistling in the booth as the Blue Jays blasted the Reds at Plant City Stadium, Marty told listeners: "When the regular players resume, we've come up with the idea of having Joe on the field whistling the *National Anthem*, accompanied by someone playing a Jew's harp." After the fake Reds made their sixth error to give Toronto a 5-3 lead in the eighth, Nuxhall tried to change the subject as Brennaman called the action.

NUXHALL: There's always something interesting to talk about around here. Ricky Stowe is out there playing jai alai. See? ... Pretty good form there, Rick ...

BRENNAMAN: He's practicing for a second career.

NUXHALL: Yeah! Oooh! He smoked him right in the nose!

BRENNAMAN: That game is about like professional wrestling, isn't it? You know what I'm talking about?

NUXHALL: That's what they say. A little tainted.

BRENNAMAN: A tad! Runners will be going here. He swings and he misses, and the inning is over. No runs, two hits, two left. We take her to the ninth ... [COMMERCIAL BREAK] Well, we have mercifully reached the bottom of the ninth. The Jays are leading 5-3.

NUXHALL: What about back-to-back ding dongs?

BRENNAMAN: Back-to-back Johnsons would be just fine to get the boys even, and send this rascal on to about 14 innings!

NUXHALL: You never know! It's that old adage:

TOGETHER: If you swing the bat, you're dangerous!!!...

BRENNAMAN: And it's grounded to third. A nice diving stop. The third baseman up and throwing, and the throw—An errant one!—Takes Markowitz off the bag and his tag—He didn't make contact.

[TO JOE] What's that going to be?

NUXHALL: A knock.

BRENNAMAN: That's a base hit?

NUXHALL: Yes sir!

BRENNAMAN: A ball hit right at him?

NUXHALL: Right at him? He dove for it!

BRENNAMAN: That will be a base hit.

NUXHALL: You said something early on about your glasses. Maybe you better get them checked.

BRENNAMAN: No, they're fine … So the Reds have now outhit the Toronto club, 10-9, but still are two runs short as James Lofton steps in …

NUXHALL: If you want a good meal, now, you're close by, go over to the dog track. In the club (dining room) they have a smorgasbord there Monday through Thursday.

BRENNAMAN: Is that right?

NUXHALL: Thirteen-ninety-five!

BRENNAMAN: It's good, huh? … Two balls and a strike. And it's in the air to center field … And the Reds are down to the last out. Of course, that stuff is like wrestling and jai alai too, isn't it?

NUXHALL: Naw, nobody ain't riding them dogs.

BRENNAMAN: I know that nobody is riding 'em!

NUXHALL: But there have been stories where they drop the gate on their tails. [LAUGHS] And they feed them, and load them down with water before they race. I've heard all these stories.

BRENNAMAN: So have I.

NUXHALL: Of course, one dog weighs 58 pounds and the other weighs 92.

BRENNAMAN: Chris Vasquez fouls it back, strike one.

NUXHALL: And I'm not sure, maybe the one that weighs 92 is a miniature what-do-you-call 'em?

BRENNAMAN: I don't know. What do you call 'em?

NUXHALL: What's that dog that Marge has?

BRENNAMAN: A Saint Bernard?

NUXHALL: A Saint Bernard! Yes!

BRENNAMAN: They'd have a hard time winning.

NUXHALL: With a good haircut!

BRENNAMAN: One strike, two outs and a runner at first …

NUXHALL: It's one of the things I've heard. I've been to the race track a couple of times, horse races, where I've heard people say, "I'd like to choke that jockey." Which is very unfair. But I've yet to hear anybody say, "I'd like to choke that dog" … But I've heard the trainer mentioned! [LAUGHS]

BRENNAMAN: … The Reds an out away from going 0 and 4. And not very impressively, I might add … A slow roller to the first base side, picked up by the pitcher. He throws on to first and that's it. The Reds have dropped four straight, falling to Toronto 5-3 … Three runs, 10 hits and a whopping six errors.

⚾ ⚾ ⚾

Sixty years with the Reds, and Nuxhall spent more than half of them sitting next to his Little Buddy. As Brennaman was retiring in 2019, when the Reds celebrated the 150th anniversary of the 1869 Red Stockings, news stories pointed out that Marty had been around for nearly one-third of the team's history. However, Nuxhall's 64 years represented nearly 43% of the club's 150 years; thanks to Brennaman's references to Joe through 2019, Joe had a presence for 75 years, or half of Reds' history.

Owner Bob Castellini called Nuxhall "the heart of the Cincinnati Reds franchise" at a Fairfield gala in 2007, seven months before he died. "Marty and Joe became a part of every Reds' fans summer nights, as their banter filled the gaps between pitches and plays."

Nuxhall savored the six decades.

"Sixty years in one organization, I'm very proud of that. I'm proud of the association I've had with this ballclub over the years, from the very first day I signed a contract in 1944," Nuxhall said in 2002, when he announced his retirement from full-time radio at the end of 2004. "The thrills I've had as a player, and in the radio booth with Marty, can't be matched in any way … I'm just thankful that I've been healthy enough and able to continue for all these years … It's been a thrill, starting out with Jim McIntyre and Claude Sullivan, and then Marty coming on. It's been a real joy to work with Marty."

In his last years in the booth, Nuxhall was a finalist for the Frick Award, but he never made it into Cooperstown. Brennaman received the Frick award in 2000—and lots of other awards—but Marty often said that doing games with Joe 31 years, and working 46 years for the same club, were his proudest accomplishments.

Brennaman has a wall filled with honors. He's been inducted into the National Radio Hall of Fame in Chicago; the National Sportscasters and Sportswriters Association Hall of Fame in Salisbury, North Carolina; and the Virginia Sports Hall of Fame. The American Sportscasters Association named him one of the Top 50 Broadcasters of all time. (He made my *Enquirer* list of Top 25 national sportscasters from Cincinnati in 2013, too.) Marty also was Ohio Sportscaster of the year 17 times, after being Virginia Sportscaster of the Year four times. Yet doing 5,600 Reds games with Nux meant more to Marty. Their 31-year partnership tied the Major League Baseball radio record set by the Dodgers' Scully and Jerry Doggett.

"The fact that Joe and I were together for 31 years, sitting together side by side, broadcasting Major League Baseball, that's the thing I'm most proud of. The rest of that stuff is fine. Being in the Hall of Fame is sensational. Being in the Radio Hall of Fame is very nice. But working with Joe and being together 31 years—and being one of five baseball broadcasters with 40-plus years with the same club—that means the most to me," Brennaman said. And being with Joe.

"Outside of my dad, he's the most special person I've ever known. And the most beloved man I've ever known."

Nuxhall spent 38 years as a full-time Reds Radio broadcaster. Brennaman was the Reds' voice for 46 years. Only five radio broadcasters spent more than 40 years in the booth with one club: Scully; Jack Buck (Cardinals); Denny Matthews (Royals); Bob Uecker (Brewers) and Brennaman. Baseball fans call them icons. Brennaman used a different word.

"We're essentially dinosaurs. There will never be another group like us. I'm the youngest of the so-called old timers," Brennaman said in 2015. "The 31 years is a record. No one will ever equal that. Our business is a transient business. Guys always think the grass is greener on the other side."

Thirty-eight years is a long time, too. Nuxhall told me in 1986, his 21st season on Reds Radio, he couldn't believe his second career was longer than his 16-year playing career.

"I figured I'd get a couple three years. I never figured I'd be here 20 years. I thought my desire to get back into the action part of baseball would be huge," he said. Nuxhall was still pitching batting practice in 1986, so he had never left the "action part" of the game.

In 1992, I pointed out he had spent 25 years as a Reds broadcaster, one more year than Hoyt (1942-65). Did he think about breaking Waite's mark when he started on radio in 1967?

"Oh God no!" he said. He was looking forward to 1994, his 50th anniversary with the Reds. "That was my goal. Fifty years."

At his home in 1996, for my "Real Mr. Red" *Enquirer* profile, he told me: "I never dreamed I'd be here that long, that's for dang sure. No way!

I thought I'd be there just a couple of years, and get run off. It's been surprising to hang around this long, without a doubt."

On the 63rd anniversary of Joe's debut, and five months before he died, the Reds honored Nuxhall, Brennaman and Hoyt on June 10, 2007, by unveiling three replica radio microphones bearing their names below the Great American Ball Park radio booth. They're flanked by the retired uniform numbers of Fred Hutchinson (1), Johnny Bench (5), Joe Morgan (8), Sparky Anderson (10), Barry Larkin (11), Dave Concepcion (13), Pete Rose (14), Ted Kluszewski (18), Frank Robinson (20), Tony Perez (24) and Jackie Robinson (42).

"This is a real honor. It's something I never expected," Nuxhall said. "To have this happen is basically unbelievable as far as I'm concerned."

A few days later, the Reds handed out a Father's Day gift to fans—an AM/FM pocket radio in a box featuring pictures of the Reds new radio team of Jeff Brantley, Marty and Thom Brennaman, and Nuxhall.

Love Letters From Reds Country

Before iPhones, tablets or computers, Reds fans sent letters simply addressed to "Marty & Joe, Cincinnati, Ohio" from all over "Reds Country, " the 38 states reached by flagship WLW-AM at nights, or 92 radio affiliates in six states.

The mail arrived at the main Cincinnati Post Office, and postal workers knew exactly where to deliver them—to the Reds office at Riverfront Stadium, or Great American Ball Park on Joe Nuxhall Way. Once when Brennaman asked a Cincinnati postal employee about the letters, the man admitted they might be "bending the rules a bit" by not returning them to the senders for inadequate addresses. "He said, 'There was a return address, but we know who it was going to, so we thought we'd just send them down to the ballpark,'" Brennaman said at his retirement press conference in 2019.

"I was blown away by that. It made me realize that we had a special thing. If that isn't the biggest compliment of all time, I don't know what is."

8

Pranks for the Memories

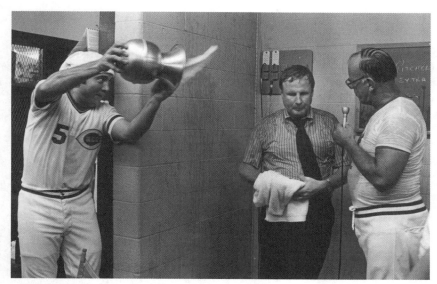

Johnny Bench tosses champagne on Joe as he interviews Reds President Dick Wagner in the Riverfront Stadium clubhouse after the Reds clinched the 1979 National League Western Division. CINCINNATI ENQUIRER PHOTO

Every September, Major League Baseball releases schedules for the next year. Players, coaches, announcers, sportswriters, scouts and their families know where they'll be the next year, whether their team will be at home or on the road. That's why Joe Nuxhall got mad to hear this message on the Candlestick Park radio booth loudspeaker: *"Long distance call for Joe Nuxhall in the main press box!"*

Everyone who knew Joe knew he was in San Francisco that hour calling a Reds game. All they had to do was turn on a radio. Yet in the first inning of the Reds-Giants game, he was being paged for a telephone call. *"Long distance call for Joe Nuxhall in the main press box!"*

The message came over the radio booth's intercom speaker. Radio booths, press boxes and media dining rooms have speakers to announce official scoring decisions, lineup changes, pitch counts and other information the media needs during a game. Joe didn't know that he was another victim of Mike Marquard, the visiting team engineer at Candlestick. With Marty Brennaman as his willing co-conspirator, of course, Marquard rigged the speaker so that the announcement was heard only in the visitors' radio booth.

"Long distance call for Joe Nuxhall in the main press box!"

Since Brennaman broadcast the first two innings, Nuxhall walked down to the press box behind home plate to take the call. Nobody knew what he was talking about. In the second inning, the announcement came over the speaker again. *"Long distance call for Joe Nuxhall in the main press box!"*

Nuxhall once more trudged down to the press box. Again, nobody knew about the call. "He went down there five times," said Brennaman, laughing as he told the story. "The fifth time he went down there, he went down there to kill somebody! You know his temper. He was HOT!"

⚾ ⚾ ⚾

As much pleasure as we had listening to Marty and Joe on the radio for 31 years, they had even more fun together in the radio booth. Who knew Brennaman was a Hall of Fame prankster? The Reds Radio booth was a funhouse at home or on the road. Most of the pranks were pulled by Marty—with help from his friends—at the expense of Joe, the nicest guy in the world with the shortest temper on Earth.

Brennaman described Marquard as one of the greatest practical jokers of all time. One night before a Reds-Giants game, Marquard suckered Nuxy with a simple note taped to the visitors' radio both door: "Attention Reds Broadcasters: Your booth has been moved to G-8." So Joe walked all the way down to G-8 near the left-field foul pole.

"All Joe had to do was turn the door handle" at the first booth. "It was unlocked. He was something, boy," Marty said.

⚾ ⚾ ⚾

Marquard engineered Marty's best prank. While Nuxhall was pitching batting practice in 1978, Marquard brought a huge Panasonic videotape machine into the Candlestick booth. The old-school '70s tape machine was the size of a large suitcase. It was so big—and the booth so tiny—that Marquard had to put it on the floor under his feet. He hooked it up to the TV monitor Marty and Joe watched during the game. Marquard cued up a tape, and they waited. And waited.

In the top of the seventh, with Nuxhall at the mic, Joe Morgan got on base. Morgan took off to steal second and the umpire called him out. Sparky ran out to argue. That's when Marquard hit the "Play" button. When Joe looked at the TV monitor, instead of a replay of Morgan's slide, he saw a scene from the pornographic movie *Deep Throat*.

"When *Deep Throat* popped up on the monitor, Joe just lost it," Marty said. "He was in the middle of doing play-by-play, and he was silent. He thought that what we were seeing in the booth was what everybody was watching back home on television. He kept poking me and pointing to the monitor. I thought he was going to crack two or three of my ribs. It was just perfect. He couldn't talk! And I am crying! Joe damn near died! It was the funniest thing in the world."

Joe got even with Marty the next year—after they both got in trouble with Reds President Dick Wagner about a story in *Sports Illustrated*. You'd think the Reds front office would be thrilled with a national magazine story on 50-year-old Nuxhall still pitching batting practice. Not Wagner.

Writer Kathleen Andria spent a weekend with Marty and Joe in the Shea Stadium booth to write "High, Fast and Forever" for the June 11, 1979, issue. She described how Joe suited up before every game to toss batting practice "to prove that, though he may have retired (from pitching), he didn't quit." *SI* reported that he threw "170-180 pitches, more than anyone would in a whole game." It also noted his two-pack-a-day cigarette habit and a diet of meat, potatoes, eggs, cheese and beer. Nuxhall told Andria that after games he liked to watch Johnny Carson's *Tonight Show* with a pound of Colby cheese, a box of crackers and Michelob beer, which he called "Mitchelobi," as Pedro Borbon called the brand.

Wagner was not happy. Not about Nuxy's diet, or smoking, or risking his health pitching batting practice. No, Wagner was upset that Nuxhall proclaimed his love for "Mitchelobi."

"Don't you know that Stroh's (Beer) is our sponsor?" Wagner asked.

Marty caught hell from Wagner, too. *Sports Illustrated* wrote that "Brennaman reads a book—not about baseball, of course—while Nuxhall broadcasts the middle innings." A voracious reader, Brennaman always brought a novel on the team bus and to the radio booth. "I'd read, and I'd watch the game. I had my headphones on, and I'd watch every pitch," he explained to me years later. Brennaman knew he was in trouble before Wagner's secretary called with an invitation to see Wagner in his office. He had the magazine open on his desk when Marty walked in.

"Wagner said, 'You've seen this?' And I said yes. And he said, 'That's accurate?' And I said, 'Yes sir.' And he said, 'Let me give you a piece of advice: This better not happen again.' He said it was very unprofessional. Usually we'd scream and shout and cuss at each other. But not this time, because he was right. And I knew he was right."

⚾ ⚾ ⚾

On a road trip to play the Montreal Expos the next week, Nuxhall got his revenge. Nux told the visitors' radio engineer that when he put his hands behind his head, the engineer should cut off the microphones, come out of a commercial break earlier than scheduled, and cue Marty to open the inning. After the second inning, Nuxhall gave the signal. The producer cued Marty, who welcomed listeners back to the broadcast and introduced Nuxhall to do the third inning. Nuxhall turned to his partner and asked, "Hey Marty, what book are you reading today?"

Brennaman stopped breathing.

"I saw my whole career flash in front of my face. I called him every name in the book," Brennaman said. "I took the cue and went right into my spiel. And Joe nailed me with it. I mean, he got me back as good as you can—and I was constantly looking for ways to play practical jokes on him."

Nuxhall was still beaming more than 25 years later when he told me the story. "He almost fell off the chair. I got him good! I was so proud of myself!"

Without a doubt, I'd guess you'd say.

⚾　　⚾　　⚾

The 1979 *Sports Illustrated* story had a lifelong impact on late-night TV star David Letterman. Twenty-three years later, out of the blue, Letterman told his CBS *Late Show* audience on April 6, 2002, about Nuxhall's beer-and-crackers postgame snack. And 15 years after that, Letterman and comedy writer Bill Scheft mentioned Nuxy's eating habits when interviewed in their Great American Ball Park diamond seats by Fox Sports Ohio's Jim Day on August 6, 2017, during a Reds-Cardinals game.

On his 2002 show, Letterman started riffing about Nuxhall when sportscaster Dick Enberg was his guest. Letterman told of listening in Indianapolis to Reds games on WLW-AM called by Nuxhall and Al Michaels in the early 1970s. He grew up a Reds fan in Indianapolis, taking a train with his dad in the 1950s to Union Terminal and walking to Crosley Field to see Ted Kluszewski.

In the early 1990s, Letterman's producers had called Nuxhall and did a pre-interview with him, a screening process for potential guests. "Some guy asked me: 'Tell me something funny that happened to you.' I don't recall what I told 'em. And that's the last time I heard from them," Nuxhall told me in 1996. Another time he told me, "They kept calling me and wanting me to come on. I told them some stuff, but I guess I wasn't funny enough."

Fast-forward to 2002, when Letterman reminisced about Nux on a Thursday night show. The first thing I did at work Friday was email the show's publicist. She sent me a transcript of Letterman's comments. Later she emailed me an edited version of his remarks as broadcast on the show, which deleted some comments about Nuxhall. Here's the full version of what he told his studio audience:

LETTERMAN: When I was back in Indianapolis, I would listen to the Cincinnati Reds games on the radio, station WLW. They'd broadcast all of [APPLAUSE]—There you go, sure. And I got to

119

listen to Al Michaels and Joe Nuxhall do radio play-by-play. That was fantastic. What a great combination those guys were. So I really felt like I was blessed, because Al Michaels on the radio doing baseball with this Joe Nuxhall, fantastic. So then I moved to Los Angeles, and on the radio doing Dodgers baseball, you had Vin Scully on the radio. [APPLAUSE] ... And while Vin Scully was working for the Dodgers, down in Anaheim doing the Angels games on the radio was Dick Enberg and Don Drysdale. So I want to tell you, for a period of about 10 years, I was in baseball radio heaven. These guys, absolutely the cream of the crop ... And then Joe Nuxhall, when he would sign off the Reds' telecast, it would be, "So until tomorrow, it's the Old Lefthander rounding third and heading for home."

Letterman also mentioned the 1979 *SI* story—although he incorrectly said Michaels was his partner, and they would "telecast" Reds games.

LETTERMAN: They had a profile in Sports Illustrated about Al Michaels and Joe Nuxhall, and Joe Nuxhall said—I just loved him for this—each night after every Reds game—and that's like 162 games—he would telecast all of them, and about 20 in spring training ... After each game, Joe Nuxhall would have a six-pack of Michelob [LAUGHTER] and one of those big quarter-pound sticks of Cracker Barrel cheese. [LAUGHTER]

Letterman ended the bit with his take on Nuxy's sign-off: *Joe Lefthander, rounding third, heading for home.*

Nuxhall laughed when I called and told him what Letterman said. He was flattered Dave remembered him and the 1979 *SI* story. But he wasn't watching Letterman that night. Nux came home from the Reds-Cubs game at Riverfront Stadium and turned on ESPN.

"I was watching *SportsCenter* to see the other scores."

⚾ ⚾ ⚾

Not every prank worked as planned. Nuxhall was the intended victim of an elaborate ruse orchestrated by Bob Trumpy at WLW-AM's old Fourth Street studios in downtown Cincinnati.

Trumpy hosted the nightly *Sports Talk* call-in show throughout the 1980s on Cincinnati radio until joining NBC Sports full time to do NFL games, golf, Olympics and other events. Instead of nailing Nuxhall, Trumpy snared Reds manager John McNamara, who replaced Sparky in 1979.

Marty and Mac were preparing to broadcast the weekly offseason *Redsline* talk show when they met a stripper and her husband hired by Trumpy to pose as a writer and photographer from *Ohio Magazine*. Brennaman was not in on the joke. Before going on the air, the attractive young woman asked Marty "all the right questions" about the show. "Everything was on the up and up," he said.

Until a commercial break. That's when the photographer commented that the studio felt warm. Brennaman said he disagreed; he was comfortable. Once back on the air, a caller asked McNamara about a rumor the Reds could be trading for Yankees pitcher Ron Guidry. Marty sensed movement to his left, and turned to see the woman "reporter" pull her sweater off, exposing her bare breasts.

"McNamara couldn't talk. He was so unnerved that he could not put a grammatically correct sentence together, to the point where he said to me on the air, 'Marty, help me!' And I said to him, 'Mac, you're on your own!'"

Listeners called the station asking why McNamara sounded incoherent, said producer Doug Kidd, who screened calls for *Redsline* and Trumpy's show. "I thought we'd all die when she sat on Mac's lap during the show. People were calling in asking if Mac had been drinking," Kidd said. Trumpy said he was "laughing so hard, I had to leave the room."

It's a good thing he did. Cincinnati League of Women Voters members meeting at WLW-AM that night wanted to watch *Redsline* through a hallway window. "Trumpy, thank God, intercepted them saying, 'Oh no! You can't go down there!' That would have been a major disaster," Brennaman said.

Longtime Big Red Machine fans still talk about the night Nuxhall interviewed comedian Jonathan Winters during a rain delay at Riverfront

Stadium in 1977. Winters, who grew up in Dayton and Springfield, Ohio, loved his Reds. He was the biggest Cincinnati fan in Los Angeles, proudly wearing a Reds hat and shirt to Dodgers Stadium. Sparky would cancel batting practice when Winters came to the visitors' clubhouse in L.A. so the players and coaches could enjoy his wacky improvisations.

Winters liked to go on Johnny Carson's *Tonight Show* playing a character, such as a park ranger or a Civil War veteran. That night Winters asked Nuxhall to introduce him as Whip Willis, a pitcher for the 1919 World Champion Reds. Nux heard wrong and introduced him as "Flip Willis," who could throw a ball through a brick wall.

WINTERS: Well, it's not really Flip Willis. It's Whip Willis. But that's all right. There wouldn't be no reason for a kid like yourself to remember me. I come to the Reds in 1919. You weren't even born. I'll tell you this much Joe. I remember your name! …

I throwed a fastball. I throwed a curve. I throwed a knuckleball. I throwed everything there was to throw. And I still didn't get a lot of money. These boys today, my lord a mercy, they're getting $25,000 in the locker room! That don't make no difference. I'm not jealous. We got two or three hundred dollars, and lived in a pickup truck, or something like that.

You said I throwed a ball through a brick wall. Well, I never did that. I don't know who told you that. I tell you what I did throw it through. I threw it through a kind a house out in the country. One of those little houses. A man came out of there like a bat out of Hades! It was just a small house. I throwed one through a Mail Pouch barn. That's how a scout one day seen me, and he said, 'I'd like to see you get into the minors and eventually play for Cincinnati.'

NUXHALL: Did you have any breaking stuff, or was it all pure heat?

WINTERS: Oh, everything I had broke. I'm broke now. I just went through everything I had. I was a fool … I put all my money in used chickens. Don't ever put your money in used chickens.

NUXHALL: Why?

WINTERS: Well, they're used! It's like used cars. They just won't lay eggs. This is Farmer's Night, ain't it? You ask them people. They don't want any used chickens ... But I'm in pretty good shape, though, for a man. I mean physically. Mentally I'm not dealing with a full deck. But I'm 82 years old. Heh, heh, heh. And I can still throw a rock, I'll tell you that. I hit a man out here in the parking lot, because I wanted to get my car in, you know?

Nuxhall finally told listeners he was chatting with "the No. 1 fan on the West Coast of the Cincinnati Reds, without a doubt, Jonathan Winters." The former Dayton WING-AM disc jockey told Nuxhall and Brennaman how he had resisted Dodgers' efforts to change allegiance in Los Angeles. Tired of being nagged by Dodgers manager Tommy Lasorda, Winters told him he'd root for L.A. if they gave him a uniform shirt.

"The Reds have given me a home shirt and a road shirt ... And then (Lasorda) gave me one, but he spelled my name wrong. So that did it for me ... It's all over. I'm back to the Reds."

Years later, Brennaman was amazed at Winters' creativity. "He was back visiting family in Springfield, and he came to the ballpark. He was Whip Willis, and all of it was spontaneous. The man was brilliant."

⚾ ⚾ ⚾

It's funny how the mind plays tricks on you. I remembered hearing Winters' hilarious conversation with Joe. For years I thought his Whip Willis claimed to be a "boneless chicken rancher." To me that's funnier than a used chicken rancher, what Winters actually said.

During my many trips to Los Angeles for the *Enquirer* to cover the TV critics' press tours, I met Winters several times. In January 1991, while promoting his *Davis Rules* ABC sitcom with Randy Quaid, Winters asked me to get him a team photo of the 1990 World Champions. I contacted the Reds publicity office, and someone promised to mail him one. In summer of 2000, I requested a one-on-one interview with him after the press conference for his PBS special, *Jonathan Winters: On The Loose,* filled with his TV clips from the 1950s, '60s and '70s.

I wanted to talk about his career; he wanted to talk about the Reds, who were about to acquire Ken Griffey Jr. I asked him about his rain delay with Nuxhall nearly 25 years earlier. He remembered it completely differently. Or was he just doing another bit?

"We did a rain delay in Cincinnati as a coach and a player. It was great. Joe Nuxhall said, 'We have Coach Meadows, third base coach Alan Meadows, how come you're up here?'

"And I said, 'Because I'm out of the rain, man! You don't want me standing down there out in the rain?'"

"Who do you think is going to be a good hitter?"

"I tell you, this young guy is not Ted Kluszewski, but he's cut his sleeves off, so he's off to a good start," Winters said. "We did stuff, I tell you. Joe looked at me, and he could hardly keep a straight face. God, I had a good time!"

Then he resumed the bit, as he remembered it: "I said that I once got beaned. My mind was gone for a month. I wasn't in a coma, I just sat in the car and listened to the radio."

It's funny how the mind plays tricks on you, without a doubt.

⚾   ⚾   ⚾

When Marge Schott was interviewed by *60 Minutes* in 1988, Marty got Joe again.

Correspondent Morley Safer interviewed the Reds owner at her Indian Hill home in January 1989. I remember it well because I got a scoop that the maître d' at the Maisonette, the city's world-renown French restaurant, refused to serve Safer. *Enquirer* restaurant writer Sara Pearce told me the blue jeans worn by Safer's producer didn't meet the dress code. I called Safer at his hotel room the next day, and he told me the restaurant was wrong. "They weren't blue jeans. They were gray trousers. It was not as if he was coming in looking like some wild pop (music) group. He was neatly dressed. So we went to a little Italian restaurant next door and it was terrific."

CBS broadcast the Schott interview on Sunday, April 3. A few days later, Brennaman and engineer-producer Dave "Yiddy" Armbruster pulled the same stunt Joe used on Marty after the *Sports Illustrated* story. Between innings, Armbruster killed the microphones and cued Marty 45 seconds before they actually came out of a commercial. Speaking into the dead mic, Marty welcomed back listeners, and then said, "Mrs. Schott was on *60 Minutes* the other night, Joe, and I'm sure you watched it."

Nuxhall put his microphone on his scorebook and silently leaned back in his chair, not wanting to make any comment about the controversial Reds owner over the airwaves. "We got him pretty good on that one. Marty would just screw with him so bad," said Armbruster, who was called "Yiddy" by his younger brother who couldn't say David, and the nickname stuck.

On the Reds' first trip to Atlanta's new Turner Field in 1997, Nuxhall ignored the no-smoking signs. So Brennaman arranged for a security guard to threaten to remove Joe from the stadium when Nuxy lit up a Marlboro Light. Brennaman also got Joe good in Atlanta in the early 1980s when Pascual Perez was dominating the Reds. When Nuxy asked his Little Buddy how well the Dominican Republic righty spoke English, Marty swore Perez could speak "the king's English." Well maybe the king of Spain.

"He brought him on the air and it was bad," Brennaman told the *Enquirer's* John Fay. "You could understand about every seventh word. It was awful. Joe was steaming."

⚾   ⚾   ⚾

Former Reds farmhand Randy Poffo visited the Riverfront radio booth on Thursday afternoon, September 21, 1989, and the crowd went wild. Reds players in the dugout cheered. Marge and Steve Schott went wild too, and not in a good way.

Most of the people at the game didn't know Poffo played 131 games for the Reds' 1974 Class-A Tampa Tarpons in the Florida State League. They knew him for his second career, as pro wrestler Randy "Macho Man" Savage, in town to wrestle at what today is Heritage Bank Center.

Poffo hit .232 as a catcher, outfielder and first baseman for the Tarpons. He started in 1971, at 18, playing for the Cardinals in the Gulf Coast

League. After three seasons, the Reds picked him up for Tampa, his fourth and final season in the minors. He quit professional baseball at 21 to try wrestling. Poffo wore his "Macho Man" outfit—purple-and-gold tights and a gold crown—in the booth.

"We talked to him about the World Champion Hulk Hogan. People weren't paying any attention to the ball game. They were looking at us, Marty and myself and Randy," Nuxhall said.

Players applauded and pointed to Savage standing between Marty and Joe in the radio booth. Eric Davis flexed his muscles for Savage in a couple of poses outside the dugout. The wrestling theatrics helped 12,522 fans forget the awful team they were watching. The Reds had lost nine straight under Tommy Helms after manager Pete Rose was banned from the game on August 24.

In the first inning, both starting pitchers were knocked out without getting an out. Jack Armstrong and Tim Birtsas gave up six runs when 10 Padres batted. Then former Red Dennis Rasmussen coughed up five runs on hits by Dave Collins, Luis Quinones, Davis, Todd Benzinger and Rolando Roomes. The Reds lost 11-7 when the Padres scored four runs in the ninth off John Franco. So the Macho Man provided a memorable distraction.

"We had a big poster of Hulk Hogan in the booth. He ripped that poster off the wall, tore it up and threw it out over the stands, and people were cheering. Oh, it was funnier than hell," Nuxhall said.

It was fun for everyone except Marge and her executive vice president. "Marge got mad," Nuxhall said, "and she sent Steve in to get that guy out of our booth."

⚾ ⚾ ⚾

Next came Round Two: Marty "The Poofy-Haired Fancy Boy" Brennaman vs. Heavyweight Steve "Shamu" Schott, cousin to Marge's late husband. Those who remember the Macho Man destroying the Hulkster's photo never knew about the rest of the drama that played in the hallway behind the radio booth, and in Schott's office.

"She (Marge) got all bent out of shape," Brennaman said. "It wasn't her idea to have the wrestler in the radio booth. Had it been her idea, it would have been fine."

Brennaman remembered seeing Steve come into the booth and speak to Armbruster. Savage left the booth, and Marty and Joe continued broadcasting the game until Brennaman had a chance to talk to Armbruster. This was Marty's account: "Yid said: 'Steve Schott told me to get him (Savage) off the air. And if we didn't get him off the air, he was going to have your job.'"

During the commercial break after the fifth, Brennaman told Nuxhall to take over play-by-play. He bolted out of the booth looking for Steve, who happened to be coming down the hall. They stepped into a nearby room. Marty provided this play-by-play: "I said: 'Let me tell you something. Don't you ever threaten me with my job again. And on top of that, you stay the hell out of my radio booth. You can't get my job.' He started crying. I said, 'Just remember what I said.'"

After the game, Reds publicity director Jim Ferguson told Marty and Joe that Marge wanted to see them in her office. It was time for Round Three.

"We walked into her office and she started in on us: 'I can't believe you put him on the air! It's not the kind of wholesome entertainment we promote here with the Reds!' I said: 'Marge, let me tell you something. You go to a wrestling match, it's family entertainment. People take their young children. There was nothing wrong,'" said Brennaman, who took daughter Ashley to WWE events.

"Then Steve pipes up and says, 'Yeah, I'll be honest with you, Mrs. Schott. I went in there and I did my best to end that interview and couldn't do it. I thought I was going to have to get physical.'

"And I turned to Steve and said, 'Why don't you shut the —— up! That guy would have pinched your head off!' And Marge said, 'That's right, Steve. Shut up!'

"It was unbelievable!" Brennaman said. "Ferguson and Yid were in the back of the room about to turn purple from not laughing."

And this one belongs to Brennaman.

⚾ ⚾ ⚾

As soon as Joe Nuxhall stepped on the team bus after the game, Brennaman hit "Play" on his cassette tape recorder. And Nuxhall hit the roof. He was livid.

It had been 15-20 years since Nuxhall had heard that tape. Brennaman somehow had obtained a copy of Joe's most embarrassing moment on Reds Radio from June 14, 1973, a year before Marty replaced Michaels. The X-rated blooper was so out of character for Joe that it was the top story on Al Schottelkotte's 11 p.m. WCPO-TV newscast.

Nuxhall shocked Reds Country by uttering a profanity during his pregame *Turfside* interview with outfielder Joel Youngblood before the Reds played their Triple-A Indianapolis Indians at Indianapolis' old Bush Stadium. *Cincinnati Enquirer* sportswriter John Erardi and Reds historian Greg Rhodes first told the story in their 2004 *Opening Day* book, and Michaels wrote his account in his 2014 autobiography. While talking to Youngblood, infielder Phil Gagliano and other players pelted Nuxy with pea gravel. Nuxhall called him an (expletive). Then he stopped the tape and started his interview all over again with Youngblood. "*Three, two, one. Hi everybody, this is Joe Nuxhall ...*"

In a hurry to shower after throwing batting practice, Nuxhall didn't cue up the tape before giving it to a clubhouse kid to run it up to the radio booth. The engineer rewound the tape to the beginning. Nuxy's pregame profanity was heard throughout Ohio, Indiana and Kentucky on 50,000-watt WLW-AM. Schottelkotte led his newscast that night with the Reds' X-rated radio broadcast from Indianapolis. Nuxhall, a Reds employee, worried that his career was over.

The next day, Wagner huddled with Roger Ruhl, the Reds promotions and sales director, to write an apology for Nuxhall to read before the game that night. Ruhl typed up a statement. He couldn't resist including a line, as a joke, for Joe to say: "It wasn't my fault. It was the (expletive) engineer."

Joe was not amused.

Over the years, Brennaman acquired another souvenir from Joe's embarrassing incident. He has a copy of the letter Wagner sent Nuxhall warning him that a repeat occurrence was "grounds for immediate firing." He will never forget Joe's reaction to his prank on the bus.

"As soon as Joe stepped on the bus, I hit the 'Play' button and it could be heard all over the bus. Joe was not happy with me at all. He got mad as hell. That was one of the few times he ever got pissed off at me. And I never played it again," Brennaman said. "There were two or three times I saw his temper. He got mad at me a couple of times, because I'd stick the needle in him about something and he'd get mad at me. But it never lasted any time at all."

Nuxhall once explained to me: "We understand each other. We kid each other, sometimes in personal ways. If he gets me, I'll get him."

The X-rated flub made a lifelong impression on a young Reds fan in Mason, Ohio. In a letter read to Nuxhall at the 2007 Fairfield charity gala, actor George Clooney recalled that when he was 12 Nuxhall once "called the players something I had never heard before. It sounded like two words. I asked my Mom about it. She washed my mouth out with soap. When I was able to speak again, I became so careful with my language and enunciation that I became a big movie star. And I owe it all to you, Joe."

On long road trips during Florida spring training, Nuxhall would drive the radio team in his roomy Ford conversion van. Armbruster would ride in the front passenger seat and Brennaman would sit in back reading a book or newspaper. Brennaman would be lost in his own little world—until a driver cut off Nuxhall on the interstate, lighting Joe's fire. Marty and Yiddy vividly remember the time a man driving a convertible with his girlfriend pulled in front of Nux on Interstate 4, which connected the Reds' Plant City headquarters to Tampa and Orlando.

"Some guy cut him off. And Joe drove 95 mph to just get abreast of this guy's car. And when he did, he lowered the window and he put the fear of God into him with a profanity-laced tirade! He was screaming at this guy going 95 mph down I-4," Brennaman said. He loved that story, and retold it his final week on Reds Radio in September 2019. "He was hotter than a match!"

"I thought Joe was going to kill the guy," Armbruster said. "If he could have stopped him, he would have. Going to or back from games in Florida, we would just laugh constantly."

Their longest drive for a Grapefruit League game—before the Reds moved to Arizona in 2010—was across Florida to the Dodgers' complex in Vero Beach. On the way back they'd stop at Yeehaw Junction, where the Florida Turnpike intersects Route 60. Whenever I passed Yeehaw Junction driving to my father-in-law's home in Palm Beach Gardens, I'd think of Joe in his early 60s, buying beer at a convenience store there.

"We'd always stop, coming back from Vero Beach, at Yeehaw Junction, and Joe would get a six-pack of beer," Brennaman said. "One year we walk into the place and there's a young lady behind the counter, and she carded Joe. And I said, *'What did you just ask him?'* And she said, 'I need to see some form of identification' for his age.' And I said, 'Ma'am, look at that face! You've got to be kidding me! You think he's less than 21 years old?'

And she said, 'I'm just doing what I had to do.' We laughed about that forever and a day."

⚾　⚾　⚾

Pitcher Tom Browning witnessed Mount Nuxhall erupt on a Plant City golf course in the late 1980s. After an afternoon Reds game, Joe and fellow lefthander Browning played nine holes at nearby Walden Lake Golf & Country Club. All went well until the eighth hole, a par 3 along a row of houses.

"We had a few beers, and we get to the eighth hole. Joe hits a big old slice into the houses. He tees up another ball, and hits another slice into the houses. Joe gets mad and throws his club," Browning said.

What went up didn't come down. Along the fairways were tall pine trees covered with moss. Joe's club got caught in the moss. So he threw a second club. And a third. And a fourth. And a fifth. He emptied his bag, failing to dislodge the club.

"After he throws the last one, he sees me sitting in the golf cart, drinking a beer snickering at him," Browning said. Nuxhall laughed too, and joined Browning in the cart for another beer.

"Then he walks over to the tree, throws one club, hits it, and brings it down. Joe picks up all his clubs, puts them back in his bag, and we play the last hole. Nuxy was such a competitor in everything! He lost it for a little bit, and then got his sense of humor back. We finished off a beer, and then we finished off the round of golf."

⚾ ⚾ ⚾

Nuxy first picked up a golf club as a kid on Hamilton's North End baseball diamonds. The game had a grip on him the rest of his life.

"I fiddled around with golf since I was 8 or 9 years old. After all the softball games were over somebody would have a golf club and we'd hit golf balls at the North End Fields. But I never took it seriously," he told me in 1996.

As a teen he hitchhiked up Ohio 4 to the Hamilton Elks Golf Club north of town. He'd earn $3 or $4 caddying, and spend it all at the hamburger stand across the road. As a radio broadcaster, Joe and his golf clubs were constant companions on road trips. He preferred the solitude on the golf course over the boredom of the hotel.

"Golf really helps pass the time on road trips. I get up early anyway. So I've got from 7:30 until 4 o'clock when the bus leaves for the ballpark. I'm not a reader. I'll read the paper in the morning, but once I'm done with that I'll go sit in the hotel lobby for a while or watch TV, and so on and so forth. So golf is really entertaining. You get out there, and there's nothing going on at all but trying to hit a little white ball straight, which is a huge problem. A huge problem."

Their first 21 years together, Brennaman didn't play golf. He read novels in his hotel room during the day and mocked Nuxhall's favorite game until 1995, when Marty's children convinced him to take up the game he had stopped playing in college.

"He used to make fun of golf. He'd say, 'That's the stupidest game! Hit a ball and chase it! That's dumb,'" Nuxhall said on WCET-TV's *Joe Nuxhall: My Life: Baseball and Beyond*. Once when Brennaman asked Nuxhall what he shot that day he replied, "I was seven under."

That got Marty's attention. Seven under?

"Yeah, seven under. I've got seven less balls than I started with," Nuxy said. "That got him!"

Golf provided "a lot of time to talk, and get us closer and closer," Brennaman said. On the road, they'd get up by 6:30 a.m., play 18 holes and hurry back to the hotel so Nuxy could get "that damn power nap," as Brennaman put it. "And we'd do it all over again the next morning."

When the Reds trained in Sarasota they'd get a 7:15 a.m. tee time and make it to the Reds complex before morning batting practice ended, as they told listeners during a game in 2006.

NUXHALL: We'll be done at 10:15!

BRENNAMAN: We'll get around there in a hurry. Of course, when you hit the ball straight, and you keep it in the short grass, it doesn't take long to play.

NUXHALL: And if you hit it in the water, you can get another one out real quick too!

Often their golf partners during the season were TV analyst Chris Welsh and clubhouse manager Rick Stowe. Welsh loves telling about playing Arnold Palmer's Half Moon Bay course outside San Francisco with Nuxy. On the 13th hole, a 153-yard par 3 with a water hazard, Joe "hit his first shot into the pond with a seven iron. He hits his second shot into the water. He hits his third shot into the water. We all told him to go back and get a bigger club, a six iron or a five iron. But no! He wanted to prove that he could still hit the ball 153 yards with a seven iron. He hit 12 balls—every ball in his bag—into the water. So he turns to Marty and says, 'Can I borrow a golf ball?' And Marty says, "No way in hell!'"

⚾ ⚾ ⚾

It took balls to golf with Brennaman. He loved to needle people. Joe's Little Buddy could be a big pain in the butt.

"I used to get Joe's goat when I criticized his etiquette on the golf course, like talking when someone was going to swing. He'd get madder than a wet hen," Brennaman told Jeff Brantley and radio listeners one day.

Marty constantly ragged Joe about his choice of golf balls. In their final season together, when Joe only did a few 2007 spring games after being hospitalized, Brennaman took his complaint to the airwaves after he noticed Nuxy signaling the radio engineer.

BRENNAMAN: You got something to say?

NUXHALL: Well, I was just going to bring up my practice ball.

BRENNAMAN: That golf ball? That's embarrassing! Honest to goodness! I'm not kidding.

NUXHALL: Those are Pro V's, man!

BRENNAMAN: If there are people listening that have access to golf balls, you can do my man a favor here. It was embarrassing!

NUXHALL: I remember you used to give me heck for using a Top Flite … The practice ball, what was that?

BRENNAMAN: It was a Pro V1. But it was the most beat-up looking thing!

NUXHALL: Who made it? Who made it?

BRENNAMAN: I don't care! Everybody knows who makes Pro V1. But that ball was UGLY! And I guarantee you that ball had bounced 15 times on the cart path, and you got it out again yesterday.

NUXHALL: Naw, I hit it in the lake.

At the Joe Nuxhall Hope Project gala in April, three weeks later, Marty gave Joe a dozen Titleist Pro V1 golf balls. "I am so tired of watching him play with bad golf balls. He's hitting Top Flites and all these crappy golf balls, I could throw up. So this is for you," Brennaman said.

When Nuxhall announced he would retire from radio after the 2004 season, Joe joked that he had to quit because "Brennaman was getting better at golf."

⚾   ⚾   ⚾

"Ring-ring-ring-ring-ring! Banana Phone!"
    For about 20 years, Nuxhall and Brennaman would "go to the Banana Phone" during rain delays and talk to callers (and a few pranksters in the

Reds clubhouse) on the radio network. When WLW-AM produced the broadcasts, the calls gave the station programming for Reds advertisers when play was halted. The fan interaction continued through 2014, when Brennaman pulled the plug on the "BP" after the team had taken over production of the Reds Radio Network.

It was called the "Banana Phone" because Don Breen, a former Reds vice president who worked for Cincinnati-based Chiquita Bands, gave them a cheap plastic banana-shaped telephone in 1987.

"It came to us as a joke. Marty and Joe said something about it, and it became legendary," Armbruster said. It was such a part of the Marty and Joe show that when rain halted play, Brennaman would refer to it by its initials. The Banana Phone was "BP" to Reds fans two decades before Brandon "DatDudeBP" Phillips was acquired from Cleveland in 2006. The phone was donated to the Reds Hall of Fame when the new ballpark opened in 2003, although they continued to "go to the Banana Phone."

It even had a theme song. The call-in segment was introduced with a speeded-up version of the "Bananaphone" song by Raffi, a children's singer-songwriter best known for *"Wheels on the Bus"*—although Yid had no clue that "Bananaphone" was a real song when someone sent him the music file.

The best calls were from the clubhouse by players pranking the guys. John Franco once called in as "Rob" to ask if Joe had gained a few pounds. Joe had no clue it was the lefty reliever.

FRANCO: We were wondering in all those Kroger commercials that you and Joe do if Joe has been eating all the bananas, because he looks kind of heavy now.

NUXHALL: You have good eyes, don't ya? [LAUGHS] You're exactly right!

BRENNAMAN: Bananas are good for you.

FRANCO: Well Joe, we're wondering if it gets windy outside, if you need anybody to hold the strings so you don't float away.

NUXHALL: Now I'm not—Now wait a minute now! Time out!

Wait a minute! Usually they float around up above us but they have engines on them, commonly called blimps.

FRANCO: I didn't say that. Joe. You did.

⚾ ⚾ ⚾

On the line was "Adam from Milwaukee." That's who outfielder Adam Dunn claimed to be when he called the Banana Phone to ask if Scott Hatteberg, his teammate at first base in 2006-08, "was a good player." The more they chatted, it became clear Brennaman had figured out who had called.

DUNN: Is it still raining in Cincinnati?

BRENNAMAN: It's just about stopped, Adam.

DUNN: Do you have your shirt on?

BRENNAMAN: The last I checked I did, yes. Why?

DUNN: Just curious.

BRENNAMAN: Listen, I'm going to let you go now, because I know you're going to get your game face on. Because we're getting ready to go back on the radio shortly. And I know you'll be listening to every word.

DUNN: I love it. Have a good one, Bro! Nice talking with ya!

⚾ ⚾ ⚾

Reds fans had no clue the Banana Phone was retired until Brennaman and Jeff Brantley didn't take any calls the first soggy night in 2015. It was then revealed that Brennaman had decided to pull the plug permanently the previous September, after a caller asked Brennaman if he ever had diarrhea while on the air and made a vulgar anatomical reference about outfielder Andrew McCutcheon. Since the Reds were producing the games at the time—not WLW-AM—the club could give the airwaves back to affiliates instead of filling time with calls.

By 2015, Brennaman, Brantley and Jim Kelch had a new fan favorite:

"The Old Coach" from Kinston, North Carolina. He was far enough away for correct pronunciations to be lost in transmission. He loved calling in to chat with "Marty Brennehan" and "Jim Belch" about his favorite players: Infielders Joey Vote-O, Scooter Gillette, Zack Mozart and Edwin Inconcepcion; outfielders Robert Duvall and Henry Winkler; catcher Tucker Barndoor; and pitchers Ray Romano, Anthony Discofanny and Bronson Oreo. (Translation: Joey Votto, Scooter Gennett, Zack Cozart, Edwin Encarnacion, Adam Duvall, Jesse Winker, Tucker Barnhart, Sal Romano, Anthony DeSclafani and Bronson Arroyo.) The Old Coach occasionally called the offseason *Hot Stove League* shows. He always ended conversations by telling Marty to say hello to his son "Thom," pronounced like "thumb."

Listeners were never told that Marty Brennehan, his son "Thomb" and "Jim Belch" were in on the hoax perpetrated by a Reds insider. You'd recognize his name if I printed it here, but he begged that I protect his identity because "Marty would kill me if I come clean and ruin the bit."

The Old Lefthander must be smiling up in Heaven when he sees the pranks continuing in the Reds Radio booth long after his passing in 2007.

On Brennaman's 73rd birthday on July 28, 2015, while the Reds were playing in St. Louis, the Busch Stadium scoreboard wished Marty Brennaman a happy 107th birthday. "I thought he (Marty) was going to pee his pants," Brantley said.

During a blustery 52-degree April afternoon game at Great American Ball Park in 2017, Brennaman assured Brantley that he'd turn on the booth's foot heaters. "The Cowboy" bent over and looked under the window ledge, but couldn't see the heaters. Why? They didn't exist. Brennaman laughed heartily while describing Brantley's misadventure after the Cubs scored seven runs in two innings off starter Cody Reed.

"We can have some chuckles up here, even when things are very dire. That's very important," Brennaman said. The Cowboy had been hoodwinked again, just like all those years the Old Lefthander was victimized by the Hall of Fame Prankster.

"I used to say that crazy things happened with Joe because we're both left-handed," Brennaman once told me, "and that automatically makes us a little bit different from other people."

George Clooney's Auditions

George Clooney won two Academy Awards, starred in dozens of movies and TV shows and twice was *People* magazine's "Sexiest Man Alive." But he didn't get the part he really wanted—playing outfield for the Cincinnati Reds.

Twice he participated in Reds' tryout camps in Lexington, Kentucky. A gifted athlete, Clooney started as a freshman on the varsity baseball and basketball teams at tiny Augusta (Kentucky) Independent High School. He would have been a football starter too, but the school was too small to field a team. There were 23 in his senior class in 1979.

"I could catch anything. I was a great outfielder in high school. But I couldn't throw well. I wanted to play pro baseball. I thought that would be it," Clooney told me in 1990 during the TV Critics Association press tour in Los Angeles, after he left Roseanne Barr's sitcom *Roseanne,* where he played Roseanne's factory boss, Booker, for 11 episodes in the first season. "Doug Flynn's dad did tryout camps in Lexington. I went down there two years in a row."

His baseball skills definitely weren't memorable. Years later, when I emailed former Reds' infielder Doug Flynn about Clooney's tryouts for Flynn's father, he said: "I have never heard that story before. Very interesting, but sorry. Never heard this before."

Fortunately, his Hollywood tryouts were more successful.

9

If You Swing the Bat, You're Dangerous!

Joe never got cheated at the plate. Here he swings and misses in a 5-2 win over the Cardinals on Sept. 22, 1963, at Crosley Field.
RHODES/KLUMPE REDS HALL OF FAME COLLECTION

"If you swing the bat, you're dangerous!"

Joe Nuxhall loved to say that when a pitcher got a hit. Years after Nux passed away, Marty Brennaman would quote the Old Lefthander's line when a pitcher reached base. As a former player, Joe knew that a pitcher who put the ball in play could help his team and stay on the mound longer. He especially delighted in talking to Reds pitchers on his *Star of the Game* show about their prowess at the plate.

Why? Because Nux could swing the bat and be dangerous. He hit 15 home runs and knocked in 78 runs in 16 years. He went deep on two Cy Young Award winners, Whitey Ford and Vern Law, and some of the best pitchers of his era. He also hit three triples and 20 doubles, and swiped three bases.

In 1953, his first full season in the Reds starting rotation, 24-year-old Nuxhall hit a career high .327 in 49 at-bats. He had three home runs, two doubles, 11 singles and eight RBI. His .928 OPS (on-base plus slugging) was second on the team to Ted Kluszewski, and would have been 10th in the National League, just ahead of Jackie Robinson (.927), had he been given enough at bats.

Nuxy also blasted three home runs again in 1954, and three more in 1955 (when he just missed a walk-off homer to win the 1955 All-Star Game). In 1961, his lone year in the American League, Nuxhall was a reliable pinch-hitter for Kansas City manager Hank Bauer. He hit .250 in 26 pinch hitting appearances with two home runs, two doubles, a triple and 13 RBI a decade before the designated hitter rule took pitchers out of the batter's box in 1973. As you'd expect, Nuxhall was no fan of the DH.

"Oh, I'd absolutely hate that. I couldn't put up with that," Nuxhall said. When pitching for the A's in the first half of 1961, Nuxhall's batting average was often the highest in the Kansas City lineup. Returning to the Reds in 1962, Nuxhall hit .269 while going a perfect 5-0. He also homered in 1962, and hit his final career homer in 1964. It was a month before his 36th birthday.

No matter your age, if you swing the bat, you're dangerous. In all certainty.

⚾   ⚾   ⚾

Kluszewski led off the fifth inning against the Pirates at Forbes Field with his 15th home run of 1953 on Sunday, June 7. Outfielder Willard Marshall and catcher Hobie Landrith followed with singles off Roy Face, bringing up Nuxhall to hit against the right-hander who would become a three-time All-Star and one of the best closers of Nux's era. Nuxhall promptly slugged a three-run homer, his first career home run.

A month later, on July 26, Nuxhall went deep off New York Giants ace Sal Maglie in the Polo Grounds. His third HR of the season was off Pirates starter Murry Dickson at Forbes Field, his favorite team and ballpark to display his power. Nuxhall hit six of his 15 homers at Forbes Field. He only hit two for the hometown crowd at Crosley Field. He also slugged a pair out of Philadelphia's old Connie Mack Stadium; and one each at Kansas City's Municipal Stadium, Yankee Stadium and the Polo

Grounds in New York, and San Francisco's Candlestick Park. Dickson and Pirates' pitcher Max Surkont twice served up bombs to Nuxhall. He also lit up All-Stars Ford, Law, Bob Friend, Howie Pollet and Harvey Haddix, and former teammates Art Fowler and Cal McLish.

The first time I talked to Nuxy at length, I told him I read he was a pretty good hitter. Nux answered in three words: "Fifteen home runs."

⚾   ⚾   ⚾

Whitey Ford was cruising. It was June 10, 1961, and the future Hall of Famer already had won eight games. Ford, who would win the Cy Young Award with a domineering 25-4 record, was unhittable the first time through the Kansas City lineup that Saturday afternoon in Yankee Stadium.

Until Joe Nuxhall, the A's starting pitcher, stepped into the batter's box in the third inning. With two outs, Joltin' Joe drilled one into the right-field lower deck. It was Nuxhall's 12th career home run, and first in the American League, on the 17th anniversary of his 1944 debut.

Ford was rattled. He walked the next batter, shortstop Dick Howser. Then Ford's old teammate, 38-year-old outfielder Hank Bauer, swatted one into the deep center field Monuments Park where three huge plaques on granite blocks honor Yankees greats Babe Ruth, Lou Gehrig and Miller Huggins. As centerfielder Mickey Mantle scrambled after the ball and finally returned to the open field to make a throw, Bauer legged out an inside-the-park home run. Ford regained his composure, and held the A's to just three more hits, winning 5-3.

Nuxhall (4-2) took the loss, ending his three-game win streak. But he kept the Bronx Bombers—Mantle and Roger Maris, who would break Babe Ruth's record of 60 home runs that year—in the park. Nuxhall's pitching line: Seven innings, six hits, four runs, one walk, one strikeout, one wild pitch and a throwing error, ending the day with a 3.61 ERA. His batting line: 1-for-2, one run, one RBI and a .353 batting average that was the highest in the A's lineup by 45 points.

The next day in a Sunday doubleheader in Cleveland, Nuxhall pinch-hit for the pitcher in the ninth with the A's down 3-2. He walked, moved to second on a single and scored on another single with a head-first dive into the plate to tie the game, which the A's lost in the bottom of the inning.

When Nuxhall faced the Yankees on June 20 in Kansas City, his name was added to baseball history books (again) when he served up Maris' 26th home run in a 6-2 loss. Maris led off the fifth and pulled a solo shot over the right field wall. Maris ended the day 1-for-5, with one RBI and a .242 batting average. Nuxhall had a better day at the plate, despite lasting only four innings and taking the loss. Nuxy tripled to right-center to drive in a run in the first, and doubled in the fourth to knock in the A's other run. Nuxhall (4-3) was 2-for-2, with two RBI and a .429 batting average.

With Nuxhall hitting better than anyone on the Kansas City roster, player-manager Hank Bauer let his pitcher swing the bat and be dangerous as often as possible.

One week in July 1961, Nuxhall reached base four consecutive times as a pinch-hitter. He singled on Sunday, July 2, against the Twins, advancing two runners as the A's rallied to take the lead, 7-6. On July 3, he singled against the Angels, moving a runner from first to third. He walked against the White Sox on Friday, July 6, and walked against the Orioles on Saturday. He also went 0-for-2 as the starting pitcher in a July 4th doubleheader against the Angels, and pitched an inning of relief on July 8 after hitting for pitcher Norm Bass.

As a Kansas City pinch-hitter, Nuxhall got five hits (four singles and a double), plus six walks, for a .423 on-base percentage and a .250 batting average. He had one RBI and scored one run.

"I don't know how many times I pinch-hit in Cincinnati. Not too often," he said. (He pinch-hit six times for the Reds in 15 years.)

Nuxy got more hits (19) for Kansas City than in his best Cincinnati season (17 in 1955), and his .292 average was second to his best for the Reds (.327 in 1953). He was the third best hitter for the A's behind Norm Siebern (.296) and Jerry Lumpe (.293). He ranked second in OPS (.798) to Norm Siebern (.859). While pitching, he also hit two homers, the shot off Ford and a three-run blast against former teammate Art Fowler in a win over the Angels on Labor Day in Kansas City.

Joe also could hurt you with his hustle and baseball smarts. Nuxhall bunted runners over to second. He knocked in runs with sacrifice flies. He pinch ran. He was patient at the plate, walking 40 times, in addition to his 152 hits. If the pitcher walked the eighth batter to bring Joe to the plate, Joe wanted to make him pay.

Batting with the bases loaded against the Pirates on June 7, 1953, he took a walk during a five-run rally in an 11-6 victory in Pittsburgh.

After Landrith walked in the eighth against the Dodgers on May 1, 1954, Nuxhall pinch-ran for Landrith and took two bases on Lloyd Merriman's single. He scored on a single to tie the game, which the Reds won 7-6 in 11 innings.

Nuxhall beat out a bunt down the third base line against the Phillies on June 24, 1955, and scored on Kluszewski's three-run homer. Nuxhall, who shut out the Phils, led off the fifth with a walk, advanced to second on a sacrifice bunt, and hustled to third on a wild pitch. A month later, he beat out a bunt in the sixth against the Pirates on July 29, 1955, and scored on Smoky Burgess' grand slam in a 16-4 blow-out. Nuxhall (10-8) pitched a complete game.

In his 1962 Reds comeback, Nuxhall got on base three times while pitching a complete game to beat the Dodgers, 12-1, at Crosley on August 18. Nuxy singled in the fourth and sixth off reliever Ed Roebuck, and was plunked by Phil Ortega in the eighth. Nuxhall (3-0) finished with 11 strikeouts and a 2.25 ERA. He got two hits and gave up four; he scored one run and gave up one. He headed to the clubhouse with a .273 batting average, a .333 on-base percentage, and a .697 OPS.

Big Joe wasn't blessed with great speed, but he knew he could be a threat by running the bases aggressively. Pitchers who didn't hustle upset him.

"It's like I say about pitchers not running out a ground ball: You expect other guys to bust their tails then you'd better do it too. If you can't run 90 feet you're in serious trouble. For a pitcher, your legs are the most important thing," he said.

If you swing the bat—and your name is Kluszewski, Frank Robinson, Gus Bell, Wally Post and Ed Bailey—you're so dangerous that you tie the NL team record of 221 home runs in 1956.

Nuxhall contributed two home runs during that magical season, when the surprisingly robust Reds blasted their way into the pennant race after 12 straight losing seasons, since Nuxhall pitched in 1944. The Redlegs wrecking crew were media darlings in 1956. Klu, Nuxy and nine other players appeared on CBS' popular Sunday night TV game show *What's My Line,* and *Sports Illustrated* put Klu, Post and Bell on the cover.

Robinson, the 20-year-old Rookie of the Year left fielder, led the team with 38 homers. Right fielder Post hit 36, and first baseman Klu clubbed 35. Center fielder Bell hit 29, followed by catcher Bailey (28); third baseman Ray Jablonski (15); second baseman Johnny Temple (3), and shortstop Roy McMillan (2). The bench provided pop from catcher Smoky Burgess (12), George Crowe (10), Bob Thurman (8), Stan Palys (2), Art Schult (1) and Joe Frazier (1).

Nuxhall contributed two, the only Reds pitcher to homer in 1956. In fact, Nuxy homered in '56 before he won his first game. He hit one into Crosley Field's right field Sun Deck on May 5 off Vern Law, his second in two years off the Pirates ace. Nuxhall (0-2) held Pittsburgh to four runs on six hits and six walks through eight without getting a decision. Bell won it with a walk-off RBI single in the 10th.

⚾ ⚾ ⚾

They were "11 guys from Cincinnati." That's what Kluszewski scribbled on the blackboard when Nuxhall and 10 other Reds were the "mystery guest" on CBS' *What's My Line* live broadcast at 10:30 p.m. Sunday, June 24, 1956.

It was a long day. They went to CBS studios in Manhattan after the second-place Reds (34-26) swept the third-place Brooklyn Dodgers in an Ebbets Field doubleheader, to pull within two games of the Milwaukee Braves. In the first game, Bailey hit three bombs and Klu hit one, giving them each 13 for the year in the 10-6 win. In the nightcap, Thurman hit his second, and Robinson belted No. 16 to put the Reds ahead for good, 2-1.

Nuxhall was 0-for-4 at the plate but was sensational on the mound. He pitched a complete game for his second win (2-5), giving up just three hits—a double to Jackie Robinson and singles by Roy Campanella and Carl Furillo.

Klu sat next to moderator John Daly on TV, while his teammates crowded behind them: Nuxhall, Robinson, Post, Bailey, Bell, Burgess, McMillan, Temple, Jablonski and Johnny Klippstein. Nuxhall, in the back right, can barely be seen in the YouTube video. Blindfolded panelists Dorothy Kilgallen, Bennett Cerf, Arlene Francis and Paul Winchell had 10 guesses to identify the "mystery guest."

At first they didn't have a "Klu." Are you a performer? Would you be seen on television? Do you work for a certain TV network? Do you wear some sort of special cover-all, uniform or costume? Do you do what you do outdoors?

Klu provided some humorous answers. When asked if he worked "for a profit-making organization," he looked at Daly and finally answered, "Yes." Daly followed with an emphatic "YES!"

Do people watch you? "At times, yes."

Does he need watching? "Yes," Daly jumped in to say. "There are a lot of fellows who think he does, I'll say that."

Would it be some sort of athletic endeavor that you're famous for? At that point Daly informed the panel that there was more than one mystery guest. Quickly they figured the guests were from a sports team. A baseball team? One of the New York metropolitan teams?

"No."

"Then you won today!" exclaimed Francis, a baseball fan who knew the Yankees, Giants and Dodgers all lost that afternoon.

After Klu introduced the team, Cerf singled out Bailey: "Can we get a special bow for the fellow who hit three homers in the first game?"

Daly thanked the players, who were scheduled to play a night game in Pittsburgh in 21 hours. "It's awfully good of all you fellows to come, and we're grateful to you. And even though this is almost heresy, being a New Yorker, but good luck in the pennant," Daly said.

⚾ ⚾ ⚾

A week after their national TV debut, *Sports Illustrated* sent writer Robert Creamer to check out the homer happy Reds. Big Klu—6-feet 2, 230 pounds—put on a show. He hit three home runs in a 19-15 blow-out against the Cardinals July 1, and three more in a July 4 doubleheader split with the Cubs to give him 20 home runs.

"The arms of Theodore Kluszewski, bare to the shoulders in the sleeveless shirt he always wears on the ball field, are one of the Seven Wonders of the Baseball World … Kluszewski is one great chunk of muscle," wrote Creamer in his July 15 story. On the cover were "Redleg Musclemen—Klu, Post, Bell."

His bulging biceps now were nationally known in an era four decades before steroids turned baseball players into bodybuilders almost overnight. "He couldn't move his arms when they (the sleeves) got wet, so one day he cut them off," his wife Eleanor said. "I don't know how they played back then in those heavy flannel uniforms."

The Reds discovered Kluszewski in 1945 when they conducted spring training during World War II at Indiana University in Bloomington instead of Tampa, Florida. Klu was a two-sport college star—an end and kicker on the Hoosiers 9-0-1 Big Ten football champions, and a centerfielder batting .443. When the Reds invited Big Klu to take some swings, he hit some monster shots and the team offered him a contract. Klu made the club in 1947 at age 22. In 1953, Kluszewski set the Reds home run record with 40. He broke it the next year, when he led the Major Leagues with 49 home runs and 141 RBIs. Klu was second in the 1954 Most Valuable Player balloting to Willie Mays. In 1955, Klu hit 47 home runs, second to Mays' 51.

Sports Illustrated pointed out that "when the pitch approaches the plate … there's not much wrist action and comparatively little follow-through. It's all arms." Nuxhall told me those burly arms lashed more vicious liners than towering fly balls.

"Most of Klu's home runs were line drives. If he would have elevated the ball, it's hard telling how many home runs he would have hit. I've seen him hit line drives that the second baseman reached for—and the right fielder caught. I ain't kidding," Nuxhall said. In the 1956 All-Star Game in Washington's Griffith Stadium, Klu hit a line drive that first baseman Vic Power reached for—and it "hit about two feet from the top of the wall down the right field line," Nux said. Klu was 2-for-2 that day with two doubles, one run and one RBI in the NL's 7-3 victory.

Kluszewski, who was Sparky Anderson's hitting coach for the Big Red Machine, was decades ahead of his time. Like Joey Votto 60 years later, Kluszewski studied motion pictures of his swing using the latest technology—home movies.

"I bought him a 16mm camera for Christmas in 1947," after his Reds debut, his wife said. "He watched the film when he was having a bad day, or a couple of bad days. And that's how it started. I could see things he was doing wrong. It worked out to his advantage."

Klu was one of the Reds' most disciplined power hitters. Votto struck out 125 times in his 2010 MVP season. George Foster whiffed 107 times in his 1977 MVP season. Barry Larkin had 49 strikeouts in his 1995 MVP season. When Klu led the majors with 49 homers and 141 RBI in 1954, he struck out only 35 times.

"Klu put the ball in play. He didn't walk that much. He didn't strike out much. If you look at his record, I bet he didn't strike out more than 80 times a season. See if I'm right about that," Nuxhall said.

Joe was right. The most Klu ever struck out was half that—40 times—when he led the National League with 192 hits and 686 at-bats in 1955. In Klu's four best years (1953-56), he had more homers (40-49-47-35) than strikeouts (34-35-40-31).

⚾   ⚾   ⚾

I never saw Big Klu hit. The Reds traded him to the Pirates after the 1957 season, when I was 4 years old. But I saw him field—in my Middletown living room. I've got pictures to prove it.

My dad shot home movies of Kluszewski showing me how to play first base when he stopped by our house en route to a 1963 Middletown speaking engagement. My dad had contacted him and offered to guide

That's me standing behind Ted Kluszewski with my sisters Karen and Kathy, and younger brother Russ, when my dad convinced Klu to stop by our house on the way to a Middletown speech in 1963.
JOHN KIESEWETTER PHOTO

him to the event in downtown Middletown if he came to our house first. Why not have the Reds greatest left-handed first baseman teach your 10-year-old lefty some fancy footwork? He only had a few minutes, but Big Klu showed me how to bend low and glove imaginary ground balls on the living room carpet.

Klu led the Major Leagues in fielding for first basemen in 1951 with a .997 percentage (five errors in 1,474 chances). He was tops in both leagues also in 1953 (.995) and 1954 (.996), while leading the NL in fielding percentage five consecutive seasons, 1951-55.

"Everybody remembers him as a good hitter, but no one remembers that he set a Major League record for fielding for a first baseman," his wife said. "I'd like to meet that gentleman in Memphis who said he couldn't catch a bear in a telephone booth … He worked hard at it (fielding). He was a natural outfielder."

⚾ ⚾ ⚾

Two outs, nobody on, and the pitcher coming to bat.

The Pirates' Howie Pollet was looking for a second straight 1-2-3 inning to keep the score 2-2. Too late. Nuxhall homered to deep right-center at Crosley Field on Friday July 22, 1956, his second and final home run of the year. Nux also singled in the sixth, scoring on Robinson's fielder's choice. After a terrible 1-4 start in '56, Nuxhall's homer helped him improve his record to 7-8.

Fast forward two months to Friday, September 21. Nuxhall won his final game in 1956 for a 13-11 record with a complete game five-hitter over the Cardinals, 9-1, at Crosley. He slapped his first career triple in the second to score two runs. In the seventh, he singled and scored on Burgess' single. With six games to go, the Reds were seven homers short of the NL record set by the 1947 New York Giants. But they'd have to do it without Klu, out of the lineup with a pulled shoulder muscle. And they did.

On Saturday, Bell hit his 28th home run and Crowe, playing first for Klu, hit his 10th in a 6-4 win over the Cards. On Sunday the Reds swept a doubleheader from St. Louis. Post hit his last two homers of the year (35 and 36). Bell hit his 29th, and Ed Bailey hit his 28th. With three games left the Reds (89-62) were 1 games behind the Braves and Dodgers, and one home run behind the NL record.

Braves ace Warren Spahn held the Reds to six singles on Tuesday afternoon, winning his 20th game by a 7-1 score. Then the Reds traveled to Chicago for their final two games. Nuxhall started Saturday and was knocked out in the third by Ernie Banks' three-run, inside-the-park homer. In the eighth, Burgess hit a pinch-hit homer, No. 221 to tie the mark. The Reds erupted for five runs in the ninth to get Nuxhall off the hook and win 9-6.

The Reds failed to homer but beat the Cubs 4-2 on Sunday to finish 91-63, two games behind the Dodgers. It was the first time Cincinnati had won more than 90 games since the 1940 World Championship. The Reds also broke 1-million attendance for the first time. The 1,125,928 fans nearly doubled the 693,662 Crosley attendance in 1955.

For years, Cincinnati fans romanticized the '56 Redleg Musclemen who brought joy back to Mudville and revived the franchise. Despite the national attention on TV and in *Sports Illustrated*, Nuxhall lamented years later that the 1950s outfielders—unanimous Rookie of the Year Robinson, four-time All-Star Bell and Nuxy's buddy Post—were overshadowed by Hank Aaron and New York outfielders Willie Mays, Mickey Mantle and Duke Snider. Or "Willie, Mickey and the Duke," as the song goes.

"Gus Bell was an outstanding center fielder, but you had Willie Mays. Wally Post was an outstanding outfielder, and we had Frank Robinson and Vada Pinson. But those fellows were in an era of Mays, Duke Snider, Carl Furillo and Hank Aaron. They didn't get their due, in my estimation," Nuxhall said.

Over the years, the exploits of Big Klu, Robbie, Post, Bell and the other men of the free-swinging '56 Big Redleg Machine grew to mythical proportions for Baby Boomers and their parents—even after the record was broken nearly 50 years later in 2005, the third year of Great American Ball Park. Although some call it "Great American Small Park," today's field only offers a significant advantage to left-handed hitters compared to Crosley Field. Centerfield (404) is 17 feet farther from home than in Crosley, and the left field pole (328) is identical. But the right field line (325) is 17 feet closer to home than Crosley (342) during the 1950s. And the "gap" in the stands behind third base needed to fit GABP into the site forms a wind tunnel for balls to right.

The 2005 Reds hit 222 home runs, thanks to future Reds Hall of

Famers Adam Dunn (40), Ken Griffey Jr. (35) and Sean Casey (9). But the "Redleg Musclemen" mystique was never matched by Felipe Lopez (23), Wily Mo Pena (19), Jason LaRue (14), Edwin Encarnacion (9) or Ryan Freel (4). Left-handed pitcher Eric Milton contributed two homers in '05, as Nuxhall did in '56. The similarity ends there. In 1956, Nuxhall was an All-Star with a 13-11 record and 3.72 ERA, and gave up 18 home runs. Milton was 8-15 with a 6.47 ERA, and gave up a NL worst 40 home runs.

In Marty Brennaman's last season, the 2019 Reds hit a record 227 bombs. Eugenio Suarez led the team (49), establishing an MLB record for third basemen and for Venezuelans (topping Andres Galarraga). Votto hit 15, while rookie Aristides Aquino slammed 19 in two magical months after Yasiel Puig (22) was traded to Cleveland. Time will tell how—or if—we remember Derek Dietrich (19), Jesse Winker (16), Tucker Barnhart (11), Kyle Farmer (9) or Josh VanMeter (8).

To be honest, Joe Nuxhall was not very dangerous with the bat in his final four seasons. After hitting .269 in his 1962 comeback, Nuxhall hit a paltry .157 from 1963 to '66 (26-for-165). That pulled down his career batting average to .198. Nuxy liked to boast about his 15 home runs but seldom mentioned his career average slipped under the so-called Mendoza Line (.200), named for weak-hitting shortstop Mario Mendoza who played for Pittsburgh, Seattle and Texas from 1974 to 1982.

Nuxhall showed flashes of brilliance at the plate in his last years. He homered off the longest name in baseball, former teammate Calvin Coolidge Julius Caesar Tuskahoma "Cal" McLish, in a 1962 loss at Connie Mack Stadium on September 22. His 15th and final home run came in a 3-2 loss to the Giants at Candlestick Park on June 17, 1964. Nux homered off Bobby Bolin in the fifth after Mays hit his 19th off Nuxhall in the first.

In 1965, Nuxy knocked Pirates starter Joe Gibbon out of a game at Forbes Field on June 29. With the Reds up 2-0 in the fourth, Gibbon intentionally walked shortstop Leo Cardenas to face Nuxhall with the bases loaded. Nux made him pay. He slapped a two-run single scoring

Tony Perez and Deron Johnson. Joe got the victory, with future Giants manager Roger Craig earning a save for the Reds. Two weeks later, Nuxhall helped win his sixth game of the year with an RBI double against the Phillies on July 15 at Crosley. Nuxhall (6-2) raised his batting average to .286, and lowered his ERA to 4.36 with the complete game. By the end of the season, a bunch of hitless games dropped his batting average to .178, while he improved his ERA (3.45) and record (11-4).

In his last season, the Old Lefthander was only 4-for-40. He hit three singles and a double, scored two runs, and knocked in two, in 1966. His final month, Nux was feared neither on the mound nor at the plate. He lost four straight in September to finish 6-8. The last of his 152 hits came in a 7-2 loss to the Cubs at Wrigley on September 22. The single to right off rookie lefty Dave Dowling lifted his average to .105. It would fall to an even .100 when Nuxhall went 0-for-2 in his final start, a 3-2 loss to the Astros at Crosley on September 29. He struck out in the fifth, his last time up.

⚾ ⚾ ⚾

His most memorable at-bat? When I asked Nuxy that question, he filled the room with that laugh his wife said started down in his toes. No, it wasn't the near home run in the 1955 All-Star Game, or lighting up Whitey Ford in 1961. Nuxy beamed at the memory from a "Hamilton Night" at Crosley Field in front of his hometown fans.

Hamilton Night always was one of the biggest Reds promotions each year. A 2-mile motorcade with 52 buses brought 3,500 fans to "Joe Nuxhall Hamilton Night" on June 21, 1955. Nuxhall was given a key to the city. The 1956 Reds yearbook devoted a full page of pictures to it, "one of the greatest spectacles ever witnessed at Crosley Field." The next year, 103 buses were needed for Hamilton Night on July 18, 1956. Nuxhall sat on the bench both games, as he did most Hamilton Nights.

His favorite Hamilton Night was on July 31, 1957, when Nuxy got his 29th birthday present a day late in extra innings against the Phillies. Tied 5-5 in the 11th, Bell doubled to right with one out. Knowing the Reds were out of position players, the Phillies walked Frank Robinson. That's when manager Birdie Tebbetts told Nuxhall to pinch-hit for Fowler. Joe sent the crowd home happy.

"I remember the one pinch-hit I got on Hamilton Night, about one o'clock in the morning, because we had a rain delay. It was the only Hamilton Night I got in. I singled to center to score the winning run," Nuxhall said.

"I hit a soft line drive. But say it was a rocket! Make it sound good!"

It was a no-doubter, when you think about it. A real rocket.

The Marge and Pete Show

Joe kisses wife Donzetta at his statue dedication on July 19, 2003, four months after Great American Ball Park opened. CINCINNATI ENQUIRER PHOTO

The big day was here. The Reds were dedicating the life-sized bronze Joe Nuxhall statue on the plaza in front of brand new Great American Ball Park on July 19, 2003. Joe's family gathered in a Reds conference room before the ceremony: Donzetta, Phil, Kim, his mother, Evelyn, and brothers Gene, Don and Bob. In came Marge Schott, still a minority owner after being forced to sell controlling interest to Carl Lindner. She handed Joe a bag.

"Hey, honey, I'm so proud of you! I brought you a little something," Kim recalled.

Joe reached into the bag and pulled out a baseball cap with droopy dog ears. It was a Schottzie cap, designed after Marge's beloved St. Bernards. Joe thanked her as the family sat in stunned silence.

"Marge liked Joe. She would always hug him and kiss him," Donzetta said. "I really don't think he liked her very much."

He didn't, without a doubt.

Sam Gingrich, the advertising manager in charge of Kroger's Marty and Joe TV commercials, recalls a frustrated Joe "nearly getting violent" talking about contract negotiations with Marge during commercial shoots. "I never heard Nux talk badly about anyone, except one person. He flat-out didn't like Marge Schott," he said.

⚾ ⚾ ⚾

When I chatted with Nux during the Marge Era, he was very guarded talking about her. After she died in 2004, at 75, Nuxhall told me that "she was a good lady, I have to admit that. She just didn't belong in baseball."

It was clear he didn't like her penny-pinching ways and many of her decisions. Such as her decision that Joe should stop pitching batting practice. He was not alone. Schott's tenure as majority owner (1984-99) was marked by front-office turnover due to her unconventional style and personality. Associated Press sportswriter Joe Kay noted that 50 of 59 staffers listed in the Reds' 1984 media guide were gone by 1996. She cut the scouting department because "all they do is watch ballgames."

"She said, 'We don't need them,'" Nuxhall said after her death.

A fifth-generation German-American, Marge made inappropriate comments about African-Americans and Jews. She praised Adolf Hitler and kept a swastika at her home. She called Eric Davis and Dave Parker "million-dollar (N-words)," for which Major League Baseball fined her $250,000 and suspended her for the 1993 season. She was suspended again in 1996, and told to sell the club in 1999.

I never discussed racial issues with Nuxhall. I'm guessing that Nuxhall—who shared the clubhouse with Chuck Harmon, the Reds' first Black player (1954), Frank Robinson, Brooks Lawrence, Vada Pinson and Lee May, and as a broadcaster rode the team bus with Joe Morgan, George Foster, Barry Larkin, Eric Davis, and Ken Griffey Sr. and Jr.—didn't approve of her slurs.

"It's sad to see such an organization that had such pride, and people thought so much of, to have the things happen the way they are," Nuxhall told me in 1996, when Larkin was coming off his MVP season. I asked

Nux if the Reds planned to celebrate Larkin's MVP with a giveaway. "Unless Barry pays for it, it won't happen. That's one of the problems down there, without a doubt. She doesn't understand that you have to spend money to make money. If this thing gets run down so far—instead of a shovel, they're going to need a steam shovel to dig us out. I worry about it. I know you run a business as economically as possible, but if you want to be successful you have to have some good chiefs sticking around. But that's not my business. I'm concerned, but there's not a damn thing I can do about it."

Nuxhall wasn't totally critical of Marge, who despite her chaos brought a World Championship to Cincinnati in 1990. He praised her for her player acquisitions. Such as when player-manager Pete Rose and General Manager Bill Bergesch went to Schott's home to ask for money to trade for Buddy Bell, father of future Reds manager David Bell, from the Rangers in 1985. Rose told me he didn't "know Schottzie that well, and she's growling like she's going to bite my [expletive] leg off. I look at Bill Bergesch and say, 'The hell with Buddy Bell. Let's get out of here!' All of the sudden, the handler came in and took the dog out. And in five minutes we had the money for Buddy Bell. But I was scared to death."

It was the "Marge and Pete Show" for Reds fans in the 1980s. Bob Howsam brought back Rose as player-manager in August 1984, and Schott took controlling interest that December. Pete broke Ty Cobb's hit record in 1985, and four years later he accepted a lifetime ban from baseball. Lou Piniella replaced Rose for the 1990 season, and the Reds won their first World Championship since 1976.

"She wanted to win," Rose told me in 2013. "She loved dogs, I have no qualms with that. But Marge was kind of a sad deal. She didn't have any family, but she had all this money, this baseball team and a big mansion in Indian Hill."

⚾ ⚾ ⚾

When I went to Los Angeles for the Television Critics Association press tour, I'd frequently be asked about Marge. Was she really that eccentric? That insensitive? That cheap? That stupid?

I assured my fellow TV writers that it was all true. Basically, they should believe every wild tale they heard about her baseball craziness. When there were doughnuts left over from a 1989 season ticket breakfast at Riverfront Stadium, Marge tried to convince the baker to take them back. Then she ordered a staffer to sell them to Reds employees for 35 cents each. Before she replaced Reds organist Ronnie Dale in 1986 with taped music, she wanted him to record his songs on cassette tapes. He refused. She could never remember players' names, so she called them "Honey" or "Sweetie." She saved money by canceling the machine that provided out-of-town scores at the ballpark and ordering the media relations department to print game notes on the back of yesterday's releases. Schott left Davis in an Oakland hospital after injuring his kidney diving for a ball, and his teammates flew home with the 1990 World Series trophy. She wanted him to find his own way home.

One of the first things she did as owner was to eliminate longtime mascot Mr. Red in favor of "the goddamn dog," as Nuxy called Schottzie. Marge insisted Schottzie, and later Schottzie 02, be included in team photos and baseball card giveaways. I was at a game in Riverfront when a fan unfurled a homemade banner reading, "*End the curse. Sacrifice Schottzie.*" Ushers quickly removed it. She took the dog to David Letterman's show in 1986 and announced Schottzie could be pregnant. She explained, "They said if their nipples get larger—"

Letterman cut her off. "I don't want to hear any more about your damn dog!"

Schottzie got a World Series ring with the team on Opening Day 1991. A few months later Marge held a news conference to announce Schottzie's death. "Pets are always there for you. They never ask for anything. They never ask for a raise," Kay quoted her saying.

Marge often was clueless. She thought the world revolved around her and her dog. She didn't care about normal polite behavior, the nuances and social graces that guide most human beings. Unlike the rest of us, she didn't try to keep up with society, and that was her fault. Ironically, her maiden name Unnewehr was pronounced "unaware."

To be fair, she had a big heart to go with her big mouth and big dog.

She insisted $1 hot dogs be sold at Riverfront Stadium. My sons Joe and David went boating on Lake Marge Unnewehr Schott at the Boy Scouts' Camp Friedlander. We bought their Eagle Scout gifts at the Marge Schott Scout Achievement Center. She funded the University of Cincinnati's Marge Schott Field for baseball, and the Cincinnati Zoo's Marge Schott-Unnewehr Elephant Reserve. She gave to animal shelters, Boys & Girls Clubs and St. Ursula Academy. (In 2020, her name was removed from UC and St. Ursula buildings after the nationwide protests over race issues. The Marge & Charles J. Schott Foundation issued this statement: "While we cannot make excuses for the rhetoric made by Mrs. Schott decades ago, we can ask you to learn from Mrs. Schott's mistakes as well as her great love for Cincinnati.")

The world only knew Marge's eccentricities. Such as when Rose wanted the Reds to sign future Hall of Fame closer Rollie Fingers in 1986. Fingers, 39, had been released by the Brewers after an awful 1985 season (1-6, 17 saves, 5.04 ERA). But the Reds insisted he cut off his trademark handlebar mustache. Recalling the story for WLW-AM's Lance McAlister, Fingers said he told the Reds: "You tell Marge Schott to shave her St. Bernard, and I'll shave my mustache."

During spring training in 1989, she settled a salary dispute with outfielder Kal Daniels by flipping a coin. He wanted $325,000; she offered $300,000. WLW-TV broadcast the coin toss live from Plant City. Marge called heads and lost. Commissioner Bart Giamatti told the *Cincinnati Post* that baseball "did not consider it a form of gambling. However ... it is a ridiculous way to negotiate a contract, trivializes the whole process and demeans the participants." As the 1989 season unfolded, Marge had a real gambling problem with allegations that Rose bet on baseball. Rose accepted a lifetime ban on August 24. The next day his picture outside the Reds' clubhouse was replaced by a photo of Marge and Schottzie.

⚾ ⚾ ⚾

My seat for the 1990 World Series was in a CBS trailer under Riverfront's right field stands. Shortly after the national telecast started, Marge walked out to the on-field microphone. The CBS folks freaked. Marge had addressed the crowd before the live TV coverage began. She wasn't scheduled to be on the field again.

Marge made the unscripted appearance to request "a moment of silence for our fighting women and men in the Far East." She apparently stifled a belch so it sounded like she asked for a "mubbub of silence" for troops actually in the *MIDEAST* after Iraq invaded Kuwait. *Cincinnati Post* sports editor Mike Bass, in his 1993 *Marge Schott: Unleashed* biography, quoted a Reds official saying she was "stumbling down the hall" drunk. People told me that if you turned up the TV sound very loud, you could hear somebody near an open CBS microphone say, "She's ——ing loaded!"

I didn't speak to Nuxhall about the 1990 season, but I've heard Brennaman, Piniella and players reminisce about the wire-to-wire championship. The former Yankees manager took over a club Pete had guided to four straight second-place finishes. Fiery Lou arrived with a sense of urgency from Yankees, where he played in four World Series, including the 1976 loss to the Reds. Lou was short and sweet in his first meeting with the team.

"There is too much talent here not to have won it by now. This is your year. Let's go out and win it. I'm here to win, too, so I don't care if you don't like me," Piniella said, according to Tom Browning. Piniella possibly was even more competitive than Nuxhall. Once when Danny Jackson started a game by throwing six straight balls, Lou uttered the words Brennaman quoted on radio for three decades: *"I've seen enough!"* Piniella ordered pitching coach Stan Williams to pull Jackson after two batters, said first baseman Todd Benzinger. Williams objected. "We can't do that. We've got nobody warming up." Piniella countered: "Dibble can warm up."

Piniella let Marge rub dog hair on him and everything else. During a hot, humid Sunday afternoon game, she gave the bat boy plastic baggies filled with Schottzie hair and ordered him to sprinkle it for good luck on the bat rack. On bats covered with sticky pine tar. "The batters had to scrape all this dog hair off them," Piniella recalled at 2016 Redfest.

The front office improved Piniella's roster by trading closer John Franco to the Mets for reliever Randy Myers. The Reds also picked up first baseman Hal Morris and outfielders Billy Hatcher and Glenn Braggs. The club won its first nine games and stayed in first place all season, going to the World Series for the first time since the 1976 Big Red Machine.

"The four years I finished second, we weren't good enough to win," Rose told me. "If you give me Randy Myers, Hal Morris, Glenn Braggs and Bill Hatcher, I'll go to the World Series four straight years."

With the 1990 pennant in sight, Marge ordered a controversial squeeze play. She forced Ken Griffey Sr., the last player from the Big Red Machine, to retire to open a roster spot for pitcher Chris Hammond. Griffey, hitting .206, was given his unconditional release on August 24. He immediately joined his son to make history in Seattle. Junior, 20, and Senior, 40, were the first father-and-son to play together in the big leagues on August 31, and to hit back-to-back home runs on September 14. Senior batted .377 for the Mariners and retired in 1991 with a .296 lifetime average.

For Brennaman and many others, the '90 team remains their favorite because nobody expected them to be playing in October, or beat the powerful Oakland A's, who were playing in their third consecutive World Series. The A's won 103 games, while the Reds finished 91-71, yet Piniella's scouts liked the match-up. "Watching a lot of films, I saw they were fastball pitchers, and we were fastball hitters. They were good at hitting the breaking ball/soft stuff, and we had a lot of power arms," he said.

Marge was upset by the sweep. Why? The Major League Baseball Players Association gets most of the ticket receipts from the first four games; the two teams split proceeds from the final three, if played. Her displeasure was evident by the absence of food at the Reds' celebration at the Parc Fifty-Five hotel in San Francisco after Game Four.

"She genuinely wanted that series to go six or seven games," Brennaman said. "We had no food. Tony Perez and I went across the street to Carl's Jr., a fast-food chain, and bought hamburgers and French fries for everybody." Benzinger, Paul O'Neill and Jeff Reed also bought burgers and watched series highlights in their rooms.

"There was nothing going on for us," Benzinger said. "It was not Marge's strength to take care of the little things like that—as Eric Davis found out the next day when he didn't have a plane."

I was on the Pete beat in 1996, interviewing Pete Rose about his nationally syndicated sports talk show broadcast by Cincinnati's new sports station, 1160 The Score. BILL RENKEN PHOTO

⚾ ⚾ ⚾

A Hollywood TV producer called me in 1991 with a scoop: Marge Schott had flown to Los Angeles to appear in CBS' *Good Sports* sitcom starring real-life couple Ryan O'Neal and Farrah Fawcett as ESPN-like sports anchors. During a break in the taping, Schott confronted Fawcett and O'Neal about living together unmarried since 1979. But he said that part was off the record; I couldn't use the info unless I got it from someone else. It was a great story: This crazy old woman from Cincinnati cornering a Hollywood power couple. When I called Marge a few days before the March 19 telecast, she proudly told me the whole story.

"That was one of the reasons I went out there," she said. As I wrote in the *Cincinnati Enquirer,* the Catholic Reds owner made it clear to O'Neal that, if she were in charge, he'd be tossed out at home. For her, it was the difference between living in sin, and living in Cincinnati. "When I met him I said, 'You'd better be glad that I'm not your mother, or I'd make you marry that girl. You'd better be glad I didn't bring a priest along!'"

The producer called again in April. He said Rose, just released from a half-way house after his federal prison term, had taped a *Good Sports,* too. Pete's May 27 sitcom appearance would be his first "TV interview" after serving five months for two felony counts of filing false income tax returns.

I was now on the Pete beat. For the next 25-plus years, I covered Rose's forays into films, TV and sports talk radio. Not able to earn a paycheck from baseball, he did a local show on WCKY-AM; syndicated radio shows aired on WSAI-AM and WBOB-AM in the 1990s; and *Pete Rose Live* on the short-lived NewSport cable network in 1995. Rose also starred in a 2013 TLC channel reality series, *Pete Rose: Hits & Mrs.,* about living with fiancé Kiana Kim and her two teen-age children, Cassie and Ashton. The kids didn't know anything about baseball or Pete's career. In my favorite scene, all four were in Cooperstown walking toward the Baseball Hall of Fame when Cassie asks: "Is this (place) sort of like the Titanic Museum, except it's all about baseball?"

TLC pulled the show after two episodes. When we spoke two months later, Rose complained about my reviews: "Hey, take it easy with my reality show, will you? Geez, give me a break. Give me a chance at another network to be successful," he said. No other network picked up the series.

Three months after *Good Sports*, Rose made his movie debut playing Ty Cobb in NBC's *Babe Ruth* starring Stephen Lang at Cleveland Municipal Stadium. I drove to Cleveland for Pete's press conference, his first media event since prison. I remember someone asking if there could be a Pete Rose movie someday.

"That's down the road," he said. "In order to have something like that—and I think you'll all agree—you have to have a happy ending. I'm working on the happy ending right now. Obviously, the happy ending would be going to the Hall of Fame."

He was still waiting 30 years later.

Nuxhall never talked to me about Pete's banishment, but he discussed it on WCET-TV in 2005. Joe supported Pete until he confessed to betting on baseball in *My Prison Without Bars*, his 2004 book.

"It's just a tragedy what happened to him, but, and I'll be honest with you, I was rooting for Pete. When he came out with his book and admitted he had done those things, then I jumped off his bandwagon." Had Pete gone to the commissioner "and said, 'Mr. Commissioner, I've messed up. I'm sorry for it. And I want to straighten it out,' I honestly believe he would possibly be in the Hall of Fame."

Without naming Roger Clemens, Barry Bonds or Mark McGwire, Nux noted that if guys "who did drugs and steroids" were allowed on the Hall of Fame ballot, then "Pete deserves to be on it. He made a mistake. He paid for it for the last 17 years now. He has done for the game of baseball more than any of the guys who are out there. That's my feeling."

⚾ ⚾ ⚾

ESPN's Chris Berman and I squeezed into the Riverfront Stadium elevator with the baseball writers for the ride from the press box to the field before ESPN's 1994 *Opening Night* telecast. As soon as the door closed, we heard the *Buzz! Buzz! Buzz!* from someone impatiently pushing the elevator call button. The doors opened at the office level. There stood Marge, Schottzie and National League President Leonard Coleman.

"Everybody out! Everybody out!" Marge shouted. "I've got to get Schottzie down to the field."

Marge got what she wanted this time. But not always. Had Marge prevailed, ESPN wouldn't have done the Reds-Cardinals Opening Night game. After she asked ESPN to put the national spotlight on Cincinnati's Opening Day traditions, she wanted them to pick another city after realizing the game was on Easter. ESPN refused, so she ordered the Opening Day parade, patriotic bunting and pregame players' introductions postponed until Monday's day game. The ESPN game drew 32,803, the only opener not to sell out, compared to 55,093 on Monday.

Marge could be a bully. And she managed to silence some of her biggest critics in town when negotiating Reds radio rights in 1991 with WLW-AM, home of talk hosts Bill Cunningham, Andy Furman, Cris Collinsworth and satirist Gary Burbank. The contract prohibited WLW-AM employees from broadcasting any remarks "that assail the personal reputation, morality, integrity or character of any of the club's partners, officers or agents." In *Unleashed*, Bass wrote that Marge tried to get Burbank fired several times after hearing about his comedy bits and prank calls. In 1994, a woman named "Marge" called Burbank's afternoon show to talk about the Riverfront Stadium lease with the city. "If council members cut me a good deal, I might let them work on the grounds crew," she said. "If I buy the stadium, Schottzie will be allowed back on the field. Who cares if she takes a dump on the field? If I own the place, I might go out there and take a dump myself."

Once Marge visited WLW-AM's Mount Adams studios with Schottzie and joked with Burbank and Collinsworth on Gary's "Sports or Consequences" trivia segment, during which the Burbank gang celebrated correct answers by chanting "We don't! We don't! We don't mess around!"

"She had the best time," Burbank said. "Marge was yelling 'We don't mess around!' And after she walked out the door I looked at Cris and said, 'Does she realize that she hates us?' And Cris said, 'Vodka is a friend to us all.'"

Burbank eventually was ordered not to talk about Marge on his show. So he began referencing "that person we're not supposed to mention on the radio." His Marge bits continued after Schott died. Sidekick John Davies, known as "Duke Sinatra," imitated Marge making calls as "Saint CEO" from a pay phone while smoking a cigarette outside Heaven's pearly gates. She'd talk about the latest person who died, or going to parties with William Shakespeare and Abraham Lincoln. The "appease Marge" philosophy also impacted sister station WEBN-FM down the hall. In 1991, the rock station produced a comedy bit mixing Marty and Joe's comments about Roseanne Barr screeching *The Star-Spangled Banner* with Schott singing *Take Me Out To The Ball Game*. It never aired.

In 1995, Marge's Reds returned to the postseason, playing the Braves in the NLCS. I was at Riverfront when her pre-game entertainment was having the Cincinnati Police horse patrol do formations in the outfield. Groundskeepers came out afterwards with snow shovels to scoop up the horse poop. As the game started, a brown smear was clearly visible on the artificial grass. I knew Reds outfielders Reggie Sanders, Ron Gant and Jerome Walton weren't going to be diving for balls in the gap.

⚾ ⚾ ⚾

"Are they allowed to do that?" Marge barked into the phone. I had called her for a comment about the USA cable's plan to make a movie called

The Marge Schott Story without her permission. It was the first she had heard of it.

The cable network had announced in December 1999—two months after Schott was forced to sell to Carl Lindner—that the movie would be based on Bass's *Marge Schott: Unleashed* and public domain material. It was one of 19 USA projects, including movies about teacher Mary Kay Letourneau's affair with a 13-year-old student and a four-hour miniseries about barbarian Attila the Hun.

We had fun with *The Marge Schott Story* at the *Enquirer*. We asked readers to cast the film, and more than 100 people gave us their best Schott: Kathy Bates, Roseanne Barr, Ernest Borgnine (*McHale's Navy*) and Dennis Franz (*NYPD Blue*). Borgnine came in second to Bates.

By Opening Day, *Marge Schott* was cut from USA's roster. "If we make a movie about someone who's so inherently unsympathetic, I'm not sure people will want to watch it," explained Adam Shapiro, USA Networks vice president. "Portraying her in a sympathetic light is difficult."

USA cable didn't have that problem with Attila the Hun.

⚾   ⚾   ⚾

I last saw Marge at the *Enquirer's* Women of the Year reception in 2002, a year after the police shooting of a young black man in Over-the-Rhine led to three days of rioting. Cincinnati news had been dominated by African-American community protests led by the Rev. Damon Lynch III, and the Catholic priest sex abuse scandal. I re-introduced myself as the *Enquirer* Tempo section editor when she was selected for Women of the Year. She looked at me and said: "I'm so tired of reading about all the Blacks and priests, and all that shit, you know, honey? And who's 'The Reverend the Third?'"

Two years after her death, when I asked Nux for his favorite Marge story, he recalled her holding up the team bus during the 1990 World Series. "We can't go because CBS wants her on the morning show. So we're all sitting on the bus waiting on her for about forty-five minutes. It didn't bother her one bit. And of course, she had the goddamn dog with her. She was the boss."

Clubhouse manager Rick Stowe told me how his father, Bernie, and Joe loved to joke about Marge. The clubhouse phone would ring, and Bernie would tell Joe that Marge wanted him to take Schottzie for a walk. Their back-and-forth usually ended when Joe or Bernie hurled the ultimate insult: *"Marge is your girlfriend!"* Followed by the response: *"No, she's YOUR girlfriend!"*

Kim has heard all the stories. He worried for years his father's candor could get him canned.

"When he would speak to some groups, he wasn't afraid to say what he thought about Marge," Kim said. "I was always worried about Dad getting in some serious trouble."

Reds Turn To Nuxhall For Media Relations

Marty Brennaman was reading the morning *Tampa Tribune* during 1995 spring training when a headline caught his eye: "Reds Turn To Nuxhall For Media Relations."

A Florida sportswriter had fallen for a joke in the Reds' game notes written by Joe Kelley on April 23, his last day as the club's public relations assistant. Kelley had turned down a chance at succeeding Jon Braude—a friend who had been fired by Marge—to work for the Cincinnati Cyclones minor league hockey team at double his salary. Brennaman told listeners Kelley had advised reporters to direct questions about the Reds in his absence to long-time employee Nuxhall.

BRENNAMAN: I see the headline of the article: "Reds Turn To Nuxhall For Media Relations." Uh-Oh! This is in the Tampa Tribune, folks. I feel sorry for the poor soul who took that line as gospel from the Reds note sheet yesterday, the final one authored by the inimitable and now legendary Joe Kelley.

NUXHALL: Would he put that in there if he didn't mean it?

BRENNAMAN: I believe he would, and did! But some poor, naïve soul picked up on it!

Joe Nuxhall: The Old Lefthander & Me · John Kiesewetter

11

The Nux Hall of Fame

*Ken Griffey Jr. and Joe share a laugh during a pregame ceremony celebrating
Junior's 500th career home run at Great American Ball Park in 2004.*
CINCINNATI ENQUIRER PHOTO

If you tried to pick an all-time Cincinnati Reds starting lineup, who's on
first? What's on second? I don't know how to do it, so I asked Nuxhall. A
year before he died, I had a long conversation with Nuxhall and asked him
to name his all-time Reds roster, position-by-position, from all the Reds
players he had watched for six decades from the field, bench or booth.

Who would he put in the Nux Hall of Fame lineup? It was 2006,
when Ken Griffey Jr. and Adam Dunn patrolled the outfield, before
Joey Votto, Brandon Phillips, Jay Bruce, Eugenio Suarez, Luis Castillo,
Johnny Cueto or Aroldis Chapman had arrived in Cincinnati. (I also

asked Marty Brennaman similar questions.) Joe's responses may surprise you. Not everyone in Cooperstown made his list.

My first question was out of left field: Who could hit a baseball farther, Dunn or Foster?

"The most power of all the outfielders was Foster," he said. "I threw him batting practice for all those years. You remember the city's club boxes (Riverfront's third deck yellow seats) in left-center field? He hit one over that box, on the center field side of it, into the fourth row of the red seats. It was batting practice, but he hit it easy, I mean with less effort than anybody I'd ever seen."

The Big Red Machine's left fielder was the National League Most Valuable Player in 1977 by leading the league in home runs (52) and runs batted in (149), and on-base plus slugging (1.013). Foster, acquired from the Giants for shortstop Frank Duffy in 1971, became a regular when manager Sparky Anderson moved Pete Rose from left to third base on May 3, 1975. The Reds were 12-12 at the time; they went 96-42 to win 108 games en route to the first of their back-to-back championships. Foster led the NL in RBIs for three straight years (1976-78) and homers for two years (1977-78). In the 1976 World Series, Foster was the second-best hitter (.429) to Johnny Bench (.533), and second in the NL Most Valuable Player balloting behind Joe Morgan. Unlike some Reds sluggers, he was very sure-handed, playing all three outfield positions.

Dunn, inducted into the Reds Hall of Fame in 2018, hit 40 home runs four consecutive seasons (2004-2007), but never led the league. His 270 homers rank fifth on the Reds all-time list behind Bench (389), Frank Robinson (324), Votto (295) and Tony Perez (287) at the end of 2020. Ted Kluszewski is sixth (251), followed by Foster (244).

"George Foster had the single greatest year of any player that I've ever seen in 1977. He hit .320 with 149 RBIs and 52 home runs," Brennaman said. "I've never seen a hitter on this club where the ball jumped off a bat the way the ball jumped off his bat. It just exploded. George was in a class by himself."

At Philadelphia's Veterans Stadium, a round multipurpose facility similar to Riverfront Stadium used by the Phillies and NFL Eagles from

1971 to 2003, Foster blasted a home run off the right-centerfield score-board in 1977.

"It was probably 25 feet up in the air," Brennaman said. "A buzz went through the press area among the Philadelphia people, because they quickly said it was the longest home run ever hit to that section of the park, by a right-handed hitter, in the history of the ballpark. The next night, he hit one 15 feet higher up on it. It was just amazing. His '77 year was just unbelievable."

How many homers would Foster have hit in Great American Small Park? Nuxhall laughed at the question in 2006, the Reds' fourth year in the new stadium. "Good gracious, Foster might have hit 55 or 60 at Great American Ball Park. He would bang them off the scoreboard, I guarantee. I'd bet my life that he would," Nux said.

⚾   ⚾   ⚾

Who would join Foster in Nuxhall's all-time most powerful outfield? Dunn? Griffey Jr.? Robinson? Eric Davis? Gus Bell?

"I'd have to take Junior. But it's tough to really pick one group of guys," he said. Interestingly, Nuxhall chose Griffey Jr., a member of baseball's All-Century Team, despite Junior having his best stats in Seattle (.292/417 HR/1,216 RBI in 13 years), not in his hometown (.270/210 HR/602 RBI in nine years). He has a .907 career OPS, 56th on the all-time list.

Next, Nux mentioned 1950's teammate Bell, grandfather of manager David Bell and father of Buddy Bell. Gus hit .288 in nine seasons for the Reds, with 206 HR, 942 RBI and four All-Star Games. He led the NL in triples (12) in 1951.

"Gus Bell had some great years. But for consistency, I'd take Robbie," said Nuxhall about Robinson, the 1956 Rookie of the Year and 1961 National League MVP. The Hall of Famer spent his first 10 years with the Reds, going to seven All-Star games. He hit .302 for the Reds, and fifth in runs (1,042) and RBI (1,009), in addition to being second in home runs. He has a career .926 OPS, 43rd all-time.

Then Nux benched Robbie for his old buddy Wally Post, whom he met at Class D Muncie (Indiana) in 1947, when both were 18. Post, the pride of St. Henry, Ohio, hit .266 in 12 Reds seasons. In 1955, he hit .309 with 40 home runs and 109 RBI, and finished 12th in the National League MVP voting. Teammate Kluszewski hit .314 with 47 homers and 113 RBI. The next year, Post hit 36 HRs, and Klu hit 35, when the team tied the league home run mark. After that he never hit more than 22 homers a year, retiring at age 34 with 172 homers in 15 years for the Reds, Phillies, Twins and Indians. He has a career .808 OPS.

Davis, whose Cincinnati stats (.271/ 203 HR/615 RBI in nine years) are eerily similar to Griffey's, didn't make Joe's short list.

"For pure power, I'd take Post. Wally could hit the ball a mile. In Crosley Field, Wally Post could reach all ports, as you'd say," he said. One of the favorite targets was the Siebler Tailors advertisement on the Superior Laundry & Towel Supply Co. building beyond the left-field wall. "You've heard about the sign on top of the laundry for Siebler suits? 'Hit This Sign, Win A Suit?' He probably got two or three suits a year by hitting that sign. That would be like way back in the second (yellow) deck at Riverfront. Wally was the best-dressed guy we had."

When I posed that question to Brennaman in 2006, he said that "from a power standpoint, I'd put Foster in left, Griffey Jr. in center field, and Dunn in right." He paused. "Darn! That's tough to leave Eric Davis out of that lineup. My fourth outfielder, a real close fourth, would be Eric Davis."

⚾ ⚾ ⚾

So who's on first? That was the most difficult question for Nuxhall. He played with four Reds Hall of Fame first basemen (Kluszewski, Frank McCormick, Lee May and Tony Perez) and loved a fifth (Sean Casey) like a son.

Klu, a feared slugger and four-time All-Star, hit 279 home runs—171 in four seasons (1953-56)—and drove in 1,028 runs. His career .850 OPS ranks 180th.

McCormick, the 1940 MVP and eight-time All-Star, helped the Reds win back-to-back pennants in 1939-40.

May, a three-time All-Star, played in three World Series (1970, 1979, 1981) and hit 354 homers for the Reds, Astros, Orioles and Royals.

Perez, the 1967 All-Star Game MVP and veteran of five World Series (1970, 1972, 1975, 1976, 1983) was inducted into Baseball's Hall of Fame in 2000 with 379 HRs and 1,652 RBI. His career OPS is .804.

Casey, one of the Reds' most popular players, batted .305 in eight Cincinnati seasons and led the team in batting six times. He played in three All-Star games.

Would it be Big Klu? The Big Dog? The Big Bopper? The Mayor? Or McCormick?

"The best answer I could give you would be either Klu or Tony. I think it's all according to how you make out the lineup," he said. Kluszewski hit left-handed; Perez hit right-handed. "Klu had good hands. His range was better than Casey's, definitely. Tony had good hands. But all around, I think Klu was a heck of a lot better ballplayer than he's given credit for, personally. Since I played (more) with Ted, and I knew the respect he got at the plate, I'll take Klu."

⚾ ⚾ ⚾

What's on second? Without a doubt, it was Hall of Famer Morgan, the back-to-back National League MVP in 1975-76 when the Big Red Machine won World Championships. In 1975 he led the majors with a .974 OPS while hitting .327, and again topped both leagues with a .1020 OPS in '76 while batting .320. He also led the National League in on-base percentage four years (1972, 1974-76).

"With second base, you have to go with Morgan." That's all Nux said.

Marty said much more in 2006, a month before the Reds acquired Brandon Phillips: "For two years, in '75 and '76, Joe Morgan was the best player I've ever seen in this game. He could beat you every possible way. He could go 0-for-3, and walk twice, hit a sacrifice fly and score two times. Every night he'd do something to help you win."

"Little Joe" retired after 22 seasons—eight in Cincinnati—as second on the Reds stolen base list (406) behind Reds Hall of Famer Bid McPhee (468), and ahead of Barry Larkin (379). Marty marveled at Morgan's aggressiveness. Morgan "knew intuitively how big a lead he could get, and still get back to first if the pitcher threw over. Riverfront had those dirt cut-outs in the Astroturf around the bases, and we'd make the comment, 'He's got both feet on the carpet!' His philosophy was that to be a good base-stealer, you could not be afraid to be thrown out. He could get thrown out twice in a game—but if he got on again, he was going to be running. You were not going to shut him down."

⚾   ⚾   ⚾

Nuxhall basically watched four great shortstops for 50 years: Roy McMillan (1951-60), Leo Cardenas (1960-68), Dave Concepcion (1970-88) and Hall of Famer Barry Larkin (1986-2004).

"With shortstop, that's tough," Nuxy said. Here's how they stack up:

In 10 Reds seasons (1951-60), McMillan hit .243 with 42 home runs; played in two All-Star Games (1956-57); won three Gold Gloves (1957-59); and was sixth in the 1956 National League MVP voting. In 1954, he set a National League record (since broken) of making 129 double plays. He led the NL in double plays turned for four years (1953-56), and was first in NL shortstop fielding percentage for three years (1956-58).

Cardenas hit .261 in nine Cincinnati seasons (1960-68) with 35 doubles, 72 home runs and 26 stolen bases; was a four-time All-Star (1964-66 and 1968); and won a Gold Glove (1965). "Little Leo" led NL shortstops two years in fielding percentage (1963, 1966), and once in double plays turned (1965).

Concepcion, who made Anderson's first club at 19, played all 19 years with the Reds (1970-88). He hit .267 with 389 doubles, 101 home runs and 321 stolen bases. He was a nine-time All-Star and the 1982 All-Star Game MVP. He won five Gold Gloves; two Silver Slugger Awards (1981-82); and was fourth in NL MVP voting in 1981 behind Mike Schmidt, Andre Dawson and Foster. He led the NL once in fielding percentage (1977), and in double plays turned (1979). He hit .351 in five NL Championship Series and .266 in four World Series.

Larkin, the 1995 National League MVP, also played all of his 19 seasons in his hometown (1986-2004). He was by far the best offensive player of this group, with a .295 average, 441 doubles, 198 home runs and 379 stolen bases. He was a 12-time All-Star and three-time Gold Glove winner

(1994-96). Larkin won nine Silver Slugger Awards, the most by all Major League shortstops, and third all-time behind outfielder Barry Bonds (12) and catcher Mike Piazza (10). He was No. 1 in double plays turned only once, in 1990 (86), but never first in National League fielding percentage for shortstops. Larkin is second to Rose in all-time Reds hits (2,340), just ahead of Concepcion (2,326).

Nuxhall's choice for best shortstop may be hard for Reds fans to accept.

"If you look for just defensive skills, I'd take McMillan, without a doubt. Like I used to tell people, on this (artificial turf) stuff they play on today, he might not ever make an error. Overall, it's pretty tough to say between Davey and Lark. But I'd take Davey. I think Davey had better range and a better arm. Offensively, he'd be very good in situational hitting type things."

Ron Oester, who played next to Concepcion and Larkin, agreed with Nux. "Nothing against Barry, I think Barry could play somewhere else because of his athletic ability. I'd still want Larkin on my team, but Davey is the best defensive shortstop I ever played with, and I've seen a lot of shortstops," Oester said at a 2005 Reds Hall of Fame event. Hall of Famer Ozzie Smith "was flashy, but Davey was just steady—especially in his younger days. He had a great arm. Barry made a lot of plays because of his athletic ability, but Davey was just a natural, defensively."

⚾   ⚾   ⚾

And I-Don't-Know is on third! Nux wasn't trying to be funny. He wasn't intentionally quoting the old Abbott & Costello comedy routine when I asked him for his all-time Reds third basemen. He actually said, "I don't know."

In all honestly, third was a revolving door for most of Nuxhall's 64 years. Some names stand out—Perez, Rose, Chris Sabo, Buddy Bell, Aaron Boone, Ray Knight, Gene Freese—but they didn't stay there long. So fans were treated to the exploits of Brandon Larson, Edwin Encarnacion, Lenny Harris, Ryan Freel, Willie Greene, Bip Roberts, John Vukovich, Rafael Landestoy, Tim Hummel, Tommy Harper and Chico Ruiz. The Reds also tried first basemen and catchers there: Bench, Paul Konerko,

Dmitri Young, Danny Driessen, Deron Johnson, Alex Trevino, Lloyd McClendon and Jason LaRue.

"I don't know who in the world I'd put at third. Probably Pete. He played first, second and the outfield. I would put Pete there," Nuxhall said.

Not a bad choice. Rose is the only Major League player with at least 500 games at five positions—first (696), second (634), third (634), left (671) and right (595). He was a 17-time All-Star playing those positions.

What about Bell or Don Hoak? Buddy led NL third basemen in fielding percentage in 1987. But he played only four of his 18 years in Cincinnati. His six Gold Gloves and five All-Star selections came with the Rangers and Indians. Hoak was a Reds All-Star in 1957, but he played just two of his 11 years in Cincinnati. As a Pirate, Hoak was second in MVP balloting to teammate Dick Groat in 1960, when Pittsburgh won the World Series.

"Buddy wasn't here very long. Hoak was good, but he wasn't here that long. I'd have to say Pete," Nuxhall said.

Over the years, the Reds also have moved slick-fielding shortstops to the hot corner: Suarez, Concepcion, Tony Fernandez, Felipe Lopez, Juan Castro, Rich Aurilia and Eddie Kasko. Brennaman told me in 2006, three years before the Reds traded Encarnacion for Scott Rolen, that Blue Jays' All-Star shortstop Fernandez played the best third base he'd ever seen for the Reds.

"Tony Fernandez and Buddy Bell would be a dead heat. Buddy was a third baseman cut out of the classic mold. He never made a bad throw. From a purely third-baseman's perspective, he would have been the best. But Tony Fernandez, to me, played the best defensive third base that I ever saw (1994). And that was amazing, because he was a shortstop. When I told that to Nuxhall, Joe said, "If all I want is defense at third, I'd put Juan Castro there."

The greatest Reds catcher? Did I need to ask?

Definitely, Nuxhall's choice was Bench. He did it all in 17 years with the Reds: Rookie of the Year (1968); two National League MVP awards

(1970, 1972); 1976 World Series MVP; 14 All-Star games; two NL home run titles (1970, 1972); three NL RBI titles (1970; 1972, 1974). He tops the Reds' all-time list for home runs (389) and RBI (1,376); ranks second in extra-base hits (794); and fourth in runs (1,091) and doubles (381).

Bench won 10 consecutive Gold Gloves (1968-1977), second all-time among catchers to Ivan Rodriguez (13). When I toured the National Baseball Hall of Fame's "Baseball As America" exhibit at the Cincinnati Museum Center in 2003 with him, Bench told me how he modified his Rawlings catchers mitts to make those one-handed tags at the plate: "I cut out all the padding in the middle so if you closed (the glove) it was just like reaching into your pants pocket. So I never really could drop the ball on tag plays and everything else," he said.

Not only was Bench the greatest catcher, he also was one of the team's Most Versatile Players. He played 195 games at third, 145 at first and 111 games in the outfield. At 22, Bench carried the club to the World Series while leading the NL with 45 homers and 148 RBIs.

In a Sunday doubleheader sweep of the Atlanta Braves at Crosley Field on May 17, 1970—six weeks before Riverfront Stadium opened—Bench caught all nine innings when the Reds won the opener, 5-1. He started in centerfield in the second game—one of his two career appearances in center—when Hank Aaron hammered his 3,000th career hit off rookie Wayne Simpson. Aaron, 0-for-4 in the first game, went 3-for-5 in the second, including home run No. 570, his 16th of the season. After Rose tied the game with a solo homer in the eighth, Bench moved from center to catcher for the 9th through 15th innings. In the 10th, Bench and May hit back-to-back jacks to tie the game again. The Reds won 7-6 in the 15th when rookie pitcher Don Gullett knocked in rookie Concepcion. Bench's day consisted of 16 innings squatting behind the plate; eight innings standing in center field; and 3-for-11 at the plate (two singles, a home run and three RBI).

Bench was durable, too. He averaged 151 games his first five full seasons (1968-72). In 1968 or 1969, manager Dave Bristol had Bench catch 54 consecutive games without a day off. Near the end of the streak, he caught a 10-inning night game at Crosley Field, and the next day was behind the plate in a 10-run blow-out. Bench was almost brain dead when lefty Gerry Arrigo came in to pitch. Arrigo, a 24-27 pitcher with the Reds (1965-69), had a good breaking ball, so Bench signaled for a curve. Arrigo shook him off. Bench again called for a curve. Arrigo said no. So Bench signaled for a fastball. Arrigo reared back and threw with all his might. Bench reached out and caught it with his bare hand.

"I was so tired. I was just beat. It was high and outside, and I just reached up and caught it barehanded with my right hand, and threw it back," Bench said.

⚾   ⚾   ⚾

After the 1981 season, Dick Wagner traded Ray Knight to the Astros for outfielder Cesar Cedeno, opening third base for the Hall of Fame catcher.

"It was miserable," Bench told the *Cincinnati Enquirer* as he was retiring in 1983. The Gold Glove catcher made 26 errors in 149 games at third. He named his fielder's mitt "E-5," baseball shorthand for an error by the third baseman. He chose to retire in 1983, at 35, after 17 seasons. At the 2019 screening for MLB Network's *Bench* documentary at Great American Ball Park, Bench admitted he wasn't the same after surgery to remove a marble-sized benign lesion from his right lung after the 1972 World Series. "I was never Johnny Bench again, but at least I got to play. I lost it, and I'm not afraid to say it. My back was killing me. I couldn't play like Johnny Bench," he said.

On Nuxhall's pregame interview with coach Tommy Helms on Johnny Bench Night in 1983, Nuxy expressed disappointment that the hot corner was too much for Bench to handle. Helms explained that "behind the plate, Johnny was blocking balls. At third base, he's probably trying to catch them too quick, to catch 'em like he's trying to block 'em. I played third base and shortstop, and it's a lot different from shortstop to third because balls come at you from a different angle. I think if Johnny started out there, he would have been a great third baseman. But being a catcher all those years, and then going over there, it had to be really tough."

When I asked Brennaman if Willie Greene, Lenny Harris or Bench was the worst at third, he said: "I'd have to say Bench, but Johnny didn't need to be told by people that he couldn't play there. It was unfair for him to be put there to begin with (by Wagner)."

Who was the worst Nux saw at third? He didn't say Bench. He didn't mention Brandon Larson, the Reds 1997 first-round draft pick who made 11 errors in 73 games at third 2001-04. Or Encarnacion, who blossomed as an American League slugger at first and as a designated hitter after five brutal years at third, with 78 errors in 490 Reds games from 2005-09.

"It was Ray Jablonski," Nuxhall said, referring to his 1955-56 teammate who made 19 errors in 155 games. "You think Encarnacion is bad throwing the ball into the seats? Jablonski would light them up behind first base big time. Big time!"

⚾   ⚾   ⚾

Bench was the greatest. Who's the second-best catcher?

As a kid, Nuxhall saw Hall of Famer Ernie Lombardi, the 1938 National League MVP and batting leader (.342) who played for the 1939-40 World Series teams. The four-time All Star hit .300 in seven of his 10 seasons for the Reds. Nux pitched to Ed Bailey, Smoky Burgess, Johnny Edwards and Bench (in spring training). After Bench, the Reds employed Alex Trevino, Bo Diaz, Joe Oliver, Benito Santiago, Eddie Taubensee, David Ross, Ramon Hernandez, Jason LaRue and dozens more.

"You'd have to go with Lombardi. I saw him play," Nuxhall said. "After that, I'd go with Ed Bailey or Johnny Edwards. They both were pretty good. I liked to pitch to Ed Bailey, and before that Smoky Burgess."

When I asked Brennaman for his back-up to Bench, he took Oliver. "Everything pales by comparison because Johnny was there for so long. And when he walked away, you had a steady parade of guys behind the plate, like Dave Van Gorder, Steve Christmas, Dann Bilardello, Alex Trevino. That's a hell of a question. I'd go with Joe Oliver."

⚾   ⚾   ⚾

Of all the Reds Hall of Famers, who would make Nuxhall's starting rotation in 2006? Would he go with teammates Jim Maloney, Jim O'Toole or Joey Jay? Big Red Machine pitchers Jack Billingham, Don Gullett, Gary

Nolan or Jim Merritt? Hall of Famer Tom Seaver? Tough-luck strikeout artist Mario Soto? Mr. Perfect Tom Browning? Wire-to-wire MVP Jose Rijo? His 1944 teammate Johnny Vander Meer, the only pitcher to throw back-to-back no-hitters?

Nuxhall's first pick was Maloney. In the 1960s, Maloney threw three no-hitters, and twice won 20 games. He's the club's all-time strikeout leader (1,592), followed by Soto (1,449), Nuxhall (1,289), Rijo (1,251) and Vander Meer (1,251). "Jim Maloney could overpower people. As long as he was getting the ball over (the plate), Maloney was hell on wheels. He had the best stuff of anybody I saw, and I'm talking about Randy Johnson and anybody," Nuxhall said.

"I'd take Maloney, Gullett, Soto," Nuxhall said. Then he stopped to think. "Joey Jay was good (21 wins in each 1961 and '62). Bob Purkey was good with his knuckleball. Oh geez, I'd absolutely have to take Rijo over Joey Jay. For my lefty, well, Merritt, that one year, was outstanding (20-12 in 1970), but I'd take Gully (91-44 for the Reds 1970-76)."

Brennaman would give the ball to Soto, Rijo, Browning, and Seaver.

"I've got scorebooks from every game of my career, and recently I found the ones from Soto's era," Brennaman said. "It was the most amazing thing I've ever seen. He'd lose games 2-1, give up three hits, and strike out 15. I've often wondered what kind of career he would have had if he pitched for good ball clubs. He could dominate a team unlike any other pitcher I've seen. He's the best great pitcher I've seen on bad teams. You had a chance to win every time he pitched, I don't care how bad you were."

For his lefty, Brennaman chose Browning because "of all the pitchers I've been associated with, no one had a better understanding, and a better game plan, each time he went to the mound, than Browning. Seaver was in the same class. To me, he and Browning were both thinking men's pitchers. They understood, and could articulate, what was necessary to be successful on a given day."

Game Seven of the World Series. The Reds are clinging to a one-run lead going into the ninth. You grab the phone to get your closer to nail down

180

the victory. Who you gonna call? One of the Nasty Boys? John Franco? Jeff Brantley? Lee Smith? Danny Graves? Or Clay Carroll, Rawly Eastwick or Will McEnaney from the Big Red Machine?

"Clay Carroll," Nuxhall said instantly. The Reds Hall of Famer saved 119 and won 71 games in eight Reds seasons (1968-75). The right-hander was named "Fireman of the Year" in 1972 after leading the National League with 37 saves and 65 appearances. He's third among games played by Reds pitchers (486), just ahead of Nuxhall (484).

Nux asked me Brennaman's choice for all-time Reds closer. I told him Marty picked Franco. "That's a good choice. Clay Carroll was tough, too. But if I had a left-handed batter, I'd go with Franco too," he said.

Nuxhall's favorite among the Nasty Boys was lefty Norm Charlton. He also liked left-handed power pitcher Randy Myers. "Randy was the guy who would come in and shut you down quick. And so could Charlton, but you never knew about Norm. He could walk two or three before he would get out of the mess," Nuxhall said. Joe had nothing nice to say about Rob Dibble, the third Nasty Boy, a two-time All Star (1990-91) who saved 88 games in six years (1988-93). "He was cuckoo. I had no use for the guy," Nuxhall said.

For the rest of the bullpen, Nuxhall went old-school. He chose lefty Bill Henry and righty Jim Brosnan, who each saved 16 games for the 1961 World Series team. "Bill Henry was nasty. He'd wind up and have the ball way up here," Nuxhall said, stretching both hands high over his head.

Why did Brennaman go with Franco? Consistency and composure, he said.

"That's not in any way to knock the other guys, but Franco just had such a great demeanor, which you have to have to be a successful closer. He was always the guy who could induce a ground ball when he was on top of his game. And he had sensational years for the Mets after the Reds traded him for Randy Myers." Franco had 424 saves—148 for the Reds (1984-89), and 276 for the Mets (1990-2004). A four-time All-Star, Franco led the National League in saves in 1988, 1990 and 1994.

"Franco was not a power pitcher when you think about successful closers. I just loved his makeup. I really believe he should be in the (national) Hall of Fame."

So do I. Without a doubt.

⚾ ⚾ ⚾

Which was the greatest team—the 1976 Big Red Machine or Babe Ruth's 1927 Yankees? Marty and Joe told us during the 1981 baseball strike. The Reds Radio Network filled some of the time with Nuxhall and Brennaman broadcasting fictional match-ups of World Series champs, including Waite Hoyt pitching for the '27 Yankees against the '76 Reds, and the '72 Oakland A's versus the '40 Reds.

The Reds did the fantasy games perfectly. They sounded very real, with crowd noise from a packed stadium. On the June 28 broadcast, Brennaman interviewed manager Sparky Anderson before the game, and Nuxhall spoke with Hoyt, who led the American League with 22 wins in 1927. "You'd better darn-side have the Yankees win," Hoyt said.

Riverfront Stadium public address man Paul Sommerkamp announced each batter. A trumpet blared "Charge!" during Reds' rallies. Nuxhall and Brennaman embellished their play-by-play for the game, which was based on the APBA baseball card-and-dice board game. They talked about the overflow crowd (56,393) and record demand for media credentials. They described Anderson, Rose, Yankees manager Miller Huggins and third baseman "Jumping Joe" Dugan arguing with umpires. When Lou Gehrig doubled in two runs in the fifth, Nuxhall noted that the "ball just missed by a foot of going out of the ballpark." After Griffey fouled a ball down the right field line, Brennaman praised a fan for "quite a catch in the seats. That will be a much cherished souvenir, I tell you." I loved hearing Joe catch Dugan's foul ball back to the booth.

NUXHALL: I got it! Don't worry, I'll take care of you.

BRENNAMAN: I told you before, that's not my job.

In the eighth, Ruth singled in the go-ahead run, 6-5, off Jack Billingham, pitching in relief of Gary Nolan and Pedro Borbon. Hoyt pitched nine innings, striking out eight, and would have won the game if he didn't give up a game-tying home run to Bench with two outs in the ninth. Closer Wilcy Moore in the 10th walked Concepcion, who scored on Ken Griffey Sr.'s single for the Reds' 7-6 win.

On their postgame show, Marty and Joe explained the extra-innings Reds victory was the best in a five-game APBA series played by a front-office staffer. Hoyt won the first game 7-4. The Reds won the others: 8-4 behind Rookie of the Year Pat Zachry; 9-5 with Nolan; and 4-2 by Gullett.

⑩ ⑩ ⑩

When you talk about your awful outfielders, Nuxhall had seen many: Dunn, Dante Bichette, Dmitri Young, Kevin Mitchell, Alex Johnson and Hal Morris. Yes, the wire-to-wire first baseman was one of dozens of outfield experiments by the Reds over the years. I was at Riverfront the first time Lou Piniella put Morris in left in 1990 so Todd Benzinger could play first.

"Yeah, that was an adventure," Nuxhall said of Morris' outfield play.

Reds fans can name the great sluggers who patrolled the outfield: Foster, Robinson, Junior, Davis, Dunn, Bruce and Dave Parker. They tend to forget all the others. Opening Day outfielders have included future Pirates manager Clint Hurdle (who hit .206 for the 1982 Reds); former MVP Kevin Mitchell; Kal Daniels, Tracy Jones; and journeymen Ruben Sierra, Chris Stynes, Jonny Gomes, Laynce Nix, Ryan Ludwick and Marlon Byrd. Reds managers also tried first basemen Votto, Dimitri Young, Paul Konerko, Terry Francona, Yonder Alonso and Lee May in the outfield; catchers Bench, LaRue, Oliver and Taubensee; and infielders Concepcion, Knight, Todd Frazier, Scooter Gennett, Brandon Larson, Willie Greene and Skip Schumaker.

Sometimes the Reds used outfielders who weren't gifted with the glove or bat, or were past their prime, which I call "Washed Up On The Banks Of The Ohio." Guys like Jim Edmonds; future Brewers manager Ron Roenicke; Corey Patterson; Vince Coleman; Dick Simpson; Tony Tarasco; John Vander Wal; Brennan Boesch; Richie Scheinblum; and Vince DiMaggio, older brother of Hall of Famer Joe DiMaggio and seven-time All-Star Dom DiMaggio. Vince hit .111 for the Reds in 1939-40.

Dunn holds the modern Reds record for being the National League's worst left fielder for four seasons: eight errors (.962 fielding percentage) in 2002; nine errors in 2003 (.959); 12 errors in 2006 (.960); and seven errors in 2008 (.966).

Nuxhall's choice for worst all-time Reds outfielder was slugger Alex Johnson, who played two years for the Reds (1968-69). Both seasons he led all National League outfielders—not just left fielders—in errors (14 in 1968, 18 in 1969). In his 13-year career, Johnson bounced around to teams the way baseballs bounded around him in the outfield, playing for eight clubs 1964-76.

Like Dunn, he was great at the plate. At age 25 in 1968, Johnson hit .312 (fourth in the NL) with 58 RBI and 17 homers. The next year he hit .315 (sixth in the NL) with 88 RBI and 14 homers. After the 1969 season, Howsam traded Johnson and infielder Chico Ruiz to the Angels for pitchers Pedro Borbon, Jim McGlothlin and Vern Geishert. With the Angels in 1970, Johnson led the American League in hitting (.329) and errors by an outfielder (12).

"Oh geez, Alex Johnson was a trip. But he could hit. He'd drive in 90, and let in 80," Nuxhall said.

In his *Charlie Hustle* book, Rose wrote about playing outfield with Johnson in Atlanta in 1969. When a Braves player hit a rocket to deep left, Johnson raced back to the wall and jumped. The ball hit his glove and bounced off. Rose, who had rushed over from center to back up the play, caught the ball for a rare 7-8 putout. Two innings later, with the bases loaded, shortstop Sonny Jackson crushed one to Johnson. The ball hit his glove waist high and fell to the ground. As the winning run crossed the plate, Johnson growled at Rose, "Where were you?"

The weirdest play Nux witnessed was by Paul O'Neill, one of the better right fielders for the Reds (1985-92) and Yankees (1993-2001). "I remember O'Neill kicking the ball right to first base, while trying to pick it up. It looked like he was playing soccer," Nuxhall said.

O'Neill was in right at Philadelphia's Veterans Stadium with the score tied 2-2 in the 10th inning on July 5, 1989. With the winning run on second, Lenny Dykstra singled to right off Franco. O'Neill charged the ball. It popped out of his glove, and bounced off his bare left hand. O'Neill swatted his glove at the ball and missed. In frustration, he kicked the ball with his left foot. It went straight to Benzinger at first on one bounce, forcing Steve Jeltz to hold at third. O'Neill was charged with an error for allowing Dykstra to take second. It didn't matter. Jeltz scored on a passed ball.

Brennaman recalled, "O'Neill kicked the ball, and it went to the first baseman. Right to him! It was almost like a drop-kick in football. There was a flare into right, O'Neill came running in and just kicked that baby right to the first baseman. It was perfect!"

My favorite awful outfielder was Bichette. Before Carl Lindner signed Ken Griffey Jr. after the 1999 season, General Manager Jim Bowden acquired Dante Bichette's big stick. He also got Bichette's glove in the deal, which didn't get much use. The Rockies' four-time All-Star had slugged 201 home runs with 826 RBI in seven seasons, including leading the National League in 1995 in homers (40), hits (197) and RBI (128). At 35, he was coming off a .294 year with 34 HRs and 90 RBI and 11 errors in the outfield, second-worst in the NL. Away from Denver's thin air, Bichette's power diminished, although he maintained a .295 average. His fielding didn't improve. As the Opening Day right fielder in 2000, Bichette struck out twice; threw a runner out trying to advance to third; made an error on a single which scored a run; and let a line drive to short right fall in for a double.

"Bichette wasn't too good," Nuxhall said. Dante didn't last the season. Bichette was traded at the Aug. 31 deadline to Boston. Despite playing a month in the American League, Bichette finished third in the National League for errors by a right fielder (8), behind Sammy Sosa and Vladimir Guerrero (10). I was at Riverfront when a fan unfurled this banner in the green seats behind him: *Bichette Happens.*

If You're Scoring at Home

Joe Nuxhall's All-Time Reds lineup (through 2006):

    1B: Ted Kluszewski (1947-57)

    2B: Joe Morgan (1972-79)

3B: Pete Rose (1963-78, 1984-86)

SS: Dave Concepcion (1970-88)

C: Johnny Bench (1967-83)

LF: George Foster (1971-81)

CF: Ken Griffey Jr. (2000-08)

RF: Wally Post (1949, 1951-57; 1960-63)

ROTATION: Jim Maloney (1960-70), Don Gullett (1970-76), Mario Soto (1977-88), Jose Rijo (1985-95, 2001-02)

CLOSER: Clay Carroll (1968-75)

BULLPEN: John Franco (1984-89), Jim Brosnan (1959-63), Bill Henry (1960-65)

BENCH: Frank Robinson (1956-65), Tony Perez (1964-76; 1984-86), Barry Larkin (1986-2004), Roy McMillan (1951-60), Ernie Lombardi (1932-41)

12

Toss Me the Salad

Marty and Joe prepare to sign autographs for fans in one of their memorable Kroger TV commercials. COURTESY KROGER CO.

"Autograph time!" said an elated Joe Nuxhall, grabbing a ballpoint pen from his suitcoat pocket. Marty Brennaman reached for his own pen as they stood behind their shopping cart in a Kroger store aisle watching wildly enthusiastic women rush their way.

"Our fans! Get ready!" Brennaman warned Nux. But the ladies didn't stop. They swarmed past the guys, turned the corner and disappeared.

"Must be the Cost-Cutter prices," Nuxhall surmised.

Brennaman picked up a couple of bananas from the kid seat in the cart and handed one to Nux. "I'll sign yours if you'll sign mine," Marty said.

It's one of my favorite moments from their several dozen Kroger TV commercials. When the Cincinnati-based grocery giant decided to be a major Reds TV sponsor in 1984, Kroger advertising manager Sam Gingrich sought the services of Nuxhall and Brennaman against the advice of his Chicago advertising agency. The Chicago marketing experts wanted Kroger to sign a star player. Gingrich held firm. He knew more about Cincinnati and the 1984 Reds roster.

The Big Red Machine had fallen apart since being swept by the Pirates in the 1979 National League Championship Series. The Reds were coming off two consecutive last-place finishes, and a year removed from a franchise-worst 101 losses in 1982. Gone were Pete Rose, Joe Morgan, George Foster, Sparky Anderson, Ken Griffey, Cesar Geronimo, Don Gullett, Gary Nolan, Fred Norman, Jack Billingham, Pedro Borbon, Tom Seaver, Rawly Eastwick and Will McEnaney. Johnny Bench retired after the 1983 season. That left Dave Concepcion, Dan Driessen, Nuxhall and Brennaman.

"The minute you hire a baseball player, and he's your spokesman, if he gets traded or leaves, everything you've invested in him goes with him," Gingrich said.

Kroger's campaign was genius. It captured their friendship and elevated their status to local cultural icons. No longer were they just Marty and Joe on the radio; they were a TV comedy team pitching the hometown grocery chain in cleverly crafted commercials. Big Joe and his Little Buddy chewed fried chicken, flipped burgers, shopped Kroger aisles, prepped for picnics and taste-tested house brands while bantering about Cost-Cutter bargains.

In 1984, nobody was sure how the Kroger campaign would fly. Gingrich said he proposed paying Nuxhall and Brennaman $3,000 each, with the hope it would lead to more. And it did, for decades. Their relationship with Kroger continued throughout their broadcasting careers—more than 20 years for Nuxhall, and 35 years for Brennaman. Marty was still doing appearances at Kroger store openings in 2019, his final year with the Reds.

⚾ ⚾ ⚾

Speaking to my Sacred Heart Church Knights of Columbus during the winter of 1994, Nuxhall said he was no longer recognized by young fans as a Reds broadcaster or former player. "Now I go somewhere and kids say, 'There's the Kroger man!'"

Their first Kroger spot was shot during 1984 spring training at Tampa's Al Lopez Field. Nuxhall and Brennaman sat on stools in front of a gray screen. Joe wore a bright pink sports jacket; Marty wore a dark suit and red tie. In walked Tony Perez, 42, re-acquired by the Reds after playing in the '83 World Series with Morgan and Rose for the Phillies.

"Hey, Tony Perez!" Brennaman said. "Are you wearing those sunglasses to hide from your fans?"

Perez flipped up his sunglasses, poked Joe's jacket and said: "No! Joe's coat!"

Soon the Kroger commercials became elaborate productions. Kroger rented a house in Tampa to film during spring training. A production truck from NBC's *Miami Vice* TV series came across the state to make three 30-second commercials in a day. Joe and Marty were on the set at 7 a.m., and sometimes didn't leave until past 2 a.m. Spotlights were needed in sunny Florida to illuminate a window for a kitchen scene filmed after midnight.

When Nuxhall and Brennaman came home from spring training, sometimes they spent all night shooting commercials in closed Kroger stores. For me, the most memorable spots exploited their contrasts: Marty's polished eloquence, Joe's folksy foibles, and their difference in stature. When Marty needed help reaching a box of crackers from a seven-foot stack, Joe waved his hand over Brennaman's head and told him that Kroger prices were perfect for Brennaman because "they're always low, Little Buddy." Another featured Brennaman laughing at Nuxhall's six-foot tall Kroger shopping cart, bigger than Marty. "You won't be laughing when I stick you in the kid's seat," Nuxhall said. After the voice-over announcement for weekly specials, it ended with Marty abandoned in the kid's seat. "Come on, Joe! Get me out of here! I was only kidding!"

To promote Kroger deli fried chicken, Brennaman interviewed Nuxhall as "a typical customer." Another time, Brennaman waxed poetic at the Kroger deli:

It makes chicken fried or barbequed, or pizza cooked the way you want it to.

Try buckets, breasts, or wings of fire, or pizza to your heart's desire.

Whole hot chicken, legs or thighs, or fresh hot pizza at super buys!

He turned to Nuxhall and boasted, "Ha! I'm a regular Longfellow, right?"

An unimpressed Nuxhall replied, "Actually, Marty, you're a regular short fellow."

⚾   ⚾   ⚾

It was no accident that Brennaman had the bigger speaking role. Gingrich learned that Brennaman, whose first career aspiration was acting, was very natural on camera. He arrived prepared; he knew the script.

"We worked with lots of actors and actresses over the years, doing commercials all over the country, and Marty was truly one of the best performers we ever worked with. You could tell Marty to be sad, to be surprised, to be angry, to be happy—whatever emotion you wanted—he could do it like that," Gingrich said.

Nuxhall couldn't. He had trouble remembering a few lines, even though the Marty-and-Joe part only ran 20 seconds. A Kroger sales announcement would be dropped into the middle of these "donut" spots, then the guys returned for the punch line. Nux never forgot a name, face or Florida highway—but he couldn't dependably deliver a couple of scripted sentences.

"They were such opposites in so many ways, including as performers," Gingrich said. "God bless him, I'll never say one bad word about Nuxy, but he couldn't always do a line very well. If we didn't get a decent take in the first five or six, it would keep going downhill. We looked for juxtapositions, or some way they could react back and forth to one another. That was the key to working with them. But you had to make the lines work for Joe, more than anything. We had to learn to write for him."

Nux had just two words in the commercial for Kroger's Senior Golf Classic presented by Fifth Third Bank at the Jack Nicklaus Kings Island Golf Center. It began with Fifth Third spokesman Johnny Bench reporting from the sixth green, then tossing to Brennaman at the ninth green, who said: "Now over to Joe on 14." The next scene was Joe missing a putt and shouting, *"Fourteen!"* He missed another and shouted, *"Fifteen!"*

The Kroger commercials were brilliant. They captured the essence of Marty and Joe perfectly. Brennaman's favorite was a phone call to the radio booth in 1988, the same year they did the banana autograph spot.

Nuxhall was doing play-by-play in a fake-looking radio booth when Brennaman answered a red wall phone behind them.

NUXHALL: It's a high fly ball!

BRENNAMAN: [ANSWERS PHONE] Yeah? Stop at Kroger?

NUXHALL: To deep center field!

BRENNAMAN: Bread, Cost Cutter specials. Right, right.

NUXHALL: [PUTS HAND OVER MIC] I can't believe your wife called!

BRENNAMAN: She didn't. It's YOUR wife!

After the Kroger product promotion, the scene returned to the booth.

BRENNAMAN: Line drive! Into left center!

NUXHALL: [ANSWERS PHONE] Yeah?

BRENNAMAN: And this one belongs to –

NUXHALL: [TAPS MARTY'S SHOULDER WITH PHONE] It's for you!

Kroger made them more than TV stars. Nuxhall and Brennaman appeared in Kroger's Opening Day newspaper advertisements; in-store announcements; in radio commercials; at the annual "bag off" competition for Kroger store baggers; and at store openings. In 1993, Brennaman announced during a Reds-Padres game that they would be at the Fairfield Kroger grand re-opening near Nuxhall's home on August 3, prompting this exchange:

BRENNAMAN: You might as well get the grocery list from Donzetta and kill two birds with one stone that day.

NUXHALL: Absolutely, I'll have it.

BRENNAMAN: I knew you would. [PAUSE] Swing and a grounder foul at first.

NUXHALL: They remodel those rascals and, you know, you have to call someone for a new (store) map ... I know where the watermelons, apples and oranges are. I know where the dairy products are.

BRENNAMAN: They're kind of easy to find.

NUXHALL: I know where the Meat Department is. But after that, it's tough.

BRENNAMAN: It sure is, pal.

At Nuxhall's on-field retirement celebration at Great American Ball Park on September 18, 2004, Kroger Cincinnati-Dayton Division President Bob Hodge thanked Nuxhall for "being a fixture with the Kroger family" for over 20 years.

"They did a great job of letting people know what kind of relationship we truly had," Brennaman said years later. "And thank God the powers that be overruled any idea of using a Reds player. The Chicago people had no clue. They didn't understand the relationship Joe and I had, which people loved. Using a player might have been fine, but I can't imagine it would have been more popular than what we did."

⚾   ⚾   ⚾

Nuxhall was hunched over the WLW-AM studio console studying a script and eating potato chips. Brennaman leaned back in his chair snacking on chips, too. Not just any chips. They were eating Marty & Joe's Potato Chips.

When I spent a day with them in August 1992 for a *Cincinnati Enquirer* story called "The Marty and Joe Show," it began with them recording radio commercials for their old-fashioned kettle-cooked chips. Earlier that year, Mumford's Potato Chips in Urbana, Ohio, about 90 miles north of Cincinnati, launched the brand in Cincinnati-area Kroger stores.

"Joe and I have an old friend in Urbana named Earl Crabtree who for years has been bringing us Mumford's Potato Chips," Brennaman told me that day. "Earlier this year, we met with Randy Peppert, whose family owns the company. That's where the idea was born. We've been munching on their chips in the booth for years."

Here's a taste of the commercials taped that afternoon before a Reds-Dodgers game:

NUXHALL: As you round third and head for home, we hope you'll stop in at your favorite grocer and pick up some for the family.

BRENNAMAN: After trying the first one, you're sure to remember: This one belongs to Marty and Joe.

NUXHALL: Wrong, Little Buddy. This bag of Marty & Joe's Potato Chips belongs to Joe!

BRENNAMAN: Hey, get back here with those!

Nuxhall and Brennaman struggled on the next spot to stick with the script while chewing chips on cue. Marty read his line, but Joe's crunching was too loud in the background.

"I can't make up my mind whether I want to eat or talk, know what I mean?" Nuxhall said.

In another commercial, Nuxhall ate part of a bag of chips on his drive to the game.

NUXHALL: Here's your half of the bag.

BRENNAMAN: The top half? Joe, this is the empty half!

NUXHALL: Hey, you get the top billing on the bag. You get the top half.

Writer Craig Bryant acknowledged the good-natured ribbing was inspired by the Kroger spots portraying Marty and Joe as "just a couple of pals spending some time together, who like to kid each other. They're very natural with it so they're easy to write. You always have to have one guy one-up the other a little bit, in a friendly way."

The salty snacking made Nuxy thirsty, without a doubt.

"Where's the Budweiser?" he asked.

⚾   ⚾   ⚾

Not everyone liked Marty & Joe's Potato Chips. During a 1993 rain delay, a caller named "Joe" rang the "Banana Phone" to complain about those "nasty-tasting, greasy Marty & Joe Potato Chips." Brennaman at first didn't recognize Jose Rijo's voice.

RIJO: They're greasy! They're horrible!

BRENNAMAN: Who the heck asked you to eat them? Nobody put a gun to your head and said you had to buy them.

RIJO: I hate these greasy chips, man! These are nasty tasting!

BRENNAMAN: You know what I want you to do? I want you to get your rest and think about your next start.

RIJO: What start?

BRENNAMAN: You know what I'm talking about …

NUXHALL: I want to tell you something, you smart aleck guy. Whatsa matter with you?

RIJO: No comprendo!

NUXHALL: You're crazy!

BRENNAMAN: Oh, go ahead and open a bag down there in the lounge, and taste them again. Nice talking to you … Come back when you can stay longer.

RIJO: God bless America!

Other consumers weren't impressed either. Sales were a titanic struggle, and Mumford stopped production after a few years. Mumford kept making chips in Urbana until closing the plant in 2018, after 86 years.

Through the years, various companies signed Nuxhall and Brennaman to pitch their products. Some worked; some didn't. They made a memorable appearance in a JTM Meats Christmas advertisement with Brennaman as Santa and Nuxhall as his huge elf. Procter & Gamble promoted its Millstone Coffee at Dairy Mart convenience stores with red plastic Marty and Joe travel mugs.

Many of Marty and Joe's other commercials sounded hokey and scripted, like this exchange for SuperAmerica gasoline on radio in 1994:

BRENNAMAN: Today I'm here with the Old Lefthander for SuperAmerica to talk about the great American love.

NUXHALL: Oh, baseball!

BRENNAMAN: That too. But today I wanted to talk about America's love affair with their cars.

NUXHALL: I love my car.

A TV commercial for Car-X in 1998 ended with Nuxhall grabbing a shiny 5-foot muffler and tail pipe assembly and saying, "How do you suppose they'd hit with this, Marty?" They both laughed, not very convincingly.

⚾ ⚾ ⚾

Laverne & Shirley. Key & Peele. Abbott & Costello. Bert and Ernie. Marty and Joe?

Their great timing and genuine bond, which kept us listening to the Reds on radio even when the team stunk, caught the attention of Multimedia Productions in the late 1980s. The commercial and TV show division of Multimedia, owners of longtime Reds flagship WLWT-TV, was dabbling in making half-hour situation comedies. The first attempt was an Earl Pitts sitcom based on a character from Gary Burbank's WLW-AM show. Inspired by Kroger commercials, the Multimedia gang talked about what a sitcom would look like for Marty and Joe, Cincinnati's best comedy team. They didn't know that radio producer-engineer Armbruster once described the radio booth craziness as "like a sitcom."

"We used to joke about doing a sitcom with them living together as Marty and Joe, kind of like Bert and Ernie on *Sesame Street*," says Deb Price, a production assistant there in the late 1980s. "We wanted to do something where they lived in a neighborhood, and it would have (car dealer TV pitchman) Jeff Wyler and Buddy from Buddy's Carpet Barn living there too." And maybe Marge Schott, Schottzie, Cincinnati radio personalities Burbank, Bob Trumpy, Andy Furman and Wildman Walker, and so on and so forth?

Definitely Kroger set the gold standard with Marty and Joe. *Cincinnati Magazine* honored them with "Best TV Commercial" in the 1990 "Best & Worst" list: "Marty and Joe for Kroger. So smooth, it doesn't seem like a local ad campaign. But is it true they are separated at birth from Gilligan and the Skipper?"

⚾ ⚾ ⚾

Before the Reds' 1993 spring opener, as Brennaman was preparing for his 20th year with Nuxhall, he was excited to tell me about four new Kroger spots he just taped with Joe.

"One will knock people's socks off. Joe is the focal point, and it's sensational," he said. Nuxhall starred in a Big K Cola ad spoofing Ray Charles' "You've Got The Right One Baby! Uh-Huh!" Diet Pepsi Super Bowl commercial. The ad opened with Nuxhall and Brennaman at an anchor desk talking about needing "a commercial like the big brands." Joe disappeared while Marty continued to talk. Then the camera cut to Joe seated at a piano while wearing a tux, bow tie and sunglasses. Nux rocked side to side to the music while holding a can of Big K saying, *Big K? Oh Yeah!"*

"Some of the commercials are so cheesy. Some were very good, I've got to say. Some of them were really, really cute," Gingrich said. "The one thing I'm most proud of in eighteen years at Kroger—and thirty-four total years in advertising—it's the crazy idea I had to use Marty and Joe as our Kroger spokespeople."

After the 1990 World Series, Kroger signed Larkin and Eric Davis to appear with Nuxhall and Brennaman. When Marty boasted at a backyard cookout that Kroger brands finished first in taste tests against national brands, Nuxhall noted: "Well, I guess that kind of makes Kroger the national champs." That's when Larkin and Davis leaned in, flashed their World Series rings, and said, "I thought we are the National Champs!"

In one outtake, played at Nuxhall's 2004 pregame retirement ceremony, a jittery Joe flipped a burger off the grill when Larkin and Davis did their line. On another outtake, when Nuxhall finally got it right after repeated flubs, Larkin exclaimed, "You've got to be shitting me!" Hodge didn't show that one on Nuxhall night.

To me, the Kroger classic was Nuxhall and Brennaman preparing for a patio cookout. Nuxhall, wearing a red apron and chef's hat, was grilling shish kabobs while Brennaman stood in the foreground at a colorful spread of vegetables. Nuxy shouted orders to his Little Buddy: Toss me an onion! Toss me a pepper! Toss me a mushroom! When Marty asked if he could help, Nux said, "Yeah, toss the salad!"

Brennaman picked up a salad bowl, glanced over his shoulder as if he was going to throw the salad on Joe, then shook his head. "Naw!" At least that's what Kroger aired during Reds games.

"You know the one with 'toss the salad?' Where I cock my arm?" Brennaman said years later. "One time I threw the salad on him."

Let's Go Krogering

Nuxhall and Brennaman did humorous Kroger radio spots, too. This one ran during the 1990 World Series:

ANNOUNCER: Hey, Marty, Joe, what are two celebrities like you doing at Kroger?

BRENNAMAN: Even celebrities have to eat!

ANNOUNCER: And you go Krogering?

NUXHALL: Even celebrities like to save money!

[PROMOTIONAL ANNOUNCEMENT FOR KROGER'S FLORAL SHOP]

ANNOUNCER: So you mean, you guys do the shopping?

BRENNAMAN: Even celebrities have to—

BRENNAMAN AND NUXHALL: Listen to their wives!

Joe Nuxhall: The Old Lefthander & Me · John Kiesewetter

Batting Practice

After retiring as a player in 1967, Joe pitched batting practice daily for nearly 20 seasons at Crosley Field and at Riverfront Stadium.

KIM NUXHALL PHOTO

Manager Sparky Anderson's Big Red Machine was sputtering in 1975. It looked more like the Big Dead Machine on May 20, after a 6-2 loss to the Mets at Riverfront Stadium. The Reds were 20-20, five games behind the Dodgers. Even after moving Pete Rose to third from left field on May 3 to get George Foster into the lineup, the Reds played .500 over the next 16 games and lost two games in the standings.

Then the Reds caught fire. Sparky's boys took first for good on June 7. By July 13, they had won 41 of their last 50 games, for a 61-29 record, with a 12 game cushion over Los Angeles. The Reds' 10-game winning streak from July 4-12 included six victories over lefties: the Mets' Jerry Koosman and Jon Matlack; Phillies' Steve Carlton and Tom Underwood; and Padres' Brent Strom and Rich Folkers. Thanks in part to the Reds special weapon, the Old Lefthander.

Most teams didn't have a left-handed batting practice pitcher. Few had a former big-league lefthander who could throw daily hitting sessions. Dozens of pitchers have retired to the TV/radio booth. None of them threw BP. Not Tom Seaver, Bob Gibson, Orel Hershiser, Curt Schilling, Rick Sutcliffe, Ron Darling, John Smoltz, Jeff Brantley, Chris Welsh, Jim Palmer, Don Drysdale or Dizzy Dean.

From the day after he retired in 1967, at 38, pitching batting practice was Nux's daily workout routine until shortly before his 60th birthday in 1988, when Pete Rose was manager. Nux was especially valuable when the Reds were going to face Carlton, Koosman, Matlock, Randy Jones, Jerry

Reuss or another lefty. On those days, he threw for at least 25 minutes.

"If we were facing a lefty, Joe was very instrumental to get us ready for a game," said Foster, the 1977 National League MVP who hit 199 home runs for the Reds from 1975 to 1980, and maybe that many off Nux during BP. "He was very helpful with my approach to hitting. If you asked him to throw inside, or throw outside, he could do it. He had control out there, so I could work on hitting from left center on over to right field. I just loved taking BP from him. People don't realize how important a batting practice pitcher is."

With Nuxhall, hitters could focus on a southpaw's release point, see "how the motion goes, and follow the ball all the way through (to the plate). Obviously it wasn't at the same speed, but you're working on rhythm and timing," Johnny Bench said.

Ted Kluszewski, the Big Red Machine batting instructor and Nuxhall's former teammate, told *Sports Illustrated* in 1979 why Nux was an ideal batting practice pitcher: "He throws the perfect pitch—a high, inside fastball. They hit it good. It loosens them up and gives them confidence." Nuxhall delivered strikes to Reds batters from behind a protective screen in front of the mound. Coaches pitching batting practice today are much closer to the hitters, throwing from about 45 feet in front of home plate,

Nuxhall was impressed that Joe Morgan, Tony Perez, Rose and Bench consistently asked him to throw off-speed pitches. "After one or two rounds of hitting when they got loose, they always asked for breaking balls—curve balls and sliders—which amazed me, because most guys want to get up there and see if they can hit it over the top of the stadium. These guys were really serious about it. I know my curveball wasn't a Steve Carlton curveball, but just the idea that they wanted to see the rotation just kind of set things up for them," Nuxhall said. He was so much a part of the team that Sparky brought him to the 1977 All-Star Game in Yankee Stadium to pitch BP.

Bench said Nuxhall kept Reds hitters alert. "He'd throw his little sinker away, or turned it over every now and then. He'd throw you a little wrinkle slider. It wasn't like you were in a monotonous situation. He was giving you a chance to think up there. You had to be ready to adjust to whatever pitches that were coming."

⚾ ⚾ ⚾

"C'mon 'O!' Let's go!"

Nuxhall was ready to throw. He ordered infielder Ron Oester to follow him from the clubhouse to the batting cages under Riverfront Stadium. It was the 1980s, 15 years after Joe had retired to the radio booth.

"He loved to throw batting practice. He did it all the time, on the field and in the cage. He used to throw to me for an hour," said Oester, the former Withrow High School shortstop who played infield for the Reds from 1978 through the 1990 World Series. A .265 career switch-hitter, Oester didn't often hit right-handed, and wanted practice facing a lefty. "Joe helped me a lot. He threw to me as long as I wanted to hit."

Oester, *Dayton Daily News* baseball writer Hal McCoy, and WLW-AM sports reporter Bill "Seg" Dennison all used the same phrase in separate interviews about Nuxhall throwing batting practice nearly every day into his late 50s. "He was amazing," they said. "At his age, and a little bit out of shape, he'd go out there and pitch batting practice every day and throw strikes," McCoy said.

Nuxhall threw 170 to 180 pitches a day, *Sports Illustrated* said. Today's starters seldom go over 100 pitches every four days. Joe was old school. He often pitched in relief between starts in the 1950s. He believed his arm got stronger by pitching a lot. Pitchers needed to pitch more and rest less, he'd tell producer-engineer Armbruster.

Tim Burman, who replaced Nuxhall as left-handed BP pitcher, said he once clocked batting practice pitchers at one pitch every 10 seconds, or six a minute. That translates into 90 pitches for a 15-minute session, 120 for a 20-minute session. *Sports Illustrated* pointed out that Nuxhall in 1979 was "throwing more pitches per season than he ever did as a player." That's saying a lot, considering Nuxy still ranks No. 6 on the Reds' list for most innings pitched (2,169).

"Dad probably threw millions of pitches. He was like a machine. Fundamentally, he had good mechanics, using his body and not throwing

201

'all arm,'" said Kim, who pitched in the early 1970s for the Reds in the minors.

In 1986, Joe complained that the new two-year experiment doing TV and radio cut into his BP schedule. "I don't pitch quite as much as I used to, every other day or so. I threw about 40 minutes yesterday. On TV (game) days, I can't throw," he said.

Bench used the word "indefatigable" to describe Nuxhall. "He'd come in from throwing, sit there and smoke a cigarette, in his sweatshirt all sweaty. Then he'd go out and throw some more. And he'd be back at it the next day. That arm never wore out."

The Old Lefthander loved to banter with batters. "He was one of the guys. He'd give it to everybody. *You can't hit this!*' And Concepcion was always the one who'd say, 'Joe, you can't geet me out! You can't geet me out' And Joe would say, 'I can get you out anytime I want,'" Bench said. Joe's competitive instincts often kicked in, as they did decades earlier. If someone took him deep, "the next pitch would be right at the noggin. He'd knock 'em down. And then he'd stand out there and laugh," McCoy said.

⚾   ⚾   ⚾

The ballpark was Nuxhall's Fountain of Youth. He was addicted. Every trip to a baseball stadium, home or away, began and ended in the club-house, even after he stopped pitching BP. He loved sitting at his locker, putting on a Reds uniform, grabbing his glove and heading out to the mound. He delighted in kidding with players, many half his age. Some people habitually go to the same breakfast or lunch place, stop at a favorite Starbucks, or hang out at a brewery or bar they find most comfortable. Nuxhall came to the clubhouse. Like the old *Cheers* TV sitcom, it was a place where everyone knew his name.

"NUX!"

In Riverfront Stadium history, only two people had a clubhouse locker all 33 years—the Old Lefthander and clubhouse manager Bernie Stowe, Joe's closest and longest friend. Stowe started as a Crosley Field bat boy and clubhouse boy in 1947, at age 12, and worked his way up to equipment manager and senior clubhouse manager through the 2015 season.

Joe and Bernie playfully ragged on each other for 50 years. Joe called Stowe "Tubby the Clubby." Bernie called Nuxhall "Marble Mouth." The trash talk was all in good fun. Joe and Donzetta and Bernie and Priscilla vacationed together.

Bernie took good care of his old pal. He knew what Joe liked to eat after BP and a shower. Stowe stocked up on hard-boiled eggs; limburger cheese; liver sausage (known as braunschweiger or liverwurst); onions; peanut butter; crackers; cookies; donuts and coffee. Joe's eating habits were as legendary as his temper. He once joined Associated Press sportswriter Joe Kay and other baseball writers for lunch before a spring game in Kissimmee with a stack of cookies and coffee. When they asked if that was all he was going to eat, Nux groused, "You sound like my doctor." During the season, Nuxhall ate his pregame meal in the clubhouse—not with Marty and Yid in the press dining room—arriving in the booth an hour before the first pitch.

Only Nuxy and Bernie ate the braunschweiger. "Players would just gag over it," said Mark Stowe, Bernie's son, who runs the visitor's clubhouse. "If there was a Vidalia onion, he'd eat it like an apple, and get the biggest kick out of it."

The Stowes ordered hard-boiled eggs "by the bucketful." Nuxhall liked them pickled and deviled, too. In the early 1960s, when Fred Hutchinson managed the Reds, Nuxhall got knocked out of a game in the sixth or seventh inning, and was thrilled to see Bernie had put a dozen deviled eggs on the post-game spread. They were Hutchinson's favorite, too, but Nuxy wolfed them all down. Hutch was livid.

"Hutch made an order right then: Nobody could eat anything off the post-game spread until the game was over," McCoy said.

The huge postgame meal from Nuxhall's playing days is a thing of the past. Players now arrive earlier and eat better. Guys roll in around 12:30 p.m. for a night game, while Nuxy's teammates didn't show up until late afternoon for an 8:05 p.m. game. Today, those in the starting lineup wait to lift weights until after the game, to conserve their energy. The Reds clubhouse staff now serves three smaller nutritious meals. No more limburger, liverwurst or beer.

Before Brantley joined Reds Radio in 2007, Joe's last season, he set the Reds record for saves (44) in 1996. "The Cowboy," who grew up in Alabama listening to Marty and Joe on WLW on the car radio with his dad, remembers his introduction to liverwurst.

"Being the closer, I got to be the *Star of the Game* often. I remember sitting in the dugout with him, waiting for the show to start, and he'd have a Budweiser in one hand and some liverwurst in the other hand. He'd eat it while he was doing the postgame interview in the dugout, and breathe on you. I wondered what he was eating. I could smell it the whole time. After the interview, I asked him what he was eating, and he said, 'Braunschweiger! Here, try some.' I said, 'No way.'"

"He loved liverwurst and limburger cheese," Brennaman said. Which is why Nuxhall, when he retired from full-time broadcasting in 2004, left one of his goodbye gifts in the clubhouse for his last game with Marty. A longtime fan made him a limburger and onion sandwich on pumpernickel rye.

NUXHALL: I really wanted to bring it up, but the response I got from the last time I had this here was not very good. It really looks great, but in respect for my partner—being this is our last day—I decided not to bring it.

BRENNAMAN: Are you going to eat it?

NUXHALL: Is there water in the Ohio River?

BRENNAMAN: Are you going to tell me Donzetta would allow that thing in the house?

NUXHALL: Absolutely. She might even have a bite!

BRENNMAN: Oh my lord. Thank God you showed some respect for me here today … It was rank! I still wake up in the middle of the night smelling it!

NUXHALL: No you don't.

BRENNMAMAN: Yes I do.

NUXHALL: Well, if that's true, then I'm gonna have them bring it up here! [JOE LAUGHS]

⚾ ⚾ ⚾

Sports Illustrated in 1979 said Nuxhall wore his baseball pants "beer-drinker style, several inches below the waist." Writer Kathleen Andria described Nuxhall, 50, as overweight and barrel-chested. "Nuxhall is now on the leeward side of 250 pounds. And the barrel has slipped a few inches on his 6' 3" frame," she wrote. By the time he was coaching Reds Fantasy Camp teams in the late 1980s at Plant City Stadium, Nuxy needed suspenders to keep his uniform pants up, said former Cincinnati radio personalities Gary Burbank and Bill Whyte.

Burbank, WLW-AM afternoon host, and Whyte, morning DJ on country WUBE-FM, were on a team managed by Nuxy in the late '80s. They lost every day. So for the final game, Burbank, White and their teammates surprised Joe by wearing suspenders with their Reds' uniforms, too. Nuxhall doubled over in laughter.

Joe's health wasn't a laughing matter to his friends, family and Reds executives. He smoked Winstons or Marlboro Lights for years. "He was a smoker—he never could kick it—and he was overweight for many years. I remember he'd walk up the steps at home, and he'd be out of breath, and yet he'd go down and throw batting practice for like forty-five minutes," Kim said.

A month shy of Joe's 58th birthday in 1986, Brennaman told me that "no one realizes what a hell of a hard job it is to throw batting practice for twenty minutes when it's a hundred and fifteen degrees on the Astroturf. Four or five years ago, he pitched BP and had chest pains. It was just a muscle spasm, but it scared him." The *Sports Illustrated* story said "friends begged him to quit" pitching in 1976 when he "was told to stop throwing" after muscle spasms.

Marge Schott finally benched Nuxhall while Rose was manager. She worried he would have a heart attack, Brennaman said. Rick Stowe, who succeeded his father as clubhouse operations director in 1997, said, "She must have seen him when he came into the clubhouse after batting practice. You know Joe sweated pretty good, and she was afraid for his health."

Kim can't remember exactly when his father was banned from BP. It was likely in late 1987 or early 1988. Burman said General Manager Murray Cook asked him to be the Reds' left-handed batting practice pitcher in May 1988. The 1971 Elder High School graduate had pitched in the Pirates minor-league system in 1975 for Cook. Burman threw Reds BP until 2016. But neither Marge nor anyone else could stop Nuxy from pitching. He continued to throw to Rick Stowe in the batting cages under the stands. That was his workout.

"I thought it would be easier to catch him than it was," Stowe said. "He was throwing screwballs, change-ups and fastballs. And he'd want to face a certain team. He'd say, 'Today we're facing the '72 Oakland A's.' And he went through the lineup—Joe Rudi, Reggie Jackson, Gene Tenace. I'd set up over here to one side of the plate, and he'd say, 'No, set up over there.' He'd tell me what was coming, and then he'd throw it. Joe would take a break, sit down in a chair, and all the sudden he'd get back up, throw a few warm-ups, and we'd do it again."

⚾   ⚾   ⚾

The last time I saw Nuxhall pitch was September 15, 1990, when WCPO-TV hosted a Big Red Machine reunion at Blue Ash Sports Center's replica Crosley Field in suburban Cincinnati. As the Reds were close to clinching the NL Western Division, most of the 1975 team (except Rose) suited up for an exhibition game against former major league players and media personalities.

I don't remember much about Nuxhall pitching that day, because seeing him on the mound was not uncommon. I was more fascinated seeing all the other old familiar faces. Paul Sommerkamp, the former Crosley Field and Riverfront public address announcer, introduced the players. Former Reds TV announcer Ed Kennedy sat at his side. Retired Reds President Bob Howsam came back to Cincinnati to watch the game. That night, Big Red Machine players—but not Howsam—were honored during a brief on-field pregame ceremony at Riverfront. Petty Marge Schott decided not to let Howsam on the field and be recognized that night for assembling the greatest team in Reds history. Schott later

***Jim Borgman sketched Nuxhall at the Big Red Machine
reunion in Blue Ash in 1990, then asked Joe to sign it.***
JOHN KIESEWETTER ARCHIVES

denied she had anything to do with Howsam's exclusion, and claimed she didn't "even know if he was at the game." Howsam said he was abruptly taken aside and told he would not be introduced with the team. He told the *Cincinnati Po*st, "I don't think they used Marge Schott's name. But I know who gives the orders around there. When you deal with small people, you have to expect this."

Cincinnati sportscaster Ken Broo will never forget the time he stepped into the batter's box to face Nuxhall during a celebrity game. Nuxhall was past 60, but could still bring it. Broo figured he had no shot. So he bunted. It rolled foul down the third-base line. The next pitch was a curveball that nearly hit Broo in the head. Joe shouted to him, "Why don't you step in and bunt on me again?"

Not only did Nuxhall keep his locker after Marge forced him to quit, but visitors' clubhouse managers throughout the NL also had a spot for him too. "He was that well-respected around the league. Everyone just loved him," Stowe said.

McCoy started covering the Reds in 1973. When he arrived to interview players in the clubhouse before a game, Nuxy already would be sitting at his locker chatting with players.

"Joe was part of the team. Marty would come in and go into the manager's office, and do his interview, and then leave. But Joe had his own locker at Riverfront Stadium with his uniform. He'd be sitting there talking to players. If anyone wanted advice, Joe was there to talk to them. He was almost like a teammate. I'm sure he felt more a part of the team than just being a broadcaster. Joe was invaluable to the Reds. He served so many capacities for the team. He was a broadcaster that everybody loved. He was the batting practice pitcher. He served as an adviser and mentor. He was a great storyteller, and was an icon to the fans. I mean, Joe was the Cincinnati Reds."

Without a doubt.

Blown Away by Belcher

Long before Aroldis Chapman blew away batters at GABP, the Reds had a pitcher who threw 105 miles per hour. As Casey Stengel said: You could look it up.

The *St. Petersburg Times* sent an intern to cover the Reds that day in 1992 or '93, when Tim Belcher started a 1:05 p.m. Grapefruit League game at Plant City Stadium. The Reds had traded Eric Davis to the Dodgers after the 1991 season for the right-hander, who was 50-38 in five seasons in Los Angeles (but only 24-20 for Cincinnati in 1992-93).

The next morning, the *Times'* story said Belcher had thrown 105 miles per hour. Reds writers were perplexed. Belcher couldn't hit triple digits on a radar gun if a hurricane ripped through Wrigley Field. A couple of Reds beat writers politely asked the young journalist where she learned about Belcher's power. She explained: "They announced it in the press box. First pitch, 105."

Good thing it wasn't 1:35 game.

Should We Keep Nuxhall?

Marty and Joe entertained baseball writers with stories about their careers when Joe announced in November 2002 that he would retire from full-time broadcasting after the 2004 season. CINCINNATI ENQUIRER PHOTO

At the 1993 Pete Rose roast at the Hyatt Regency in downtown Cincinnati, Sparky Anderson joked about everyone at the head table—Pete, Marty Brennaman, Dave Parker, manager Davey Johnson—except for Joe Nuxhall. Sparky had nothing but praise for Joe, then a 50-year Reds employee.

"As far as the great Nuxy, there's nothing that you can say about Joe Nuxhall except that he's the only man I've ever seen that could put his feet up on Dick Wagner's desk, and no way could Dick Wagner fire him," said Anderson at the "Riot in the Hyatt" on September 2, 1993, some 15 years after Wagner fired the Reds' winningest manager. "Joe Nuxhall was the only person I know in the game of baseball who can't be fired. They would kill 'em, right here in the city, if you fired him."

What nobody knew then—or until this day—was that Wagner considered getting rid of Nuxhall in fall of 1970. If Wagner had his way, Nuxhall wouldn't have been on radio when Brennaman was hired in 1974. There would have been no Marty and Joe.

After the 1970 World Series, when the Reds were searching for Jim McIntyre's successor, Wagner flirted with replacing Nuxhall too. The Reds had just hired John Soller—later general manager of WKRC-AM in the 1980s—as the club's first broadcasting director. In Soller's first weeks on the job, he said, "I remember Wagner asking me if we should keep Nuxhall."

Should we keep Nuxhall?

"I was stunned at the question, and defended strongly the reason to keep Nux," Soller told me. Others in the front office supported Joe, too, so he was retained and paired with Al Michaels.

⚾   ⚾   ⚾

No Marty and Joe? Say it ain't so! But it's true.

More than a dozen times, events could have prevented or terminated the Marty and Joe team long before they tied the Major League radio record of 31 years. Reds Radio would have sounded very different if Wagner had prevailed in his numerous clashes with Brennaman; if penny-pinching Marge Schott had prevailed in negotiations; or if Commissioner Peter Ueberroth had carried out his threat after Marty and Joe's descriptions of the Riverfront Stadium crowd when Rose shoved umpire Ron Pallone.

You've heard about lucky breaks needed to win a ballgame? That's what happened leading up to the day Marty met Joe in 1974. First, Wagner considering dumping Nuxhall before hiring Michaels. And Michaels wasn't the first choice. The Reds wanted Harry Kalas. What if Kalas came to Cincinnati in 1971, and stayed to win his Frick Award here in 2002, instead of in Philadelphia?

Michaels balked at moving from his Hawaiian paradise to the cold, gray Midwest. What if he fell in love with Cincinnati and stayed until going to ABC Sports in 1977? What if Brennaman stuck with basketball? At his 2019 retirement announcement, Brennaman said he "never expected to be broadcasting big-league baseball anyway. I was doing pro basketball in the old American Basketball Association, and I loved it … This thing fell into my lap, and fortunately, I got the job."

What if Nuxhall uttered another expletive that resulted in his firing?

Once Nuxhall and Brennaman had established themselves, and Marty had network World Series exposure, other clubs noticed Cincinnati's talented young announcer. Teams made pitches to the future Hall of Famer from baseball's biggest markets: the New York Yankees, Los Angeles Dodgers, San Francisco Giants, Boston Red Sox and both Chicago teams.

Before the Cubs hired Thom Brennaman, after he did Reds TV 1988-89, they had an interest in his dad. In the early 1980s, Marty also got a call from an assistant to White Sox President Eddie Einhorn, for whom Marty did college basketball telecasts in the 1970s. She wanted him to know that when Marty's contract expired in a year that Einhorn, "a big Reds fan, would like to talk to you about coming to the White Sox,'" Brennaman said. At spring training years later, Einhorn told him, "I tried like hell to get you to the White Sox."

The Dodgers were interested in Brennaman when the seat came open next to Vin Scully, the voice of the Dodgers dating back to Brooklyn's Ebbets Field, Jackie Robinson and Red Barber in 1950. Instead, the vacancy was filled by Los Angeles sportscaster Ross Porter for the 1977 season—which meant the Dodgers had approached Marty after the 1976 World Series. So Marty could have left Joe after three years, as Michaels did. Brennaman's departure would have coincided with the Tony Perez trade to Montreal, and Don Gullett leaving for free agency to the Yankees, the first steps in dismantling the Big Red Machine.

The Dodgers' pitch? Brennaman, 34, would take over when Scully, 50, retired.

"I realized correctly, as it turned out, that Vinny was never going to leave, and I'd always be No. 2," Brennaman said. Scully finally retired in 2016 after 67 years, prior to his 89th birthday. Brennaman would have been Scully's sidekick for 40 years before succeeding him.

Scully, a close friend, gave Brennaman advice in the mid 2000s which probably added years to his career. "Vinny once asked me when we were out in Dodger Stadium: 'How many games do you take off?' And I said I don't take any off. And typically in Scully fashion he said: 'You don't labor under the delusion that they can't play if you're not there, do you? Let me give you a piece of advice: If you want to hang around forever, or as long as you want to, start taking time off.'"

Marty did, after Joe retired.

"And this one belongs to the Red Sox?"

On the wall of Brennaman's baseball room is a framed, hand-written offer to become the voice of the Boston Red Sox. After the *Redsline* call-in show at WLW-AM on January 17, 1980, station owner Joe Scallan tried to poach Brennaman. His Cincinnati-based Mariner Communications had just purchased Boston's WMEX-AM, which owned Red Sox radio rights.

"I sat in his office down on Fourth Street, and he wrote out a five-year contract to come to Boston and be the voice of the Red Sox," he said. Scallan offered $80,000 a year. "I had interest from Boston, Pittsburgh, the Yankees, White Sox, Cubs, Giants and Dodgers. The only one I seriously considered was the Red Sox deal."

During Brennaman's on-field retirement party in 2019, Giants broadcaster Jon Miller—who did ESPN's Sunday night games for years with Joe Morgan—thanked Marty in a video for turning down the Boston job in 1980, which Miller got. Morgan, Perez, Pete Rose and Sparky Anderson were gone by 1980. How would Reds fans have reacted to the loss of Brennaman too?

It's hard to image a world without texts, Twitter, Facebook, Instagram, cellphones, laptops, tablets or other devices with instant connectivity to all the information in the world. When Marty and Joe were in their prime, people got their news and sports from TV and radio newscasts; evening radio sports talk call-in shows; or morning or evening newspapers. Sportscasters—and especially newspaper baseball beat writers—provided dependable reports. However, the best way to learn every Reds move was listening to Marty and Joe. Marty's pregame conversation with the Reds manager, Joe's pregame interviews, and their banter during the game were the best sources for Reds news before the Digital Age.

Brennaman's blunt, inquisitive style—asking questions that were on the minds of Reds fans—made him unique among announcers employed by Major League clubs. In a 1992 story, I suggested that "Brennaman's reputation for fairness and hard work … could conceivably earn him a plaque in Cooperstown in the next century." Sure enough, the National Baseball Hall of Fame announced February 3, 2000, that Brennaman would receive the Ford C. Frick broadcasters' award that July, when Perez and Anderson were inducted into the Hall of Fame.

When Brennaman first met manager Lou Piniella on the 1990 Reds Caravan, he warned Sweet Lou that their daily pregame interview show would be far more critical than the New York media.

"I'm going to ask you questions you've never been asked before. There will be questions concerning strategy that you might have used last night that backfired, and may have cost the club a game. Never will I ask you a question to make you look bad. The purpose of the radio show is to inform people … Most managers or coaches don't like to be asked tough questions. But this show will be a piece of crap if I can't ask what I want to ask. Pete would say, 'If you ask me a question I can't answer, I'm going to dance.' And I said: 'That's fine, but at least I'm going to ask the question.' The guys who were insecure were the guys who get prickly if you ask them tough questions."

By the time Sparky was fired, five years into Marty's tenure, Marty had established his outspoken style. Wagner wasn't happy about it. When John McNamara replaced Anderson, Wagner canceled the manager's pregame show so he wouldn't be subjected to Brennaman's scrutiny. The ban continued until Rose replaced Vern Rapp in 1984.

"Pete came back, and we've been doing it every day since then. I enjoy doing the (manager) show. It gives me a better understanding of the way the guy approaches his craft," he explained in 2015.

When gambling rumors swirled around Rose in 1989, sometimes his interview with Brennaman was his only comment before a game. So beat writers would ask engineer Armbruster to play the tape to them before it aired. "Pete always talked to Marty because it was part of his deal," Armbruster said.

Reds fans listened to Marty and Joe because they told it like it was. Reds CEO Bob Castellini praised Brennaman at the 2014 Nuxhall Ball for the Nuxhall Foundation by saying: "Marty is the voice of the team. He's the voice of the fan. He tells it straight." Nuxy, the former player, was the good cop with a constant cheery outlook, uncomfortable criticizing a player; Marty was the bad cop with the negativity when necessary. Brennaman often said that "the one thing I'm going to have when I leave this business is my credibility, and that's the most important thing in the world to me in my profession. If I sugar-coat everything that happened, then nobody can believe anything I said." When we spoke in 1996, nearly halfway through his Reds' career, Marty added, "If people get upset because I try to be as honest as I can be, I'm sorry."

By "people" he meant Reds players who didn't like Brennaman's stinging criticisms heard across 38 states on WLW-AM. Such as when the 1992 Reds won 90 games, but finished eight games out, in Piniella's last year. The team was in transition, with Barry Larkin, Chris Sabo, Joe Oliver, Hal Morris, Paul O'Neill, Jose Rijo, Tom Browning, Norm Charlton and Rob Dibble from the World Series team, joined by Bip Roberts, Dave Martinez, Reggie Sanders, Willie Greene, Freddie Benavides and Tim Belcher.

"The majority of players in the clubhouse, if they were honest, would admit that they don't care for me a whole lot. And that's fine with me. I respect them for what they do for a living, and I would hope they would respect me. Whether they like me or not is immaterial," Marty said in 1992.

During his first Reds season, Pirates announcer Bob Prince gave him advice he used throughout his career. Any time players were upset over something he said on the air, Prince suggested that Marty ask them how many times they thanked him for complimenting them.

"In every instance, that ended the conversation," Brennaman said.

It was a two-way street. If Brennaman praised guys for playing well, he reserved the right to describe how they weren't.

"I've never had a personal vendetta against any player. A lot of players I didn't particularly care for, personally, but I think you have to put that aside when you walk into the radio booth, because if you don't, that's where the professionalism goes away," Brennaman explained. "Anybody who has listened to us knows that, individually and collectively, the thing we want more than anything is for the Reds to win. Because we both have great, great love and affection for this organization. But if criticism is due—and I think that people have come to expect that over the years, since I've been in the booth with Joe—that's the way it is. I think many feel like it's a personal attack on them, and it's never been that way ... And fortunately, I've been allowed to broadcast the way I broadcast."

Nuxhall didn't always agree with his Little Buddy. He would wince and grouse when Marty made a critical comment in the eighth or ninth inning while listening in the clubhouse waiting for the *Star of the Game* show. When Marty said something negative, Joe would tell clubhouse manager Rick Stowe, "He wouldn't have said that if I was up there."

A reporter asked Brennaman at a 2002 press conference if his contract contained restrictions on criticizing the team. "There's nothing in my contract. If there was, I wouldn't be standing here today ... I cannot be a cheerleader, and I don't criticize guys who are. If the time ever came when I was told by anybody in this organization that 'You've got to stop broadcasting the way you broadcast,' then I'd have to leave."

And he almost did in the early 1980s.

⚾   ⚾   ⚾

Marty and Joe ... and Dick?

Without telling Nuxhall and Brennaman, the Reds announced late in the 1980 season that Dick Carlson would be added to the radio booth during a three-game weekend home stand as an "experiment" for cable TV games. Carlson was doing Reds play-by-play for ON-TV, a local pay-TV subscription service started that season, 11 years before the Reds launched a cable TV package. Brennaman was reduced to four innings, so Carlson could do the fifth and sixth. Before Carlson entered the Riverfront radio booth on Friday, September 12, publicity director Jim Ferguson and broadcasting director Jim Winters risked their jobs by telling Brennaman the truth: This wasn't a cable TV experiment. It was Wagner's way of telling Marty and Joe he was fed up with their critical comments.

Brennaman—the guy Wagner thought "had no balls" during the 1974 hiring process—spent the weekend ripping him. "I did everything to get fired," Brennaman said.

The three-men-in-the booth controversy was the *Cincinnati Enquirer's* top sports story the following day ("Reds-Hot 3-Way Scorches Marty And Joe"), not the Reds 5-2 loss. The paper quoted Nuxhall saying: "I just don't like it, period. I think it's bleep-bleep. That's just what I think."

Marty and Joe had been called on the carpet by Wagner twice in the previous five weeks. He visited the booth in Philadelphia August 3 to have "a lengthy discussion" about their comments on George Foster's play. "I didn't think we had been overly critical at the time, and in retrospect, I don't think we were overly critical now. George isn't fielding well and wasn't hitting. We said that," Brennaman told *Enquirer* writer Ray Buck. Foster, hitting .254, failed to make the National League All-Star team after four consecutive years on it. On September 6, Wagner complained about their criticisms of Ray Knight's 10th inning error in a 4-3 loss to the Cubs. Nuxhall told the *Enquirer:* "I think we've been very honest. I've never had one player complain to me yet."

The feud festered through the weekend, then Wagner summoned Marty, Joe and Winters to a Monday meeting. Wagner died in 2005, at age 78, so all I have is Brennaman's account. After an awkward silence, Marty called Wagner "a lying son of a bitch," he said. "For thirty-five minutes, it was me and Dick. The other two never opened their mouths. Dick said, 'You think you're so goddamn good? I've got a credenza back here with cards and letters that would be contrary to what you think about your work!' And I said, 'Let me see them!' ... He never did. So we accomplished nothing."

When the Reds headed to Los Angeles on Friday, Brennaman was convinced Nuxhall would need a new partner after seven years. He met Wagner in his L.A. hotel suite. Wagner asked him: "If you're so unhappy, why don't you resign?" Brennaman remembered what he learned from Sparky: If you have a contract, don't quit; make them fire you and pay you. As Brennaman talked with Wagner that day, he had a change of heart and asked out of his contract.

"I don't know whether I can do that or not," Wagner replied.

Two weeks after the season, Wagner told Brennaman he could not get out of his contract. Wagner reminded him that, unless he let Brennaman out of his deal, Marty couldn't work for another club. Brennaman told him: "You have a chance—right now—to let me out of my contract to go somewhere else. You've chosen not to, so I'm going to do the games the way I want to do them."

And that's what Marty did, in all honesty.

The Titanic struggle was over, for now. Nuxhall and Brennaman were back at the mic during the strike-shortened 1981 season. It was a frustrating year, with the Reds compiling "The Best Record In The NL" (66-42) but failing to make the playoffs because they had finished second in each half. The next year, Marty and Joe were the only reason to follow the Reds when the 1982 team lost an unprecedented 101 games under managers McNamara and Russ Nixon.

As their 10th season started in 1983, Brennaman's war with Wagner resumed, placing the Marty and Joe team in jeopardy again. Brennaman told Winters during spring training he wanted a contract extension. Wagner said he didn't negotiate contracts during the middle of the season.

"That's a damn lie! You want me to tell you the names of players whose contracts you've negotiated with during a season?" Brennaman said. He started naming them.

"Let me put it this way," Wagner replied. "I'm not going to negotiate *YOUR* contract."

Brennaman gave Wagner an ultimatum: "If I'm not signed by August 15, I'm going to call a news conference at (a local restaurant) The Precinct and announce that I'm leaving, and why."

Brennaman no longer was intimidated by Wagner, unlike his first few years here when he was "scared to death of Wagner," he told me. Just as Nuxhall and Brennaman could be "good cop/bad cop" in their comments about players on the radio, so could Bob Howsam and Wagner in the 1970s.

"Howsam was like your granddad, and Dick was like Hitler, and Dick reveled in it. If he jumped your ass he could do it better than anybody I'd ever been around," Brennaman said.

Brennaman and Wagner didn't speak during the 1983 season about the extension. The Reds were stumbling toward a second-straight last-place finish without George Foster, Tom Seaver, Ken Griffey and Ray Knight when Brennaman got a call from Winters on July 11. Limited partners Bill and Jim Williams had just fired Wagner. Howsam agreed to return as chief executive officer and general manager. Brennaman's world changed in a flash.

"I was convinced to this day that I was done here, that Wagner wasn't going to bring me back," he said. Twenty-five years later, Brennaman acknowledged that his contentious relationship with Wagner wasn't very smart. Wagner "had an idea of how he wanted games broadcast, and I had an idea the way I wanted to broadcast, so we were at odds with each other. And I was kind of stupid, because I took him on, and it was a no-win situation, because he could fire me any time he wanted to."

When Howsam came back to Cincinnati, he was very generous to Brennaman, as if "he was trying to undo all the bull—— that went down between me and Wagner." Marty and Joe "never had a problem since that day in 1983 that Dick Wagner was fired. They respect that we are established baseball announcers, and … they've allowed us to be ourselves," he said in 1986.

⚾   ⚾   ⚾

"Well, Marty, Dave Pallone, he's the worst umpire in baseball."

Nuxhall was cautious about criticizing players, but he wasn't shy when he thought someone was an embarrassment to the game. Tops on his list was Dave Pallone, the umpire who poked Rose in the face during a 1988 argument at Riverfront which resulted in Marty and Joe being summoned to the commissioner's office.

Pallone was on Nuxhall's radar for years. He was behind the plate on September 8, 1985, when Rose tied Ty Cobb's all-time hit mark of 4,191 in Wrigley Field. Rose opened the game with a single, hit No. 4,190. Dave Parker singled. Pallone next called Nick Esasky out looking, prompting this exchange:

NUXHALL: Well, Marty, Dave Pallone, he's the worst umpire in baseball.

BRENNAMAN: Worse than (Paul) Runge?

NUXHALL: Well, they're both—They tie. They make a good twosome. That ball on Esasky was six inches below his knees. Now, you watch Pallone—and Runge is the same—and how they can see a pitch low, that's over the plate? There's no way in the world. They're terrible.

Nuxhall also didn't like the "replacement players" fielded by the Major League teams in spring of 1995 during the players' strike. When union leader Donald Fehr declared that minor league players would be considered strike-breakers, club executives scrambled to sign softball, college and former high school standouts. The Reds started 0-3, prompting Nuxy to tell listeners, "I'll be honest with you, I've just about had enough." After a fourth loss—5-3 to the Blue Jays on six errors on March 5—Nux said on his postgame *Clubhouse Report* that the replacements threatened the integrity of the game.

NUXHALL: You try to be positive about things … but I haven't seen one guy—in my opinion—that you could absolutely say this kid is going to be in the major leagues in the next two or three years …

219

I want to see baseball. But you want to see the game carry on with the respect that it had, and right now, I think it's losing a lot of it.

Nuxhall was right. Not one of the Reds replacements made the majors. Their names, statistics and records were erased from history after the strike ended March 28. The 1996 Reds media guide only lists stats for the "real" players and their 12 exhibition games before the '95 season started three weeks late on April 26.

When the Cubs beat the Reds 7-1 on Opening Day, a plane flew over Riverfront Stadium pulling a banner that read, "Owners & Players: To hell with all of you!"

And then there was Marge. Nuxhall and Brennaman were almost thrown out at home by Schott after the 1996 season, as they were completing 23 years together.

On Monday, September 23, Brennaman told WLW-AM listeners that he and Nuxhall "have been jacked around" by Schott, who rejected their August deal with Reds President John Allen. "We don't have signed contracts for next year. I don't know if either one of us will be back next year … We don't know if we're dealing with John Allen, or if we're dealing with Marge Schott." He gave Marge a deadline.

"If I don't have a signed contract by the last out next Sunday (September 29), I'm outta here. This club preaches loyalty all the time. I don't know of two people who have been more loyal to the organization. I've repeatedly turned down offers to go to New York, Chicago, Los Angeles, Boston, San Francisco and Atlanta. I just feel we deserved a little bit better than the way we've been treated so far … I've kept quiet long enough, and I'm not really pleased with the way it's going. But from the club's standpoint, they don't give a damn if I'm happy or not. Compared to what we're asking for, compared to what the players are making, we're not asking for anything. I just feel like we're being jacked around."

Brennaman's blast worked. He and Nuxhall got new three-year deals.

Five words, that was all it took for Nuxhall to create a huge controversy in 2001.

"Barry is losing it, folks."

Nuxhall honestly described how 37-year-old Barry Larkin failed to throw out an Astros' batter who grounded to shortstop on Saturday, June 23.

> NUXHALL: The first pitch is swung on and it's bounced to Larkin. He fields, throws and (crowd noise) I hate to say it—Barry is losing it, folks. It hurts to say that, but Barry Larkin makes that play anytime. Not anymore.

Larkin was not happy about Nuxhall's uncharacteristic rip. Reds manager Bob Boone was displeased. Brennaman told the *Enquirer* that his radio partner, at age 72 and in his 35th on radio, "is more opinionated. I don't know why. Maybe he's going through a midlife crisis."

Nuxhall was just calling 'em as he saw 'em. "I'm not trying to bury or belittle Barry Larkin. Heck, I love Barry. But that's what we see. The people have trusted Marty and I enough to say what we see," Nuxhall told *Enquirer* baseball writer Chris Haft.

A year earlier, owner Carl Lindner had given Larkin a $27 million three-year contract in July 2000, a few days after General Manager Bowden had tried to trade the hometown favorite to the Mets. The trade deal fell through because the Mets wouldn't offer Larkin a contract extension. Larkin then started the 2001 season by hurting his right groin in an exhibition game, and went on the disabled list May 18 to June 15. Five days after Nuxhall's criticism, Larkin aggravated his groin again slipping on wet Wrigley Field grass going after Sammy Sosa's grounder. Before Larkin returned to the disabled list June 29, the Cincinnati baseball icons had patched things up.

"It's water over the dam, or under the bridge," Nuxy told the *Enquirer.*

When Nuxhall announced his retirement in 2002, Joe acknowledged that he "got in trouble a couple of times, because I said what I thought." Brennaman added, "Actually, in the last couple of years, he's gotten more like me, and I've gotten more like him! I mean, I've been out of the controversy for the last couple of seasons."

①　①　①

Twenty-five years after the 1988 Pete Rose-Ron Pallone incident, I got one of my biggest scoops for the *Enquirer*. In doing a 25th anniversary story about Nuxhall and Brennaman being summoned to the Major League Baseball office in New York City, Brennaman revealed to me that Commissioner Peter Ueberroth had threatened to banish them from baseball. I was stunned. Nuxhall and Brennaman could have been permanently barred from the game a year before Rose!

Ueberroth was angry about their on-air comments after player-manager Rose was ejected for shoving umpire Pallone when they argued about his delayed call at first base during the Reds' 6-5 loss to the Mets on Saturday, April 30, 1988. Rose told me years later he pushed Pallone after the umpire poked him in the face while making a point. The call allowed the Mets' winning run to score from second.

Nuxhall called Pallone a "liar," "a rotten umpire" and a "scab," in reference to Pallone working during the 1979 Major League Umpires Association strike. Brennaman called him "incompetent." They described fans throwing debris on the field while radio listeners could hear the crowd booing and shouting "bull——!" during a 15-minute delay. I was listening to WLW-AM while helping my neighbor's brother drive a U-Haul truck home from Marion, Indiana. Marty's candor didn't surprise me. But I was shocked to hear the Old Lefthander lambaste his least favorite umpire, providing a rare glimpse into Joe's hot temper from his playing days. At work Monday, WLW-AM refused to release the Reds' game broadcast to me, so I found another Reds affiliate to play it over the phone so the *Enquirer* could publish a partial transcript.

NUXHALL: Marty, unless I'm blind, Dave Pallone called him out.

BRENNAMAN: Pete Rose has just bumped Dave Pallone, and made no bones about it!

NUXHALL: Well, I'll tell you, Pete shoved him but Pallone hit him with a finger in the shoulder or in the face, one or the other. Well, Pallone is a liar—I don't know what else you can call him, because he definitely called him out ...

BRENNAMAN: ... And folks, I want to tell you, Dave Pallone absolutely stinks. He is a terrible, terrible umpire on any level of this game. And all you folks who umpire at home, don't take umbrage at what I'm saying. I am specifically citing one umpire, and he is bad news ... I cannot believe that the powers that be in the National League allow an incompetent like Dave Pallone to continue working in this league! It amazes me! ...

NUXHALL: ... You know you hate to see things like that happen, but I tell you, Pallone brought it on himself. And well, he's—he's a rotten umpire. I guess that's the best way to put it ... Pallone deserves it. You know, an ump like that doesn't belong in the league. He's a scab in the first place. And he's just been terrible ever since he's been there. There's just no question about it ...

BRENNAMAN: ... I tell you, this is as angry as I've ever seen a crowd in this ballpark in the fifteen years I've been here, and with good cause I might add.

NUXHALL: I have not seen anything like this in Cincinnati, I'll be honest with you.

National League President Giamatti fined Rose $10,000. Two days later, Giamatti summoned Nuxhall and Brennaman to New York after issuing a statement blaming the "extremely ugly situation" on the Reds broadcasters "inciting the unacceptable behavior" with their "inflammatory and completely irresponsible remarks." As they prepared to board a 6:30 a.m. flight the next day, Brennaman told a bleary-eyed Nuxhall, "I bet you never had this much fun working with Al Michaels!"

The meeting with Giamatti, who banned Rose 17 months later, went very well. Brennaman described it as "almost like three guys sitting in a bar drinking and talking. He allowed us to express our difference of opinion, that it was impossible for anybody (in Riverfront) to hear us on a radio because it was so loud in the ballpark. He never challenged us or threatened us," Brennaman told me in 2013.

The tone changed when Uebberoth entered the room. Nuxhall's temper flared at an inopportune time. "Joe really got into it with the commissioner.

And I thought, 'Joe, you've gotta back off.' Ueberroth brought up the name calling, and said, 'You referred to him as a scab.' And Joe said, 'That's what the hell he is!' And I'm thinking, 'Joe, just shut up! Let's endure this and shut up!' Ueberroth threatened us with kicking us out of the game, taking our jobs away from us," Brennaman said.

While switching planes in Pittsburgh on the way home, Brennaman called his attorney. He gave Brennaman good news and bad news: If the commissioner banned or suspended them, the attorney would file a First Amendment lawsuit "that we could not lose," Brennaman said. By suing baseball, however, they'd never work again as Major League Baseball announcers. He told Brennaman, "Believe me when I tell you, this is not going to happen."

Before the Expos game at Riverfront that night, Nuxhall said he regretted making comments "in the heat of the moment." Brennaman, who approached the baseball writers with tape over his mouth, said he was "embarrassed" that he "belabored the point about how angry the crowd was. Given the situation over again, I wouldn't have said those kinds of things." However, they never mentioned their possible banishment.

Two weeks later, Marty and Joe each received a letter from Ueberroth saying he wasn't taking "any action." And 25 years later—seven years after Joe's death—Brennaman revealed their threatened expulsion. He called Uebberoth "the most pompous jerk I've ever met."

⚾ ⚾ ⚾

After Marty said "no" enough times, clubs stopped trying to pry him away from Nuxhall. He loved the Queen City and its great college basketball, restaurants and music venues.

"Every time I thought about making more money going someplace else," he told the Reds Hall of Fame Joe Nuxhall Chapter in 2018, "the quality of life meant more to me than anything,"

And Nux.

"It was a combination of factors: Working with Joe, liking it here, and the kind of acceptance I got from the people who listened to our broadcasts. I've had chances to go everywhere. And every time I had to pull the trigger, I couldn't. I never hesitated ... Working with Joe for 31 years, and being one of five guys with 40-plus years with the same club, that means the most to me."

⚾   ⚾   ⚾

That dreaded "R word." Retirement. Much was made about when and how Brennaman would retire as he approached his 45th season in 2018.

But it was Nuxhall's talk about retirement that shook Brennaman in the 1990s, as they battled Schott over contract renewals. Nuxy told me in 1992, after he had missed part of spring training due to prostate cancer, that he was contemplating quitting or cutting back his radio schedule.

"The only thing that bothers me is the travel," he said. It was August 1992, a month after his 64th birthday, six months after cancer surgery, and a year before his contract expired. "I'd have to say there's a sixty percent that I will be back and forty percent that I won't. I don't know. It's hard to make up my mind."

In 1996, four months before Brennaman went public about their contract fight with Schott, Nuxhall again told me he was "really seriously" considering retiring because of the road trips. "The other day I was sitting in San Francisco, on a Sunday, and I asked myself, 'Do I enjoy this?' And my immediate answer was '*NO!*' ... I enjoy going to the ballgame, but not the travel. Probably Donzetta and I will talk about it sometime this summer, and see what we can come up with."

Such talk made Brennaman nervous, even though he believed Joe couldn't walk away from the Reds any more than he could. He knew how much Nuxy missed baseball while recuperating from cancer surgery. Nuxhall told me that "was worse than trying to make the ballclub (as a player). You're sitting at home, and you can't do anything. That's the thing that worries me about if I ever do decide to retire. I'll miss the camaraderie of baseball, there's no doubt in my mind."

Nuxy knew the day was coming. He summed it up this way to me in 1992: "Everything comes to an end. When it does, it's over. That's been proven many times."

Without a doubt, in all honesty.

⚾   ⚾   ⚾

They survived Wagner, Schott, the commissioner, and Marty's multiple enticements. But not Carl Lindner.

To his dying day, Nuxhall believed Lindner, who bought controlling interest from Schott in 1999, pushed him into retirement. The Cincinnati financier best known for bringing Ken Griffey Jr. home to the Reds was in charge of the franchise when Nuxhall signed his final contract after the 2002 season, which limited him to 60 games his last year (2004), a nod to his 60 years with the club. Publicly, Nuxhall was a loyal employee. At his 2002 Riverfront Stadium press conference, Nuxhall talked about retiring after working for the Reds 60 years. "I'm looking forward to being able to be one of the few people who were able to work in all three of the ballparks ... I'm proud of that," he said.

That remained the story for nearly two years, until an event at the main public library in downtown Cincinnati to promote his new biography with Greg Hoard, *Joe: Rounding Third and Heading for Home*. Nux said the Reds forced him out.

"I had to get it off my chest ... It's been on my mind ever since it started," said Nuxhall, according to John Fay's front-page *Enquirer* story. "They didn't want to do (2004), honestly." However, his attorney, Reuven Katz, negotiated the 60-game deal for 2004 with John Allen, Reds chief operating officer. By midway through the 2004 season, Nuxy's workload had grown to 78 games.

"Nuxhall absolved Allen of blame," Fay wrote. "But he would not say that chief executive officer Carl Lindner was the one who is forcing his departure. 'It wasn't John Allen is all I'll say,' Nuxhall said. Lindner is the only one in the organization above Allen. So was it him? 'I don't know who it was,' Nuxhall said. 'I'm not going to comment until I find out.'"

Nuxhall's book with Hoard did not blame Lindner. It suggested Reds executives might have wanted to change announcers because Joe was "too slow," made too many mistakes or was "caught on camera sleeping in the booth." Kim stressed to me years later that his father "absolutely didn't want to retire, although he wanted to back off some."

226

The next day, the Reds tried to extinguish the firestorm by announcing Nuxhall would broadcast "some spring training games and regular-season games in the future." The club said there was a "mutual misunderstanding" that Nuxhall's 2004 season would be his last. Nuxy ended up doing games with Brennaman for three more years before he died in November 2007.

After he started that limited work schedule, Nuxhall would remain seated in the booth long after games ended, quietly looking down at the field. "It seemed as if he didn't want to leave for fear that it might be the last time," said Russ Jackson, former Reds Radio producer.

My final breakfast with Nuxhall at Bob Evans was March 23, 2007. He was thrilled about being back on radio for Opening Day. "I think I've got two innings, but I'm not sure. I'm looking forward to it. It's a big deal. Since 1952, I've only missed two openers. Right now, I'm scheduled for 17 games. I'd like to do more, but it's that time to cut back."

To Tell the Truth

Marty Brennaman's commitment to tell the truth, the whole truth and nothing but the truth met its match in 2017. Brennaman wasn't totally honest during the popular "Ask Marty" segment in the eighth inning one day.

A listener submitted this question: "How did Yiddy and Seg get their nicknames?" It referred to radio engineer Dave "Yiddy" Armbruster, and WLW-AM sports reporter Bill "Seg" Dennison.

Brennaman explained that Armbruster had been called "Yiddy" since childhood by a younger brother who couldn't say "David." Then he danced around the origin of Seg's nickname. Why? Because he couldn't tell the truth without risking a Federal Communications Commission fine for every Reds network station. Brennaman knew that Bob Trumpy, the former WLW-AM *SportsTalk* host and NBC announcer, in the 1980s dubbed Dennison "SEG," an acronym for his "Shit-Eating Grin."

For the first (and maybe only) time on radio, Brennaman was speechless. He fumbled through several vague explanations, telling listeners to think of someone with a really big smile.

For years, Dennison has been just "Seg." He told me at 2017 Redsfest that he's almost exclusively known by his nickname. "It's gotten so I never answer to Bill," he said.

The Next Nuxhall

Joe, Donzetta, Phil (left) and Kim posed for Jack Klumpe at Crosley Field in 1960. RHODES/KLUMPE REDS HALL OF FAME COLLECTION

Joe Nuxhall was throwing a baseball with his teenage son, Kim, at spring training in Tampa in the late 1960s when they caught the eye of Reds scout Rex Bowen. Just 14, Kim was already five feet eleven, four inches shy of his dad's height when Joe made his debut at 15.

"Let me see your hands," Bowen said to Kim. Bowen was impressed.

"I had hands back then as big as I do now," Kim recalled nearly 50 years later. "I remember him saying that he liked the size of my hands, and that I had a live arm. They saw Dad. I'm sure they were thinking that I was going to grow. But I didn't."

Kim, the younger of Joe and Donzetta's two boys, played baseball, basketball and football for Fairfield High School. Kim had what he calls an average year pitching his senior year at 17. At the Reds' suggestion, he committed to pitch for Gulf Coast Junior College in Panama City, Florida, before the Reds would draft him. It was all set, until he attended an open tryout at Riverfront Stadium after high school graduation in 1972. His stuff was electric.

"I just had a phenomenal day. Dad was on the road, and I remember going home and telling Mom, 'They want to sign me.' In the back of my mind I'm thinking, 'They want to sign me because I'm Joe Nuxhall's son? Or do they really think I have it?' Then they offered me $5,000. So that told me they were serious. We talked it over, and I signed and was off to Bradenton," Kim said.

Born on September 10, 1954, Kim didn't turn 18 until he finished his first professional season pitching for the Gulf Coast League Reds. He was 1-3 with a 5.71 ERA in 10 games, including seven starts. In 40 innings, he gave up 53 hits, 37 runs and 28 walks, and struck out 20. Among his teammates was future Big Red Machine pitcher Manny Sarmiento, just 16. The Reds sent Kim back to the Gulf Coast Reds in 1973, and he did worse. Kim was 1-2 with a 10.29 ERA in eight games. He gave up 31 hits, 24 runs and 19 walks in 21 innings with only two strikeouts. Kim also played 11 games in the outfield, and four at third, hitting a microscopic .067 (3-for-45). He also played five games at shortstop in 1974 for the Seattle Rainiers, the Reds short-season Class A team in the Northwest League, hitting .231 (3-for-13) with five strikeouts and two errors. His Major League dreams ended in Seattle at 19.

Like his father's minor league years, Kim struggled with his control. "I couldn't throw enough strikes. It must be some sort of genetic thing," he said with a laugh.

⚾   ⚾   ⚾

After Joe made baseball history in 1944, the Reds' search for the next Nuxhall continued for 30 years, until Kim washed out of the low minors.

Joe's younger brother Bob Nuxhall signed with the Reds out of Cedarville College. Born in 1931, Bob pitched four years in the Reds farm system. Bob, also six foot three, made his debut with the Ogden (Utah) Reds in the Pioneer League in 1954 (10-9, 5.16 ERA). When Joe made the All-Star teams in 1955-56, Bob bounced around from the Sunbury (Pennsylvania) Redlegs to the Duluth (Minnesota) Dukes, Wausau (Wisconsin) Lumberjacks and Savannah (Georgia) Redlegs. At 25, after going 7-5 with a 4.07 ERA in 1957 for Class A Savannah, he quit with a 29-24 record over four seasons.

Don, the youngest of Joe's three brothers, pitched two years in the Milwaukee Braves system. Born in 1933, Don attended Indiana University on a football scholarship, and transferred to Miami University to play basketball. He was 4-9 in 22 games over two years (1956-57) with the Topeka (Kansas) Hawks and Lawton (Oklahoma) Braves when his big league dreams were cut short at 24 by a pinched nerve in his right (pitching) arm. So he switched to softball. Don was inducted into the Butler County Softball Hall of Fame in 1984, and Butler County Sports Hall of Fame in 1996. When we met in 2007, he was playing third base at age 70 for a traveling slow-pitch team. His wife Myrna said Don was "batting between .600 and .700" and one of five players chosen for an All-World Team.

When Phil Nuxhall attended Fairfield Junior High School, basketball coaches salivated at the chance to develop his skills. They knew Joe loved basketball as much as baseball, maybe more. Joe often worked the offseason at Hamilton's Estate Stove Co. or Mosler Safe to play on their Shop League basketball teams. Joe told me in 1996 that he worked very physical jobs every winter until 1963, which would have been before his last three seasons with the Reds.

"They'd just put me wherever they needed someone. At Mosler, I worked in the receiving department, receiving all the steel. Railroad cars would come in with plates to make safes out of, three-fourth inch steel plates. We had to center the magnet for the crane to lift them. Me and another guy used to rue the day when the flatbed truck pulled into the dock loaded with one-hundred pound bags of cement. We didn't have a forklift or anything. We had to handle those things ourselves. At Estate Stove, over on East Avenue, we took small wood-burning, pot-belly stoves from train cabooses off the line, and stacked them in the warehouse. Them things were dead weight."

After regaining his amateur status in 1946, two years after his Reds debut, Nuxhall was captain of the All-Ohio basketball team. When he struggled in the minors in 1950, Nuxhall thought of quitting baseball to work in Hamilton and play Shop League basketball, according to his *Joe: Rounding Third & Heading For Home* book. Donzetta talked him out of it.

"That was the big thing, the (company) basketball team," Donzetta told me. "He was very good. He could have played pro basketball. He loved basketball."

Phil didn't love basketball. He had his dad's height, as one of the tallest kids on the junior high school team. That was it. Not wanting to miss an opportunity, his Fairfield coach invited one of the Miami University basketball coaches to transform Phillip Joseph Nuxhall into the next Nuxhall star athlete. Phil was furious.

"It ticked me off. No. 1, I hated basketball. No. 2, I was absolutely horrible at basketball. I had no business being on the team. And No. 3, I did not like the special treatment. I said, 'You either have him coach everybody on the team, or I'm done.' That was the end of that. I quit."

Fifty years later, Phil was still ticked. "They wanted to create the next Nuxhall, pure and simple. They should have figured that out really quick that nothing could make that happen, because I don't have any ability for basketball."

Phil, who topped out at 6-foot-1, made it clear his famous father or loving mother didn't push him into sports. "I just felt pressure from the community. I don't remember my dad or mom ever saying, 'You should do that.' I just felt like I had to do it," he explained.

Same with golf. Joe loved golf; Phil didn't. He never felt comfortable playing with dad at Potter's Field in Hamilton as a teen. He wasn't very good, and didn't like being rushed to hit a shot. "The minute I saw people waiting on us, that was the end of that," he said. Phil liked running track in junior high school, but had to quit when the family went to spring training. He played on the high school tennis team until coaches tried to alter his grip on the racquet.

"Dad used to love telling these stories: 'Phil played every sport for like a week, and then he quit!' Then he'd laugh. Thank God he thought it was funny."

⚾ ⚾ ⚾

Kim didn't get his dad's height or durable arm. Phil didn't get his dad's passion for sports. At the 2018 Nuxhall Ball to benefit the Joe Nuxhall Miracle League, Cincinnati TV news anchor Sheila Gray pointed out that Kim and Phil "inherited a lot from their dad: His sense of humor, his sense of decency, his kindness, his character, respect, honesty, his giving spirit, his passion."

Joe Kelley, former Reds publicity assistant, said the general public "didn't know what a kind soul he was." Kelley described Nuxhall's pregame ritual for road games, when they'd leave the clubhouse for the press box 30 minutes before the pregame show. Nux said hello to each security guard; chatted with the elevator operator on the ride to the press level; and joked with the press box credential checker. Eventually they had to leave the clubhouse 40 minutes before the game to get upstairs on time.

Once a Cincinnati police officer gave Nuxhall a speeding ticket driving to Crosley Field. Joe thanked him. "That's the kind of person Joe was," said Judy Switzer, the officer's daughter. If Nuxhall caught a foul ball in the Riverfront Stadium booth, he'd look down at the Plaza-level green seats and toss it to a young fan. If an adult intercepted Joe's toss, you could hear him on the radio shouting, "Give it to that kid! That kid right there!"

Kim and Phil also got their father's famously flowing tear ducts. Tears ran in the Nuxhall family. All of the Nuxhall men cried at emotional moments. And sometimes at not-so-momentous occasions.

"I'd tell him that he'd cry when the sun comes up, or when a door opens," Brennaman told me in 1986, a year after Rose set the all-time hit record. "When Pete broke down and cried at first base, Joe was crying too. He's the most sentimental guy I've ever known." When Nuxhall called Bench's home run on Johnny Bench Night, "he broke down and started crying on the air," Brennaman said.

Joe's dad gave his wife a diamond ring one Christmas, and his brothers "just sat there and sobbed. It was so sweet. I'm the same way, too," Phil said.

After dropping out of sports, Phil found his calling onstage. He sang with the Fairfield High School Choraliers show choir and performed in school plays. "When I was in *The Diary of Anne Frank*, Dad was sitting in the front row, and he was just sobbing," said Phil, who earned a speech pathology degree at Ohio University and worked 30 years for the Hamilton County Board of Mental Retardation and Development Disabilities.

Kim earned a degree from Miami University and taught elementary school physical education in Fairfield schools. He also ran the Joe Nuxhall batting cages and golf range in Joyce Park, which straddles Hamilton and Fairfield. When Kim talks about his dad publicly, he chokes up. At the 2017 Joe Nuxhall Miracle Ball benefit for the family foundation, a week before the 10th anniversary of Joe's death, Kim's first words were: "Where is the Kleenex? There's supposed to be a big box here. It's going to be a tough night."

Donzetta isn't surprised to see him cry. "Kim is almost a clone of Joe, except for (Joe's) temper. Kim's quieter. He's got a whole lot of Joe in him. Thank goodness."

Working with Joe rubbed off on Brennaman. When Nuxy's "Little Buddy" announced his retirement in 2019, he cried several times speaking to the media. "Of all the things I learned from Joe Nuxhall in 31 years"—his voice quivered as he spoke—"the one thing I learned is: There's nothing wrong with crying, and it's masculine to cry."

⚾ ⚾ ⚾

Whenever I ran into Joe around Fairfield, I would introduce myself in case he didn't recognize me away from the ballpark. Some days the Reds Radio booth can be busier than the CVG concourse with sponsors, radio affiliate members, celebrities and other visitors popping in to meet Marty, Joe, Jeff or whomever was doing the game. Joe always greeted me as if he remembered exactly who I was. It wasn't an act, I found out long after his death. Kim said his dad had a photographic memory. Joe seldom forgot a name or face—and he met a lot of folks in 64 years with the Reds. Phil called his father "a savant" for his ability to tell stories for hours with no notes. Rick Stowe called Nuxy "a human GPS" for his knowledge of Florida roads driving to exhibition games or golf courses.

Fans felt they knew Nux from listening to him on the radio. And if Joe met someone, he never forgot them. During a San Diego road trip in the early 1990s, Nuxhall played golf with Reds publicist Kelley and Kelley's uncle Jerry Roof. Years later, after Kelley left the Reds, Nuxhall saw him and asked, "How's your Uncle Jerry doing out in San Diego?" Donzetta couldn't believe how well Joe remembered people's names. "And he'd ask about their brothers and sisters!" she said incredulously.

People talk about someone's intelligence quotient (IQ) or emotional quotient (EQ). Kim thinks his dad had "a very high emotional quotient, where he connected with people that way. That allowed him to remember names, because it meant something to him to meet people. People meant a lot to him."

He loved calling Hal McCoy, the Dayton sportswriter, "Harold." When McCoy was introduced to Joe in the 1960s by Dayton *Journal-Herald* sports editor Ritter Collett, "Nuxy thought he said 'Harold McCoy,' which is my real name. But I hate it. I never go by it," said McCoy, whose family called him "Bubby" as a kid in Akron. "I never let anybody call me Harold but Nuxy, and I never corrected him. Joe just got a kick out of calling me Harold."

⚾   ⚾   ⚾

Little Kim Nuxhall was standing in the kitchen of the Nuxhalls' Fairfield home in January 1961 when his mother broke the news: Dad was just traded to the Kansas City Athletics. Kansas City here we come! Kim, who turned 6 the previous September, wasn't on board.

"I'm going to stay here and live by myself!" he declared defiantly.

Long before Kim came along in 1954, his mom was a nomadic baseball wife. She followed Joe to every minor-league town. Early in their marriage, in the offseason, Joe and Donzetta lived with her parents, or Joe's parents and brothers. "That was a trip, moving in with those four boys," she said.

Donzetta Houston had met Joe at LeSourdsville Lake amusement park north of Hamilton in the summer of 1946, after she graduated from Hamilton High. They married October 4, 1947, four months after Joe graduated from high school. They were the same age, but Joe was a year behind in school. He repeated fourth grade after missing most of a year recovering from a ruptured appendix.

Joe and Donzetta eventually bought a house on Arlington Avenue, in Hamilton's Lindenwald neighborhood on the south end of town. In 1957 they built a home two miles down the road in Fairfield. When Nuxhall packed up for spring training every February, and for Kansas City and San Diego, the family went with him. Donzetta said she "loved San Diego and the weather. All I did was sit by the pool. But we were happy to come home. Joe was lucky to be able to do that."

Joe loved the spotlight, enthralling fans with his stories. Shy Donzetta was content in the shadows. She didn't mind people constantly interrupting their meals in a restaurant. Fans "pretty much came up whenever they wanted to, even when we were eating. But it never bothered him, because he'd eat and talk at the same time! He loved being around people. He got a lot of attention, and he loved it. I'm glad I didn't have to talk to a lot of people, or do any of that," she said.

She was used to doing things on her own. Joe wasn't present either time she gave birth. He was pitching for the Tulsa Oilers when Phil was born August 18, 1951. When she delivered Kim in September 1954 the Reds were on a nine-game road trip to Philadelphia, Pittsburgh and Brooklyn. Joe, 9-4, was having his breakthrough year.

"My neighbors had to take me to the hospital for Kim. Joe got to bring me home because I didn't want my brother to have to bring me home with my baby," she said.

At their Fairfield tri-level, Joe built the deck around their above-ground pool. He loved to cut the lawn on his riding-mower. "It's abhorrent to me, but Joe genuinely loves to get on his John Deere. I've never seen a guy who loves cutting grass more than Joe," Brennaman said in 1996. "In the wintertime, he uses it to clear the snow off his driveway, and everybody else in the neighborhood. He's truly a wonderful neighbor."

Nuxhall loved to garden. He planted green beans, cucumbers and tomatoes, of course. He also tended the roses, his mother's favorite, and snapdragons. When I spent a day with him in 1996, he had bought four dozen dwarf snapdragons to put in planters around the pool deck.

"Chances are they won't grow because I planted them. Anybody else plants them, and they'd be all right—but me. Probably only four will survive."

Donzetta ran the house and raised the kids while Joe was busy with the Reds. She decorated their paneled den downstairs with his memorabilia, and made scrapbooks chronicling Joe's career. She framed the photo of Joe and herself reading the *Enquirer* headline on June 18, 1956: "Nuxhall Puts Redlegs Second—Blanks Giants In Nightcap After Locals Drop Opener 7-6." She hated the picture.

"She wasn't happy with this. She doesn't go for that stuff," Joe explained, kind of sheepishly. "And she's real photogenic, too."

As outgoing as Nux was, that's how shy Donzetta was—except around me. She was always talkative when we'd meet at events. She'd ask me about my three sons. We exchanged Christmas cards. In preparation for this book, we talked in her kitchen for three hours. Phil was flabbergasted. *Three hours?* I took a selfie with her in 2015 at the inaugural meeting of the Reds Hall of Fame Joe Nuxhall Chapter in Hamilton. It's one of my favorite photos.

When Joe announced his retirement from Reds radio in 2002, he thanked Donzetta during the press conference in his inimitable style: "We've been married 55 years, and … when you think of a wife—and 55 years of baseball—and she's still with you—she's a pretty good girl, without a doubt."

Seven months before his death, at the Joe Nuxhall Hope gala in Fairfield, Joe tearfully praised his wife of 59 years.

"I've taken a lot of accolades, and a lot of nice things have been said, but I can't tell you"—he choked back tears as his voice cracked. "You're a wonderful woman, Donzetta."

This One Belongs to Phil

As soon as Phil Nuxhall walked into the room, he knew he had found his new home in 2016. Realtor Barbara Druffel had suggested he check out a condo in suburban Madeira with a framed baseball print on the den wall.

"I could see that it was Crosley Field. And as I got closer—Oh my God!—There's Wally Post and Klu! And then there he was. Dad was right in the middle, looking straight out at me."

Phil had never seen the "1956 Redlegs Wrecking Crew" by artist Bill Purdon, commemorating the home run record-tying team. Purdon drew Frank Robinson, Gus Bell, Roy McMillan, Johnny Temple, Post and Kluszewski casually standing around home plate with their bats. In the center was Nuxhall.

"I knew it was my place the absolute moment I walked in here. I never felt anything like it before," Phil said. "I love telling the story because it's so unbelievable."

The seller agreed to leave the print. Druffel gave him the keys with a note saying, "Here's to you, Phil, and your new home, where your beloved Dad gave approval and his blessing as added serendipity."

Star of the Game

On "Johnny Bench Night," Joe did his postgame interview with the future Hall of Famer at home plate on Sept. 17, 1983. MARTY PIERATT PHOTO

Joe Nuxhall packed up his scorebook and headed to the visitor's clubhouse in San Diego's Jack Murphy Stadium after calling the seventh inning of the Reds-Padres game on Monday, September 21, 1981. Nuxy knew who he wanted for his *Star of the Game* interview—the Padres' rookie who was pitching a three-hitter. It couldn't be more perfect. The Padres pitcher was a fellow lefty, and a 1973 St. Xavier High School graduate who grew up near Moeller High School. He singled in the third, and walked with the bases loaded in the sixth, when San Diego scored six runs. Joe loved a pitcher who helped his own cause.

"If you swing the bat, you're dangerous!"

His name? Chris Welsh, Reds TV analyst since 1993.

"People ask me if I was ever on Joe's *Star of the Game* show, and I was on one time," said Welsh, who was 22-31 with a 4.45 ERA for San Diego, Montreal, Texas and Cincinnati. "I pitched a shutout for the Padres against the Reds in 1981. After that game, he got me on the *Star of the Game*. It was the highlight of my career."

◊ ◊ ◊

For at least half of his radio career, Nuxhall did two interviews a day—one recorded for the pregame show, and the live postgame conversation. By 1993, Joe's 24th year on the air, the *Star of the Game* had morphed into *Reds Wrap-Up* after visiting players stiffed him too often.

At Riverfront, he'd take the elevator down to the clubhouse and follow the game on radio. If the Reds won, he'd grab a player to be his guest in the Reds' dugout. If the Reds lost, he would ask the clubhouse manager to call the visitor's clubhouse and request one of several players. He rewarded guests with gift certificates for Montgomery Inn, Burbank's Real Bar-B-Q, Honey Baked Hams, Sears, Richter & Phillips Jewelers or other companies.

On the two shows, Nuxhall introduced listeners not just to stars from the Reds' and visitors' lineups, but also up-and-coming rookies, veterans, coaches or some of the baseball lifers Joe knew from his playing days. During batting practice, he'd hold court with his old buddies in the dugout.

"It was something to watch. He'd sit in that dugout and players would come over to him, or wave to him, every time they came into town," said Bill "Seg" Dennison, who started helping on Reds Radio broadcasts in 1978 while a Northern Kentucky University student. Dennison still calls the home plate end of the Reds' dugout, where Nuxhall did his postgame show, "Joe's office."

"Riverfront Stadium or Great American Ball Park, it doesn't change. That's Joe's office. That's the way it's always going to be as long as I'm around," he said.

Only two Reds refused to do interviews with Nuxhall: Reggie Sanders and (for a while) Dave Concepcion. As a former player, Joe had sympathy

240

for Sanders, the center fielder who led the National League with 114 strikeouts in strike-shortened 1994. Although he was an All-Star the next year, hitting .306 with 28 home runs, 99 RBI and 36 stolen bases, he was dismal in the Reds' playoff games against the Dodgers and Braves. He whiffed 19 times, going 4-for-31 (.129). Nuxhall didn't take the refusal personally. "I understood why. He was going bad, so on and so forth," Nuxhall said.

Concepcion, after hitting a grand slam in Wrigley Field to beat the Cubs, was upset that Nuxhall picked somebody else for the postgame show. "I can't tell you who I had on ... but Davey thought he should have been on, and he gave me hell. Finally I said, 'OK, if you don't want to be on anymore, that's OK. We've got plenty of guys to talk to.' It wasn't long when Davey came up and said, 'Joe, I sorry!'"

⚾   ⚾   ⚾

Joe knew the game so well that he could get great responses from veterans and rookies alike. The questions might be convoluted in Nuxy's unique syntax, but the result was always insightful information Reds fans wanted to know. When Tom Seaver no-hit the Cardinals at Riverfront on June 16, 1978, Nuxhall opened the interview with the obvious question.

NUXHALL: Tom, you look at the ballgame, and at any time during the course of the ballgame were you really thinking no hitter?

SEAVER: I knew from the third or fourth inning that I didn't give up a hit. And, of course, the fans from about the sixth inning on were starting to acknowledge that there were no hits. I've been close before ... If you pitch long enough, and you have good stuff, you're bound to pitch one sooner or later.

In Nuxy's inimitable style, he elicited a great comment about the wonderment of the moment.

NUXHALL: When you think of no-hit ballgames, and I'm sure the thrill of this probably will hit you a little later on, when you talk to Nancy and see the two girls, it's something you just don't believe right at the moment.

SEAVER: It certainly hasn't hit me yet. I'm glad to win the ball game. Maybe tomorrow or tonight ... I think I'll go home and call my mom and dad, because my mom never thought I'd pitch one. [BOTH LAUGH]

After the Reds opened the 1995 National League Division series with a 7-2 win over the Dodgers in Los Angeles, Nuxy talked with catcher Benito Santiago.

NUXHALL: A two-run homer in the first, and Benny, what a big inning for you guys, and a big hit for you.

SANTIAGO: It was great. I've been waiting nine years to be in the postseason, I have to do something, because for me, it was too long. We scored four runs in the first inning and it takes a little pressure off my teammates ...

NUXHALL: How did you feel starting off? Were you a little nervous about it or not?

SANTIAGO: Not really, not really. To me it was like another game. I have four All-Star Games ... It's always exciting being in the All-Star Game ... I don't want to put any pressure on myself. I just want to go out and have fun.

On the last day of the 1997 season, Nuxhall chose rookie Aaron Boone for his postgame interview instead of a pitcher who had swung the bat dangerously. In Nuxy's mind, Boone's 4-for-4 trumped Mike Remlinger getting three RBI on a double and a bases-loaded walk. Remlinger also took a perfect game into the seventh, and finished with a four-hitter in the 11-3 win.

"It was just a big day for the youngster," said Nuxhall about Boone, who managed the Yankees after playing 12 years for the Reds, Yankees and four other teams. Nux asked if the four hits indicated he was more comfortable hitting, compared to his brief June call-up. (In possibly the first MLB transaction of its kind, he came up to the Reds when his brother Bret was sent to Indianapolis on June 18.)

BOONE: The last few days I've been able to relax and trying to find my swing back. I'm going to go to Arizona and work on things, and get ready for next year, and try to come into camp and win a job.

Nuxhall also offered constructive criticism, in his own way, about Boone at the plate.

NUXHALL: Aaron, one thing, the strike zone, and I noticed—and I think you'd agree with me—you swung at quite a few bad breaking balls away, and that certainly says you're a little anxious, maybe.

BOONE: Yeah, definitely. I was doing that a lot up here, especially early in the count. I was getting a little anxious, like you said, and working out those nerves of coming up to the big leagues. That's something I need to work on.

One of my favorite interviews was Joe's conversation with future Hall of Famer Ozzie Smith during Smith's retirement weekend in St. Louis in 1996. Joe got the Wizard of Oz to talk about developing from a defensive star into a .272 hitter; refusing to have surgery; doing his trademark back flip; and Cincinnati hospitality.

NUXHALL: When you boil this thing all down, and think of the number of years you've played, and really I guess the only serious injury you had, what, two years ago?

SMITH: Actually in 1985 I tore my rotator cuff diving back into first base ... I didn't have any surgery. I wanted to let Mother Nature take its course ... My rotator cuff is still torn, but I've been able to incorporate my weightlifting, and build the muscles around it ...

NUXHALL: I guess a lot of people are listening to this are saying, "Well, Joe, ask Oz when he started doing that, as we call it, the back-over-flip?"

SMITH: ... When they had Fan Appreciation Day, (they) asked me, "You know what would be great ... if you would do your flip when you're going out to the field. And I said no ... I played with flair, but it wasn't to show anybody up. But people loved it so much that they came to expect it.

NUXHALL: ... I know I speak for every baseball fan on WLW and our network that we congratulate you.

SMITH: I'd just like to say thank you to all the people who have been very hospitable to me when I've come to Cincinnati ... Some of my fondest memories of Cincinnati will always be having the opportunity to play against Pete Rose, Johnny Bench, Joe Morgan and Tony Perez. That Big Red Machine was something to behold.

Producer-engineer Dave "Yiddy" Armbruster said people "don't think of Joe being a great interviewer, but he talked about all kinds of stuff with players, and he talked to everybody."

When I chatted with Nuxhall in 1996, as he was starting his 20th year on radio, he surprised me by saying the job wasn't easier after about 6,000 interviews. "I admire guys who are in the business and doing that kind of thing every day, doing two interviews every day. There are just so many questions you can ask, in that line, because your time is limited."

⚾ ⚾ ⚾

There are just so many questions you can ask, in all honesty, but you've got to have someone to interview. As years passed from his playing days, Nuxhall had more trouble getting opponents to be his *Star of the Game*. Younger players didn't know Nuxhall. Or they were paid so well they didn't care about a $50 gift certificate for ribs, rings, watches or wrenches. By the early 1990s, the *Star of the Game* show went the way of Sunday doubleheaders, 25-cent scorecards, Father-Son games and Farmer's Night. Joe's postgame was renamed *Reds Wrap-Up* after too many no-shows.

After a loss to the Braves on May 25, 1993, he told listeners that his guest "might be Tom Glavine, it might be David Justice, and it might not be anyone." Justice, a Covington Latin High School graduate, had homered in the eighth at Riverfront. Glavine held the Reds to five hits in seven innings.

NUXHALL: [RETURNING FROM COMMERCIAL] Well, apparently we're not going to have a guest with us on the Star of the Game. We apologize. All you can do is ask. But if no one accepts it, that's the way the old cookie crumbles ... I guess this is getting to be old hat for us. That's the way it goes. So until tomorrow night, this is the Old Lefthander rounding third and heading for home. Good night, everyone.

⚾ ⚾ ⚾

Joe had a hunch the Reds weren't going to beat the Pirates at Three Rivers Stadium one night in the early 1990s. As Nuxhall and publicity assistant Joe Kelley headed to the clubhouse in the top of the eighth, Nux asked Kelley to get outfielder Andy Van Slyke for the postgame show.

Walking to the Pittsburgh clubhouse, Kelley saw the Pirates coming off the field. He called to Van Slyke, and asked if he'd be the *Star of the Game*.

"No, get somebody else," Van Slyke replied. He turned and walked away, then stopped. "Is that with Joe Nuxhall? Where do I need to be?"

Kelley had said the magic words: Joe Nuxhall. But not even Harry Potter could conjure a spell to make Barry Bonds cooperate with the media. I was on the field at Riverfront for visitors' batting practice once when Bonds was in town. When WCPO-TV's Dennis Janson asked Bonds to do a quick interview, Bonds replied, "Call my agent in Beverly Hills."

Bonds, baseball's all-time home run leader, gave Nuxhall the brush-off, too. Nuxy was in the visitors' clubhouse at Riverfront asking players to donate autographed items for his annual golf outing to fund college scholarships. He asked Bonds to sign a bat. Bonds refused. Nuxhall explained it was for his charity. Bonds didn't care. Nuxy walked away, fuming big time, you could say.

Another year, visitors' clubhouse manager Mark Stowe went through the room getting a bat signed for Nuxhall's fund-raiser when Cy Young Award-winner Doug Drabek was the Pittsburgh ace. "I asked Bonds to sign, and he said, 'No.' And then Doug Drabek goes up to him and says, *'It's for Nuxhall!!'* Drabek got on him, and he signed it," Stowe said.

⚾ ⚾ ⚾

The 1994 Major League Baseball strike is remembered as the year the World Series was canceled for the first time since 1904. The work stoppage on August 11 also meant that Reds' network stations lost lucrative advertising revenues. So Nuxhall and Brennaman were sent to Birmingham, Alabama, to broadcast a weekend series between the Reds Double-A affiliate Chattanooga Lookouts and the White Sox's Birmingham Barons at Hoover Metropolitan Stadium.

With help from Barons manager Terry Francona, who played for the Reds in 1987, Nuxhall interviewed Michael Jordan, the NBA superstar playing outfield for the Barons, before the game on Saturday, August 20.

NUXHALL: Has it been a surprise in a sense, Michael, the work it takes to play this game?

JORDAN: I knew it would be a lot of hard work. I think one thing that was under-estimated was baseball players being athletes ... I was like most fans from the outside (thinking) that they may not have the physique of an athlete ...

NUXHALL: You look at hitting, and everybody says, "What the heck, it's not that difficult." But you get up there. You've experienced it ...

JORDAN: One thing about hitting is it's so mental, you know, each and every time that you swing the bat. One thing that I don't have in my favor is the repetition of a good swing ... What I'm trying to do is to know on any pitch how to react ... Your great baseball players are somewhat similar to a basketball player: You make adjustments at all times. And I think the quickness of response of seeing the ball—and then making those adjustments—divide the great baseball players from the average baseball players.

NUXHALL: You did a lot of hitting, from what I read, off of a machine ... And all of the sudden a live arm shows up and it's a totally different game.

JORDAN: It changes a whole lot, the pick-up of the ball ... You can't get the rhythm off a pitching machine that you can get off of a pitcher.

NUXHALL: ... I really appreciate you chatting with us. As Tony Perez says about hitting, "See dee ball, hit dee ball."

MICHAEL: He's got it. That's the easiest advice I'd had this far.

⚾ ⚾ ⚾

The ballpark was locked. That didn't stop Nuxhall. While in Birmingham in 1994, he wanted to see Rickwood Stadium, where he made his minor league debut 50 years earlier, after his Reds debut. Nuxhall, Brennaman, Armbruster and WLWT-TV reporter Jeff Hirsh drove Sunday morning before the Lookouts game to the 1910 stadium. The former home of the Barons and the Negro League Black Barons had been used that spring for *Cobb*, Tommy Lee Jones' film about Ty Cobb. Abandoned in 1987, "America's Oldest Ballpark" had been placed on the National Register of Historic Places in 1993.

The guys climbed over a six-foot fence and walked around the old stadium. Hirsh interviewed Nuxhall on the mound about his Barons' debut with the vintage outfield advertisements as a backdrop. On their way out, Brennaman, Armbruster and Hirsh hopped over a collapsible accordion fence and headed to the cars. Nuxhall, 66, was halfway over when a leg cramp left him straddling the fence, paralyzed with pain. The longer he took, the more paranoid Brennaman got about breaking into the historic landmark.

"It took Joe forever to get over," Armbruster said. "We're sitting in the car, and Marty said, 'If the cops come, we're leaving him so we don't get arrested! We're leaving him here!'"

⚾ ⚾ ⚾

Bernie Stowe knew what Nux needed. At home or on the road, "Joe would always come down here to the clubhouse after the seventh inning, and the first thing my dad usually did was hand him a beer," said Rick Stowe, clubhouse operations director. *Sports Illustrated* reported in 1979 that Nuxhall did his *Star of the Game* with a "beer in hand." Tom Browning says that after his perfect game, Nuxy greeted him with two beers, one for each of them, for the postgame show.

Joe also didn't round third and head for home after the *Star of the Game*. He went back to the clubhouse to unwind over a few more beers, as he did during his playing days. Oester, Browning and Nuxhall would "sit around and tell baseball stories all night. We had a cooler, and we'd put in two or three cases of beer every night," Rick Stowe said. (That doesn't happen today. Beer is banned in the clubhouse, and players don't stick around for postgame bull sessions.)

The one place you didn't see Nuxhall with a beer was in the radio booth, said Brennaman, Oester, the Stowes, McCoy, Armbruster and Dennison. McCoy called it "an urban legend that's not true. Someone starts a story by saying, 'Nuxy was slurring his words late in the game, because he was drinking beer.' No he wasn't." The Stowes called it the biggest misconception about Nuxhall. "I asked about it once, and Joe said, 'Never!' Don't get me wrong. He loved beer. But he didn't have one until he was waiting to do his postgame interview," Mark Stowe said.

In my first extensive conversation with Brennaman in 1986, Marty made it clear: "He doesn't drink beer on the air, and gets testy when fans persist in thinking he does. Because he's been so closely identified to brewery sponsors—dating back to the days when the announcers were signed by the beer company, not the ballclub—people assume he drinks on the air. He's never done that. He's professional enough not to do that."

⚾ ⚾ ⚾

On his last postgame show in 2004, at the conclusion of Nuxhall's final full season in the booth, Joe chatted with a very special guest—his Little Buddy. It had been planned all year, and Nuxhall and Brennaman stuck with the plan even when Barry Larkin ended his 19-year career that afternoon. Nuxhall was at the mic in the top of the fourth on October 3, when manager Dave Miley sent rookie Anderson Mechado to replace the future Hall of Famer at shortstop. Nux didn't realize the significance.

NUXHALL: Apparently Felipe Lopez is going to leave the game. Machado is going to take over, but for what reason? Or Larkin, rather, is leaving the game. [CHEERS] Well, Barry Larkin leaving the game! [CHEERING SWELLS] Barry being given a hug by each of the members of the starting team. And hopefully it's not the last time we see Barry Larkin here, but we never know. A pretty touching moment. The crowd standing, and Barry is waving his hat."

In the bottom of the fourth, Larkin visited the booth to thank Joe and Marty "for everything you guys have done. You guys are the voice of the Cincinnati Reds, and I appreciate it." Then he explained his early exit from the game.

LARKIN: I wanted to get up here before Joe got off the air. I went to Miley and told him what I was thinking. And he wasn't in approval of me coming up here, but I told him I wanted to do it.

BRENNAMAN: That was a nice gesture on your part. We appreciate it.

NUXHALL: We appreciate it, Lark … Thank you.

LARKIN: Thanks to the fans. Hopefully I'm back next year. We'll see what happens.

NUXHALL: We're counting on you, pal … Well, a class act for Barry Larkin, without a doubt. That was very nice.

Larkin, 41, did not play again. But Nuxhall returned to call games in 2005, 2006 and 2007.

ⓑ　ⓑ　ⓑ

Nuxhall and Brennaman never spoke about their final broadcast before the game ended that day at Great American Ball Park. They didn't want to be "confronted with the reality, that this was going to be it," Brennaman said years later.

The postgame show sounded like they were having a few drinks after playing 18 holes. They recalled their favorite moments in a shorthand version of the Marty and Joe's Greatest Hits you've read in this book. They talked about their first meeting in 1974; Marty's "Al Michaels Field" flub; Joe's compulsion for crying; the *Deep Throat* video; and Nuxy pranking Marty about reading in the radio booth. Brennaman had mentioned some of these things in a story that morning by *Enquirer* sportswriter Kevin Kelley.

In all honesty, the lack of detail and context in their conversation (particularly the *Deep Throat* incident and the long-distance call for

Nuxhall) must have been frustratingly cryptic for even their biggest fans. Yet it was pure Marty and Joe, and fans had to love eavesdropping as they nostalgically circled the bases before Joe headed for home one last time as a full-time broadcaster.

NUXHALL: Back at Great American, the Reds losing 2-0 to the Pirates this afternoon, the final of this 2004 season, and, um, I'd guess you'd say the final of the good old *Star of the Game* show. Marty's been after me. He said, "Why can't I get a Montgomery Inn gift certificate, and one from Frontgate Catalog?" [MARTY LAUGHS] So in order to satisfy Marty, we're going to sit and chat after these messages. [COMMERCIAL BREAK]

NUXHALL: Marty, thirty-one years, pal, and I guess we go back to the first day in Bradenton, Fla., when you joined the ballclub. That was OK. And then we move up to Al Lopez Field in Tampa, Fla. ...

BRENNAMAN: That's correct. And I felt as loose that day as I feel today. I'm so loose today I could almost fall asleep.

NUXHALL: Well, I know the Montgomery Inn –

BRENNAMAN: I'm all fired up now, because I'm getting those freebies! And the next day—I remember like it was yesterday. The Chicago White Sox. You and I sitting up there at the top of the stands. I'm here. You're over here. And I welcome people to Al Michaels Field. I mean, good Lord! And I get no help from you. That's about the only time you hung me out to dry in thirty-one years.

NUXHALL: I was laughing!

BRENNAMAN: I know you were!

NUXHALL: I couldn't talk!

BRENNAMAN: As soon as we go to the commercial break, you said, "I'll be damned. We haven't even got to the regular season yet, and I've got material for the banquet circuit next fall" ...

NUXHALL: And of course, I go back to my first day with Claude

Sullivan and Jim McIntrye, and I thought I had to describe every pitch. You would have enjoyed that. You wouldn't have got any words in, as much as you like to talk … Finally I realized that their duty was to talk, too. But, you look back on it, Marty, and we go to that eventual day in Dayton, Ohio, when you joined us on the Reds Caravan. I think we had to go to a studio, wasn't it, to get a picture taken?

BRENNAMAN: … You and I met with Jim Winters at the photography studio in Dayton. That's the first time we ever laid eyes on one another.

NUXHALL: And we didn't realize we were left-handed, did we?

BRENNAMAN: Well, I knew you were left-handed because, like I said, the first thing I said to you was, "I had your baseball card."

NUXHALL: That was nice. You and Vice President Cheney.

BRENNAMAN: He said that too, didn't he? I thought about that too when we had him in here on Opening Day [in 2004]. And that's the truth. And that—uh—Well, I mean—[LONG PAUSE] We're going to have a hard time getting through this thing.

NUXHALL: Oh, we'll make it, I think. You know it's—

BRENNAMAN: We haven't talked about it all year, and we chose not to, because we knew this day was going to come. [VOICE CRACKS]

NUXHALL: And it's here!

BRENNAMAN: It's tough.

NUXHALL: You know, it's—it's—You know, it's—I don't know to explain it. I really thought that by doing just a few games during the course of the year that it would make this particular game a lot easier, but it hasn't. But what the heck, we'll go on and—I've got to bring up some of the things I thought were hilarious for us this year—

BRENNAMAN: [CRYING] You're supposed to be doing this, not me!

NUXHALL: I'll get to that, don't worry! I had mine when I walked into the booth today. But I guess—I know you mentioned to Kevin Kelley about the little fiasco in San Francisco with the film? The movie?

BRENNAMAN: In my open letter to you in the Enquirer this morning.

NUXHALL: … The other was the PA deal in San Francisco [press box public address announcer] and I said, "The next time they mention my name, there'd better be a phone call or"—

BRENNAMAN: You were going to clear out the press box.

NUXHALL: And there wasn't any more phone calls. And then the time in Montreal, when you—

BRENNAMAN: When I was reading, but I really wasn't!

NUXHALL: And we set this thing up with the engineer … I said, "Now when I put my hand behind my head, you turn these mics off because we're going to get Marty, and get even with him." Which we did.

BRENNAMAN: You did. You asked me what book I was reading, and Mr. Wagner had already said to me, "If I ever hear about you reading a book while you people are working again [JOE LAUGHS], you're going to be in trouble." You dropped that on me, and my whole career flashed in front of my face. You cannot imagine what I was saying about you.

NUXHALL: It's been thirty-one years and we've had some great times together. I guess you look back on the '70 ball clubs, and then the '90 club which no one really expected that much out of, to go wire-to-wire, and sweep the Oakland A's in four games. What a—What a great time we had!

BRENNAMAN: In the old ballpark—and in being here in Great American Ball Park for two seasons now, and as wonderful as this facility is, and as devoted as it is exclusively and one hundred percent to the game of baseball—it will be hard pressed to equal the run of years that that ballpark next door had, I mean with players, and teams, and moments. You know, I've been lucky, because I've been here through the most fruitful period in the club's history, and of course, sitting side-by-side with you for thirty-one years. One nice part about it all is that you are going to do some games next year.

NUXHALL: Well, I look forward to that. [NERVOUS LAUGH] Now you got me [CRYING].

BRENNAMAN: …You know, I told people I think—I think that's the most macho thing a man can do. And I told people for years that Joe can cry at door openings, at the sun coming up, it doesn't make any difference. And I knew it wouldn't take long to get you …

NUXHALL: Well, you know—It's just—Well, it's been my life! Six decades. Sixty years of playing and watching the game of baseball, and all with the same club. I hope people understand how difficult this is to say goodbye to you, in a sense, as far as sitting in this booth, and the players, the association with them. It's tough! And we're going to get through it. But, boy, I'm going to miss you.

BRENNAMAN: Well, like I said in the paper today, there's golf to be played and laughs to be had. And hopefully a lot of that will be with me down the road, because I'm going to be around and—and—thirty-one years! In our business, and I don't know if people realize it, this is about as transient a business as there is. Guys are always looking for a steppingstone to something bigger and better. And to have two people sit side-by-side for thirty-one years—which, by the way, is one thing I'm as proud of as anything I've ever accomplished … I don't think anybody will be together that long again, and that says something. I'm very proud of that.

NUXHALL: Ditto here. I think our relationship has been outstanding. You look back on some of the things we just talked about, and when you think of thirty-one years, sitting in a booth side-by-side, that you'd have some disagreements. And I think we can honestly say that we've not had one serious one … the day I got trapped in the Astrodome.

BRENNAMAN: Well, now that's a stretch. You didn't get trapped!
[JOE LAUGHS]

NUXHALL: In my opinion I did.

BRENNAMAN: You just decided not to come back.

NUXHALL: Well, they kept tying the score!

BRENNAMAN: And the game went sixteen innings, and I'm hotter than a match! [JOE LAUGHS] I mean, I was not real happy.

NUXHALL: I got to be honest with you. I started back up there about four different times.

BRENNAMAN: I know you did. And somebody would score, and the other team would counter. And I kept looking at the scoreboard, and now it's at twelve (innings), and now it's at fourteen, now it's at sixteen, and I saying, "Where in the hell is he?" And he never came back!

NUXHALL: They wouldn't let me out on the field to look up and say "Hi" or anything.

BRENNAMAN: No, they wouldn't call time out so you could wave at me! That would have really lit me up, if you would have done that.

NUXHALL: Well, Marty, again thank you. It's been—

BRENNAMAN: No, thank you, Joe. Thank you. Thank you. It's been the best! I guarantee you there's been nobody that's worked together in this business that derived as much fun out of—out of—broadcasting a ballclub's games as we have had over the last thirty-one years. It's impossible. And this is a business where you're working together every day for six months. If you don't like the guy you're working with, this job can be absolutely hell on earth. And thank God, two lefthanders came together in February of 1974, and we were off and running from that point.

NUXHALL: Well, it's been great. I want to wish you the best … It's been a joy, and we'll see you later, pal.

BRENNAMAN: OK, pal, thanks. [COMMERCIAL BREAK]

NUXHALL: Marty Brennaman has been our guest on *Reds Wrap-Up*, and his one desire has been answered. He, of course, gets a gift certificate to Montgomery Inn, home of the world's greatest ribs …

But really, we thank Marty for sitting here and chatting with us, as we said, it's been a great thirty-one years. And personally we're sorry to see it come to an end, but it has. This will be kinda it, I guess. A lot of people we want to thank before we leave the air … [He mentions sponsors, the media, players, "Yid" and "Seg."] And certainly to Marty who has been my pal for thirty-one years and will continue on certainly in that vein, and hopefully we can match up in a golf game here and there, and I'm sure we will.

And not to leave you folks out, you fans. You've been absolutely unbelievable, and we appreciate every bit of support you've shown to us and to the ballclub. It's been a glorious career, and I mean that sincerely. And for last Saturday night, what a big night that was for my family [INHALES DEEPLY, THEN SILENCE] and I want to thank you for it. [VOICE CRACKS] It's been great.

For the last time, this is the Old Lefthander rounding third and heading for home. Good afternoon, everyone.

A Very Honorable Legacy

Hamilton paid tribute to Nuxhall in 2017 with a mural of young and old Joe on the north wall of Clark's Sporting Goods, 15 South B Street.
JOHN KIESEWETTER PHOTO

Next to Opening Day, there was nothing Joe Nuxhall enjoyed more than awarding scholarship checks every May to high school seniors from 14 Butler County schools.

"That's my favorite day of the year, when we give out the scholarships," he told me in 2007.

Nuxhall left a long legacy—the Fairfield baseball complex for developmentally disabled children and adults, the character education fund, Rookie Success baseball program for underprivileged youths, and the streets, signs, statues, ballfields and bobble heads in his honor. My favorite is the Joe Nuxhall Scholarship Fund. The man who never went to college would pass out $28,000 in scholarships every year to seniors at

14 schools. The program, funded by a June golf outing, has continued after Nuxy's passing. By 2021, the scholarship fund has distributed more than $900,000 in 36 years.

"To see the smile on those kids, and when I think of what public education costs nowadays, it made me feel extremely special," Nuxhall said. He was very grateful that his baseball career fulfilled his dreams for his family. When he announced his retirement from full-time broadcasting in 2002, Nuxhall noted sons Phil and Kim were college graduates "because of baseball, and my association with this ballclub. It's something that I pride myself on, because that's what I wanted for them, and we were able to get it for them."

Joe regretted not getting a college degree. "That was the big thing he thought he missed. He thought he should have gone to college. But I believe he did all right," Donzetta said.

Donzetta, Kim and Phil attend the Joe Nuxhall Memorial Scholarship lunch every year. As recipients' names were called at the 2019 ceremony on Miami University's Hamilton Campus, their academic achievements were read along with their volunteer activities—not their athletic accomplishments. They were honored for helping at food pantries, nursing homes, soup kitchens, day care centers, homeless shelters, and programs for the developmentally disabled.

"From the day he signed that first Reds contract, he got the sense of such gratitude that he always wanted to give back. He knew he was lucky to have a talent playing baseball," Kim told recipients in 2019. "He was a totally egoless person. He never turned down an autograph. He never said no to a kid. He was always so appreciative. He was always so thankful."

In the first years of the scholarship fund, Reds players and coaches drove to the Hamilton Elks Golf Club north of Hamilton on an off day to play in what Kim calls "Dad's baby." After Joe's death in 2007, more than 100 golfers have continued to play in the golf outing—but no current players. Marty Brennaman, Ron Oester, Tom Browning, Chris Welsh, Billy Hatcher, Dave Miley, Scott Williamson, Jeff Shaw, Jon Warden, Jim Tracy and other Nuxhall baseball buddies usually play, along with former Bengals, Olympians, media personalities and area golfers.

"All the celebrities who come back year and year, and repeat players, are a credit to the memory of Joe. You know what a worthy cause this is," Brennaman told golfers before teeing off in 2018.

⚾ ⚾ ⚾

The Cincinnati Reds don't hide their affection for the Old Lefthander.

The team plays in Great American Ball Park at 100 Joe Nuxhall Way. Everyone walking to the stadium from Main or Third streets can read Nuxy's signature saying—"Rounding Third And Heading For Home"—in lights atop the Reds offices. People driving Interstate 71 through town see the sign, too.

The last thing people pass going into the main gates is the life-sized statue on Crosley Terrace of Nuxy pitching to batter Frank Robinson and catcher Ernie Lombardi. Inside the park, a replica microphone with Nuxhall's name is displayed beneath the Reds on Radio booth, along with ones for Brennaman and Waite Hoyt, and players' retired numbers.

Fans year round can visit the Reds Hall of Fame and Museum on Joe Nuxhall Way, next to the ballpark. Inside is the Marty and Joe Broadcast Exhibit, which opened in 2019 as part of the Hall of Fame makeover for the club's 150th anniversary. The displays include eight photos of Nuxhall, mostly with Brennaman, plus posters of Joe promoting Wiedemann's Beer and a 1973 Reds Radio advertisement for Nuxhall and Al Michaels. A sign under a display explains that Nuxhall and Brennaman were "the most beloved broadcasting team in Reds history … From their initial pairing in 1974, until Joe's retirement in 2004, for many fans, Marty and Joe were the Reds. Players might come and go, and some years the Reds played better than others, but a welcome constant was Marty and Joe."

In one corner is an interactive display where visitors can play about 50 Reds TV or radio highlights. The collection features two Nuxhall classic calls: Bench's home run on Johnny Bench Night in 1983, and Joe Oliver's 10th inning single to win Game Two of the 1990 World Series. And he's heard shouting *There it is! There it is!* when Brennaman calls Rose's record-breaking hit in 1985, and cheering *Get outta here, baby!*

when Michaels calls Joe Morgan's homer in the 1972 National League Championship Series.

Atop one wall is Marty's "And this one belongs to the Reds." Across the room is "Rounding third and heading for home." Long before Marty headed into his final season, the Castellinis talked to him about the broadcasting exhibit; serving as Opening Day parade grand marshal; and being the first broadcaster inducted into the Reds Hall of Fame. The Reds wanted to name the exhibit in Brennaman's honor. He refused.

"I said, 'No, unless you put both of our names on it.' We spent 31 years together," he told me. "Just naming it for me was not right. It needs to be both of us."

And that's why this one belongs to Marty and Joe.

⚾   ⚾   ⚾

When Hamilton or Fairfield schools, police agencies or social service providers needed to pass a tax issues in Butler County, they counted on Joe Nuxhall. His support for Butler County tax levies goes back to at least 1974, after his first season with Brennaman, when he chaired the successful Board of Mental Retardation levy. In 1994, he vigorously campaigned and spoke to countless groups for a bond issue to build a new Fairfield High School.

"I doubt that it would have passed without his support. Joe Nuxhall the humanitarian far exceeds all the things he has done as a baseball announcer and player, with his scholarship program and character education program," said Charles Wiedenman, Fairfield superintendent at the time. As the high school was being built in 1996, Nuxhall told me he endorsed "levies and stuff that I think are important. The school was one of the proudest things I've done, although I didn't do anything but speak for it. It was something the city really needed. Things like that you feel happy to be part of."

It was common to see photos of Nuxhall with his 97-year-old mother, Naomi Purdy, on billboards and campaign literature for Butler County Elderly Services levies in the late 1990s. "A lot of people need help. That was nice to be able to help the older folks," he said in 2007, at age 78. "I keep saying, 'older folks.' And I'm one of them!"

Nuxhall has been honored throughout Hamilton and Fairfield. Since 2017, a wonderful mural depicting young and old Joe graces the side of Clark's Sporting Goods in downtown Hamilton as part of Hamilton's StreetSpark public art program. Joe Nuxhall Boulevard in Hamilton's North End passes the Joe Nuxhall Fields in L.J. Smith Park, where Nux was discovered by the Reds. Joe Nuxhall Way runs through Joyce Park on the Fairfield-Hamilton border. Diamond No. 1 at Fairfield's Waterworks Park is named Marty and Joe Field. Behind the backstop is a life-sized bronze statue of Nuxhall showing two children how to pitch by sculptor Tom Tsuchiya, who also did the statues outside Great American Ball Park. Down the street from the statue are the Joe Nuxhall Miracle League Fields.

Joe's generosity wasn't known beyond Butler County on purpose, Brennaman told me in 2007, before Nux died. "Unlike a lot of people, he doesn't do things and then pat himself on the back, and make sure everybody in captivity knows what he's doing. He legitimately would not care if anybody ever knew about it, because he derives enough satisfaction by himself, in doing what he does, that he doesn't need for everybody to know about it ... He gives his time (to a cause), he doesn't just put his name on it. He talks the talk, and he walks the walk. It doesn't get any better than that."

⚾   ⚾   ⚾

Sean Casey loves to tell about receiving a letter from Kim Nuxhall. "I didn't know Nuxy had a daughter," he said with a laugh.

Casey soon learned that Joe's son was the force behind the Nuxhall Foundation programs in Fairfield. Kim sought the All-Star first baseman's help in 2003 to launch the Joe Nuxhall Character Education Fund. The goal was "to create a more respectful society" by teaching responsibility, kindness and self-control to grade school students across the U.S. Kim has distributed thousands of character-themed baseball cards featuring Casey, Reds employee Teddy Kramer, WKRC-TV anchor Sheila Gray, NBA player Luke Kennard from Franklin and pitcher Brent Suter from Moeller High School.

"Kim got tired of the kids not respecting each other at his school, and so on and so forth, and he started this with Sean Casey," Joe said. "He will tell you that he's seeing the kids show respect with 'Yes Ma'am, No Ma'am.' It's for everyone, not just elders. When you look at it that way, I know we will achieve progress."

After Joe was hospitalized with four leg tumors during spring training in 2007, Kim announced the ambitious $7.65 million Joe Nuxhall Hope Project. Family and friends wanted to establish Joe's legacy through five projects: a Cincinnati Reds Community Fund Rookie Success baseball league for underprivileged youth; the scholarship and character education programs; and a $2.4 million gym and all-weather Miracle League baseball field for developmentally challenged people of all ages.

"The total goal of what we're trying to do is make our nation better. And it starts not with twenty-year-olds, it starts with six-and seven-, and four- and five-year-olds," Nuxhall said at the April 5 dinner seven months before he died.

Joe had told me two weeks before the fundraiser, over breakfast at Bob Evans, about his commitment to kids. "I don't like to blow my own horn, or anything like that, it's not my nature. But years ago Rollie Schwartz from Cincinnati, the old boxer, we used to have baseball and boxing clinics. I remember doing them in Hamilton and Cincinnati on Sunday in the offseason while I was still playing in the '50s and '60s. For the kids. Rollie would talk to them about boxing and conditioning, and I'd talk baseball. It was fun. That's basically how I got involved with kids," he explained.

What was it about kids that you love?

"Well, you know, you'd like to feel that you've helped them succeed in some capacity. It doesn't have to be sports. I think a lot of times that sports will teach you a lesson in adversities. You know, if you can't get the job done there, you've given your best, and then it's time to move on. Which you understand that hard work is what will get you to certain places, and there's no shortcut either."

Part of the plan involves the Reds Community Fund starting a Rookie Success League in Fairfield? And to teach baseball to under-privileged kids?

"That's going to be inner-city stuff. The Fairfield little league (Youth

Baseball Association) has given Kim permission to use those diamonds, so hopefully they get interested (in baseball)."

You're happy to pass on a love for baseball?

"Yeah. For the kids."

And kids with disabilities?

"Yes, there's the Miracle League. It's all going to be good. All of it is for the kids, and handicapped kids, and adults, too. There are some handicapped adults that like to do some things, I would think. So it's going to be really first class around here."

Why do you want to build a gymnasium?

"These special-ed kids and the disabled, from what I understand, they have a rough time finding a place to play games. Plus it would have other advantages for them, a place to play indoors in the winter. It would be really nice if we could get that done."

Your first effort was the college scholarships, right?

"I wanted to do scholarships. We started off giving them to Monroe, Middletown, Hamilton, Badin and Fenwick (high schools). Five scholarships. And now we've built it up so every high school in Butler County gets a $2,000 scholarship. And the Character Education Fund is not just for Hamilton or Fairfield. Kim wants to get all schools involved. It works. Kim will tell you that. It's not for me or anybody. It's for the kids, so they become good citizens."

Are you trying to establish things that will be around after you're gone?

"I guess that's what Kim has in mind. It's very nice to have people feel that way about you. But like I said, it's not about me. It's for the kids. You can take my name off of (the gym) if someone wants to donate $2 million. They can put their name on it real quick. But it's nice to have people feel that way."

That would be a pretty cool legacy?

"Yes, it would be very honorable, I'd guess you'd say."

⚾   ⚾   ⚾

Joe and Kim also were motivated by another Nuxhall, someone you'd never heard about: Shauna Nuxhall, daughter of Bob Nuxhall, Joe's brother who pitched in the minors for the Reds. Shauna and Kim were born one day apart in September 1954. Their lives couldn't have been more different.

Kim caught fly balls with Reds players during Crosley Field batting practice. He pitched in the Reds' farm system; sat in the radio booth with Marty and his dad; and was inducted into the Butler County Sports Hall of Fame in 2017.

Shauna is a person with a significant disability who spent her childhood in programs for developmentally disabled. She has lived the past 20 years in a county facility.

"I've been so fortunate," Kim said. "People ask why I cry so much, and I think it's for two reasons. My dad gave it to me; and I have a cousin who was born almost the same day as I was. Shauna was born with what back then they called 'mental retardation.' She's living in a home, and I got to do experiences that kids only dream of. That's always been on my mind.

"And my dad, too, seeing Uncle Bob dealing with having a child like that. And a lot of people also didn't know that Dad had a sister Evelyn who passed away," Kim said. Evelyn Nuxhall was 2 when she died of pneumonia March 2, 1944, two weeks after Joe signed with the Reds. "I think his sister and niece are what touched his heart to do things for kids the rest of his life."

⚾ ⚾ ⚾

Nuxy's friends responded generously to the Joe Hope Project. Butler County's Rookie Success League started that summer at Waterworks Park.

Nuxhall's rubberized field of dreams opened on Joe's birthday in 2012, five years after his death. Just like in the Major Leagues, players from age 4 to 74 see their faces on the outfield video screen and hear their names announced over speakers. Special devices allow batters with limited muscular control to hit the ball. People of all ages who never envisioned playing baseball can round the bases before heading home from the Joe Nuxhall Miracle League Fields.

"I just wish the Old Lefthander could have lived a little bit longer to see the startup of the Miracle League Fields, to see that the kids can play baseball just like all the other kids do," said Dennison of WLW-AM.

Marty Brennaman holds his "NUXY," the award given to the Nuxhall Miracle Ball honorees designed by sculptor Tom Tsuchia. JOHN KIESEWETTER PHOTO

In 2021, the gym remained on the wish list. Estimated to cost $6 million, the facility next to the Miracle League Fields would house programs for people with intellectual and physical disabilities, offices for the Character Education program, and a Joe Nuxhall memorabilia display.

Kim talks about the gym at the Miracle Ball every November, benefiting the Miracle League and other Nuxhall Foundation programs. At the ball, Kim has presented humanitarian awards to Brennaman, Casey, Reds Community Fund director Charley Frank, Bengals Hall of Famer Anthony Munoz, Sheila Gray, and the family of Iraq War fallen hero Lance Corp. Taylor Prazynski. The award designed by sculptor Tom Tsuchiya featured four letters stacked on top of each other: The NUXY.

"When I go around speaking," Brennaman said when honored in 2014, "people are more interested in my thirty-one years with Joe Nuxhall than the current plight of the team. I hope the Big Guy is up there smiling and looking down. This is a big deal to me."

Artist C.F. Payne, whose illustrations have appeared on the covers of *Time, Sports Illustrated, Boys Life* and dozens of other magazines, has contributed original illustrations of Marty and Joe, Munoz and Nuxhall pitching to Musial in 1944 to the foundation. He also drew a huge Old Lefthander waving from atop the leftfield wall at the Miracle League Fields since 2016.

"I've been lucky. I've been doing this for forty-plus years, and I've done some pretty cool assignments, like *Time* magazine covers," Payne said. "But when you do a *Time* magazine cover, it's on the newsstand for a week and it's gone. That picture of Joe waving from the outfield wall is going to be there for years to come, for all the kids and people to see."

No doubt about it.

⚾ ⚾ ⚾

Joe Nuxhall lost by a landslide, I'd guess you'd say.

Open online voting for the 2008 Ford C. Frick Award coincided with Nuxhall's funeral in 2007. Nuxy blew away the competition for the award presented to a baseball announcer for broadcasting excellence, "reverence within the game, popularity with fans and recognition of peers." He received 82,304 votes, more than two-thirds of the 122,000 total. He had 10 times more than the second-place finisher, A's voice Bill King (7,659). But the award was given to Dave Niehaus, the Mariners' play-by-play man since 1977.

The previous year, Nuxhall led online Frick nominations with 8,000 of the 75,000 votes. The 2007 award was given to Denny Matthews, Royals' voice since 1969. The year after Nuxhall died, he won the fan ballot with 19,547 votes. Retired NBC sportscaster Tony Kubek was given the 2009 award.

Why do they let fans vote to nominate Joe for the Frick Award, but not for the actual winner? That was a question for Brennaman at the 2015 Joe Nuxhall Memorial Sports Stag in Hamilton.

"Because they're damn stupid," Brennaman said.

Several times since Nuxhall's death his name has been on the ballot. He was one of 75 on the 2012 ballot, competing against Al Michaels, Waite Hoyt, Joe Morgan, Joe Buck, Tim McCarver, Phil Rizzuto, Jon Miller and Thom Brennaman. Longtime CBS and Fox TV analyst McCarver got the award. The Hall of Fame changed rules in 2017 to rotate every three years among Major League Markets (team-specific announcers); National Voices (network broadcasters); and Broadcasting Beginnings (radio/TV pioneers). Bill King won in 2017. NBC veteran Bob Costas received the 2018 award. Former Reds announcer Al Helfer (1935-36), who also worked for the Pirates, Yankees, Dodger, Giants, Phillies, Houston and Oakland from 1935 to 1969, was honored posthumously in 2019. White Sox announcer Ken Harrelson was selected in 2020, and Al Michaels for 2021.

Nuxhall never will get into Cooperstown. It's not just his lack of national notoriety. There are too many radio and TV announcers ahead of him—active, retired or deceased. Nux has no chance.

What Nuxhall has are plenty of other accolades that would mean more to him, beyond the streets, statues, mural and Miracle League Fields. The annual UC-Xavier baseball game is called the Joe Nuxhall Classic. The Cincinnati chapter of the Baseball Writers Association of America annually presents the Joe Nuxhall Good Guy Award to a Reds player. Bronson Arroyo, Tucker Barnhart, Jose Rijo and Casey won it multiple times. Hamilton's Knights of Columbus Council 968 raises money for charities through the Joe Nuxhall Memorial Sports Stag every January.

Nux even has a baseball team named after him: The Hamilton Joes. Brennaman and Ford Frick don't have that. College-age players in the summer wood bat league wear the word "Joes"—replicating Nuxhall's distinctive signature with a sharp peak on the cursive J—on their hats and jerseys. Nuxhall's photo is on pocket schedules and game programs for the Great Lakes Summer Collegiate Baseball League team which plays at Hamilton's Foundation Field. Founding executive Mike Brennan had three suggestions for the team name in 2009. When Hamilton Mayor Pat Moeller heard the first one, he didn't need any other options.

"The name 'Hamilton Joes' was perfect because he's our favorite son.

Both Joe and Hamiltonians are hardworking, big-hearted, and give one hundred and ten percent in everything in an old school, blue collar way," said Moeller, son of *Hamilton Journal-News* sports editor Bill Moeller, Joe's biggest supporter. "Joe Nuxhall would have loved these young men enjoying the game with dreams of playing in the big leagues."

⚾ ⚾ ⚾

This golf course is a very inclusive club. The wheelchair-accessible 18-hole Joe Nuxhall Miracle League Fields Mini-Golf course has three automated putters for those unable to swing a club. Kids love seeing the huge Frisch's Big Boy, a giraffe from Trader's World flea market in Monroe Ohio, and a life-sized Joe Nuxhall bobblehead at the 18th hole. Printed on the guide wall is: "Until next time, this is the Old Lefthander rounding 3rd & heading for home."

Marty and Donzetta christened the golf course in October 2019 with a ceremonial first putt. Donzetta, 91, hit first. Her ball rolled against the curved wall and plopped into the hole.

"What can I do for an encore?" Brennaman said. I immediately thought of Marty and Joe's first Opening Day, after Marty had called Hank Aaron's record-tying 714th home run, when Joe asked him: "What the hell are you going to do for an encore?"

At the mini-golf opening ceremony, Brennaman praised the Nuxhall family. "What Kim and Bonnie have done—with the help from a lot of people—is keep fresh the legacy that Joe set, by offering scholarships to young kids coming out of high school and to deal with special needs children. Every time I drive up to this facility, I'm in awe. It's something that's going to be here for all time."

⚾ ⚾ ⚾

Meet me at Nuxy. That's where I tell friends to gather outside Great American Ball Park when we go to Reds games. I'm not the only one. Many meet their friends at the iconic Nuxhall statue in Crosley Terrace on Joe Nuxhall Way. When I interviewed Hall of Fame baseball writer Hal McCoy for this book, he wasn't surprised about Nuxhall's lasting legacy.

"Ten years after his death, and we're still talking about Joe Nuxhall. And years from now they'll still be talking about him—about Joe Nuxhall Way, and his statue," McCoy said.

Joe Nuxhall would be surprised, no doubt about it. He never thought of himself as special. He considered himself a regular Joe.

"As I tell people: I look at my career as maybe you look at yours, or somebody that worked at Fisher Body for thirty-five years looks at his. I'm no different. It just so happens that baseball has been my life. It makes me no different than anybody. I like to walk down the street feeling like I'm just one of you folks.... I just like to treat people like I want to be treated. It's about as simple as I can put it," he told Dennis Janson on WCET's *Joe Nuxhall: My Life: Baseball and Beyond* in 2005.

The four-part series ended with Janson praising Joe for all he did after his historic Reds debut.

"It's always a nice feeling to be appreciated, by not just a few, but everybody, if you can. And that's something I'm proud of. Many places I go, and they say, 'Well, we've got a celebrity here.' Naw! Naw! That's a lot of malarkey. 'Celebrity' I don't go for because—again, I'm no different than you are. I just had a different profession that put you in the limelight. But I appreciate it, and I've enjoyed it.

"I just want people to think of me as one of the regular guys."

Heading for Home

Fans placed baseballs, ball caps, Budweiser bottles, personal notes and flowers at Nuxhall's Great American Ball Park statue after his death on Nov. 15, 2007. JOSEPH KIESEWETTER PHOTO

By the time my wife Sue and I arrived at Fairfield High School, the line for Joe Nuxhall's visitation wrapped from the arena door up the sidewalk and looped twice in the plaza outside the main school entrance. The parking lot was nearly full. Almost 2,000 people were there when the doors opened at 4 p.m. on Tuesday, November 20, 2007.

Standing quietly in the cold were Reds fans of all ages from throughout Greater Cincinnati. We all came to say our final goodbye and thanks to the beloved Reds icon. An hour before the public viewing, Marty Brennaman, Barry Larkin, Johnny Bench, Sean Casey, Bob Castellini, COO John Allen, Ken Griffey Jr. and Sr., Pete Rose and Pete Jr., Bernie Stowe, Chuck Harmon, Tom Browning, Billy Hatcher and others met privately with the Nuxhall family. Also coming to Fairfield to pay their respects were sportscaster Bob Trumpy; retired TV newsman Nick Clooney; Hamilton native and former Dodgers, Pirates and Rockies manager Jim Tracy; Bengals Hall of Famer Anthony Munoz; and Furniture Fair spokesman Ed Hartman.

Once inside the gym doors, the line circled the entire basketball court. Several hundred Nuxhall photographs and other memorabilia were displayed on tables along the perimeter for people to look at until they reached the family. Donzetta, Kim and Phil personally greeted each of us next to Nuxhall's open casket. Joe's and Kim's breakfast pals—Dale Lierman, Dan Hare, Bob and Janet Evans—set up the display after breakfast at Bob Evans Restaurant up the road.

Flowers surrounded the casket. The scoreboard above it read, "Rounding third and heading for home. We love you, Joe."

Griffey Jr. praised Nuxhall as a first-class person. "He was down to earth. He was a guy you could talk to about anything, and I think that, you know, baseball was second, and how you were doing was first," Griffey told reporters. "If he could help you in any way, he would do it. I think, you know, that's what we're going to miss the most … He didn't give you a hard time about your performance. He wanted to help you, any way that he could."

Castellini called Nuxhall "one of our most beloved citizens," and instantly corrected himself. "There are no adjectives. He *IS* our most beloved citizen. I think we all feel that, and it's showing itself tonight."

Brennaman choked back tears when he spoke to reporters after lingering at the casket. "Coming through the door was tough. You know, this brings back a lot of memories, the times that we had, and the things that we did … and how much people related to him," he said.

Nuxhall was embarrassed in 1992 by the hundreds of get-well cards and notes from Reds fans after his prostate cancer surgery, which caused him to miss part of spring training. "He was legitimately blown away. He could not understand to the point that I said to him, 'You really don't get it.' He said, 'What are you talking about?' And I said, 'You simply don't understand the way people feel about you,'" Brennaman told me in 2015. "It never dawned on him that he evoked the kind of love that he did from people. I mean, nobody has ever said one negative thing about him, to my knowledge."

Brennaman had told me the same thing in 2007, but he added this comment: "When the day ever comes that I walk away from this business, the one overriding thing that I will be thankful for is the fact that I spent thirty-one years in the radio booth with him."

Surrounded by reporters not far from Nuxhall's casket, Brennaman said, "Truly, if he is looking down on us today, he's not going to believe what he's going to see for the rest of this day."

It was an amazing sight. School officials estimated that between 7,000 and 8,000 people attended the visitation. At 8 p.m., funeral home officials and police capped the line and turned newcomers away. People were still in line when I drove back to the high school at 10 p.m., to monitor the proceedings for the *Enquirer*. Kim and Phil were still standing by the casket, refusing to sit in tall boy chairs available to them. At 11:15 p.m., the Nuxhall family shook hands with the last people in line, the school janitorial staff working that night. After the family left, I helped the breakfast bunch pack up the pictures and carry them out to their minivans.

Many who drove to the high school on Ohio 4 passed tributes to Nuxhall on signs for businesses and schools.

"We Will Remember Our Favorite Left Hander" read the sign at Meyer's Garden Center. "Central Remembers Joe Nuxhall Our 'Hero of Character,'" was posted at Fairfield Central Elementary School, where Kim created the character education program. At Nuxy's favorite Bob Evans, the sign simply stated, "Joe We Miss You." Jungle Jim's International Market replaced its video board advertisements with more than a dozen Nuxhall photos. Periodically the pictures were interrupted with this message: "Jungle Jim's Customers: Sorry for the inconvenience. Joe was a great man. Please excuse us while we help remember him. —Jungle Jim."

Outside Great American Ball Park, a shrine appeared around the Old Lefthander's statue, which the club covered with a huge canopy and lighted at night. Reds fans expressed their gratitude and sympathy by leaving handmade signs; dozens of Reds hats and baseballs; bouquets;

a baseball glove; miniature bats; plastic Reds' concession cups and mini batting helmets; photographs; a golf club; Gapper doll; wreaths; rosaries; crucifixes; candles; and dozens of Budweiser bottles and cans.

Drawings include everything from Jim Borgman's *Enquirer* cartoon of Joe doffing his cap entering heavenly clouds to a redesign of the Reds' logo with "Joe" inside the wishbone C. One sign read, "Good Bye Joe. Say Hello To Marge."

Many scrawled messages on their hats and balls: "Our Extraordinary Ordinary Joe" … "R.I.P. Nuxie" … "NUX" … "Nuxhall A Reds Radio Icon" … and "Thanks for my love of baseball." My favorite was the baseball signed "Joe, Rounded 3rd & Headed To Heaven."

⚾   ⚾   ⚾

At my last Bob Evans breakfast with Nux, on March 23, 2007, we chatted about his health before talking about the Joe Hope Project. He had spent a week in a Sarasota hospital in February due to shortness of breath. Doctors discovered blood clots in both lungs and legs. They also found four cancerous tumors on his left leg, a return of the lymphoma which sent him to Fairfield Mercy Hospital the previous June.

"I've been feeling pretty good up until the last three days. I don't know what the hell is going on," he said. "I go to the doctor this morning for another (chemotherapy) treatment. That will be my eighth one. All my lumps, so to speak, are going down, so that's good news."

I had called Kim in February when I heard Joe was in a Florida hospital.

"Dad had trouble breathing walking from the clubhouse to the field," he told me, according to notes in my Nuxhall file. The last line in my handwriting noted Donzetta's wishes: "Mom didn't want much out."

Nuxhall's health always made headlines. Reds officials were so relieved he beat cancer in 1992 they gave him the honor of throwing the ceremonial first pitch on Opening Day. Nine years later, he suffered a heart attack at age 73 in a Sharonville restaurant on December 17, 2001. Cancer returned in fall of 2003, when he had a 3-hour surgery in October to remove a lump on the side of his face near his ear, followed by eight chemo treatments for non-Hodgkin's lymphoma. Nuxhall told *Cincinnati Enquirer* sportswriter John Erardi the prognosis made him "very confident. We apparently got the lymphoma in the early stage." Erardi noted Nuxy spoke at the Elder High School Sports Stag hours after getting chemo, which prompted Brennaman to tell Erardi: "Joe's amazing. I would have been home in bed."

My story announcing that "Lymphoma Returns For Nuxhall" ran atop the *Enquirer* sports page May 31, 2006. He had been admitted to Fairfield Mercy for double pneumonia and radiation for a tumor on his tonsil found by his dentist. Joe had ignored the tonsil for two weeks, putting up with his aches and pains while maintaining an active schedule heading into Memorial Day. He played golf four consecutive days and broadcast the Saturday Reds-Diamondbacks home game with Brennaman. On Memorial Day, he cut the lawn and grilled out for the family.

"He was winded when he came up the steps (at home). He didn't eat, and dad loves to eat. He just wasn't right—but he's got that old stubborn German in him," Kim told me at the time. So at breakfast on Tuesday, Kim insisted Dad see a doctor. He was hospitalized by 11 a.m.

"I felt something was wrong with him for two weeks," Brennaman told me back then. "I played golf with him and he had trouble catching his breath. But he simply wouldn't go to the doctor."

The recurrence of cancer in 2007 was deflating for Joe, a perpetual optimist. Kim told me in February, after talking to his dad in Florida, that "he was bummed. He felt he had it licked."

⚾　　⚾　　⚾

"It's not a good day."

I jotted that comment from Kim on a legal pad October 10, 2007, five weeks before Joe passed. At 79, Joe was back to chemotherapy treatments after doctors found three more spots on his side, near his ribs and lungs. One cancerous tumor was removed. At the *Enquirer*, we sensed the end was near. My job was to keep in touch regularly with Kim and Donzetta, and prepare biographical info and stories about Joe's Fairfield life.

For the Nuxhall family, it was a roller coaster ride. He led the Zinzinnati Oktoberfest chicken dance on Fountain Square in September. He surprised

Kim on his 53rd birthday with a new Ford F150 King Ranch pick-up truck. In the same conversation, Kim told me his dad had fluid on the lungs and a low white blood cell count. On October 22, Kim said his dad was playing golf and "doing fine." We talked about the statue of his father being made by Tom Tsuchiya for Fairfield's Waterworks Park.

Joe rapidly declined three weeks later. He went back to Fairfield Mercy Monday November 11 with pneumonia, a low white blood count and slow pulse rate. Donzetta said he was very weak and had lost his appetite. Again his hospital room filled with flowers and get-well cards. Some contained checks for the scholarship or character education programs.

"I can't believe it. It's kind of overwhelming. Everyone I talked to and see says, 'We're praying for him.' I know prayers work," Donzetta told me Thursday.

He died that night.

On Friday morning, the regular gang hurried to Bob Evans and talked about their dear friend. Joe "set the standard for all of us. He's probably the best person I've ever known," said Dane Hare, formerly of Fairfield Township. Dale Lierman, a Hamilton attorney, called him "the perfect example of what a human being should be." Fairfield remodeler Mark Lewis said Nuxhall was an inspiration because "he kept going and going. And the most he'd say was, 'I'm tired.'"

Donzetta admired her husband's courage. After Joe died, she found full pill bottles, including pain medication, in his bathroom. "He never, ever, said anything hurt. He just never talked about it. He seemed to be healthier than he was, I guess, because he never complained," she said.

After the visitation attended by thousands, private services were held at Zettler Funeral Home in Hamilton. On the way to his final resting place at Rose Hill Burial Park in Fairfield Township, Nuxhall's body took one last trip past special landmarks: the Fairfield Kroger store (where Joe shopped); Fairfield West Elementary School (where his sons attended); the Joe Nuxhall Golf Center on Joe Nuxhall Way in Joyce Park; Hamilton's East Side ball diamonds (where the Reds discovered him in 1943); Hamilton's Greenwood Cemetery (where his father was buried); and the old high school stadium on Fair Avenue (where Nuxhall played football).

A month after Nuxhall died, my son Joseph and I designed a special card for friends at Christmas, an Old Lefthander baseball card. On the front were photos of Nux with my sons Joe and David from 2004 and the baseball signed "Joe, Rounded 3rd & Headed To Heaven." The back featured stats from his 1944 debut and 16-year career. For his teams, we listed his radio teammates: Jim McIntyre, Claude Sullivan, Al Michaels, Marty Brennaman, Steve Stewart, Thom Brennaman and Jeff Brantley. And we included this vital information: THROWS: Left. BATS: Left. DRINKS: Bud. ROUNDS: Third. HEADS: Home.

⚾   ⚾   ⚾

A week before Opening Day 2008, I visited the Reds Hall of Fame and Museum to write about "The Ol' Lefthander" exhibit which had just opened. Nuxy was remembered with his old Reds jerseys, hats, plaques, photos, golf clubs, microphone, the Banana Phone and Elvis Presley bust from the Reds Radio booth, and the life-size JTM Meats cardboard poster of Marty as Santa and Joe as his huge elf. Fans could choose from 36 audio clips from his Reds play-by-play, color commentary, interviews or banter with Brennaman. A 10-minute film featured some of Marty and Joe's Kroger commercials, and the two singing *Take Me Out To The Ball Game*, which ended with Marty planting a big kiss on Nuxy's cheek.

Many stopped to read the June 10, 1944 newspaper story announcing that Nuxhall, 15, would be in uniform that day—and the adjacent box score from the young lefthander's ugly debut.

On Opening Day, Kim drove his dad's 1989 Lincoln Continental in the Findlay Market Parade with signs reading, "Win Nuxie's Car." (It was raffled off to benefit the Nuxhall Foundation on Hamilton Night, when 30,000 fans received a bronze replica of Nuxhall's Great American Ball Park statue). All of the Reds—manager Dusty Baker and coaches too—wore "Nuxhall 41" jerseys for the pregame introduction. All the jerseys were donated to the Joe Nuxhall Character Education Fund. Major League Baseball gave starter Aaron Harang permission to wear "No. 41 Nuxhall" the whole game. It's in the Reds Hall of Fame. All season the Reds wore a round "Nuxy" patch on their uniforms. A matching "Nuxy" magnet was included with the April magnetic schedule give-away.

Enquirer sportswriter John Erardi wrote on Opening Day: "Nuxhall, who since moving to the radio booth in 1967 (after a 16-year playing career), never had anybody say anything bad about him in life, now takes the streak into eternity." No question about it.

⚾   ⚾   ⚾

As long as Marty was calling Reds games, Joe's spirit was in the booth, too. Brennaman frequently would quote his longtime partner's favorite phrases, or tell Brantley a story from working with Nuxhall.

"I think about Joe all the time, particularly during the season," Brennaman told me in 2015 before going to Arizona. "Countless times during the course of the year something will occur to make me think of Joe, and all of the sudden it will stimulate a story in my mind that needs to be told again, and again, and again. It's a memory that will never die, thank God."

Brennaman told Reds Radio listeners the same thing four years later on what would have been Nuxhall's 89th birthday on July 30, 2017: "There's not a day goes by, particularly during the baseball season, that something happens that makes us think of the Old Lefthander."

Brennaman was especially reflective in 2019, as he was rounding 46 years and heading into retirement. Often the "Ask Marty" segment, when Brantley read questions submitted by fans, resulted in Brennaman reminiscing about Joe—like his reaction to Marty calling Hank Aaron's record-tying homer on his 1974 Reds debut ("What the hell are you going to do for an encore?"), or recalling how letters addressed simply to "Marty & Joe, Cincinnati, Ohio" were delivered to the ballpark. Working with new announcer Tommy Thrall in spring training, Brennaman described Phillip Ervin's two home runs off Brewers' pitchers this way: "Both of them—in the words of the late, great Joe Nuxhall—were no-doubters." In the opening game of a Memorial Day doubleheader against the Pirates, Marty reminded listeners: "As the Old Lefthander would say, 'You can't win two if you don't win the first.'"

Halfway through his last season, as Brennaman approached his 77th birthday, Marty told a Dayton radio station that Joe's deteriorating health their last years together was "the biggest single reason I decided to quit when I did. I announced it in January, but I knew three or four years ago. When Joe retired, he was physically incapable of doing a lot of things that he wanted to do, and that made a tremendous impact on me. I decided then that I'm going to retire when I have my health about me, when I can go places and do things and not have to worry about some physical infirmity."

Going into Brennaman's final series on September 24, Brantley asked Marty to tell some of his favorite Nuxhall stories during the game. Marty recounted Joe's road rage on Florida's Interstate 4, and nearly running over a security guard who wouldn't let him park near the visitors' clubhouse at the Blue Jays' spring park in Dunedin, Florida. "Joe was hotter than a match!" Brennaman said. After his final broadcast September 26, fans gathered around him on the field for a "Marty Party" celebrating his career. Brennaman first thanked the fans for their support; fellow broadcasters; his wife, children, grandchildren and other family members; and concluded by turning to face the Nuxhalls.

"Last but not least, Kim and (wife) Bonnie are here. And it would not be complete without you two. I hope you know that the thirty-one years that I spent with your dad, Kim, there was nothing more special," he said as his voice cracked. "And the thing I learned from him, and the way he welcomed me—he could have made it very difficult for me when I came here in 1974, but he welcomed me in—and it created inroads for me immediately that might have been tougher to travel, had he not embraced me the way he did. And the longer we were together, the closer we got. So close, as I've said a million times, that I could stop a sentence in the middle of it, and he could finish it … I hope you know how much I love the Nuxhall family, how much I love you Kim, and you Bonnie, and your brother Phil, and certainly your mom Donzetta. The family has been wonderful to me. Your old man was absolutely the living, breathing best."

⚾   ⚾   ⚾

Marty and Joe were together the last time – golfing, of course – a few days before Joe died. MARTY BRENNAMAN PHOTO

The photograph is framed in Brennaman's basement baseball room. He sees it every day. Joe and Marty have their arms around each other while playing golf at Kenwood Country Club. It was their last time together, in November 2007, days before Joe died.

They were golfing with two men who had won a contest to play 18 holes with the Reds broadcasters. It was a beautiful, sunny November afternoon, 57 degrees. Nuxhall was extremely weak but insisted on keeping the commitment. He couldn't play all 18. He rode in the cart, and hit a ball every two or three holes, while entertaining their guests with great baseball stories.

"After nine holes, he was worn out. I said, 'Let me take you back to your car.' And he said, 'No, I'll be OK.' At the 14th tee box, we were sitting in the cart and he said to me, 'We really had a good time together, didn't we?' And I said, 'Yes, we really did.' It was so out of character for him. And I'm convinced that he intuitively knew this would be the last time we'd see each other. Four days later, he died."

Brennaman first told me the story in 2015, when he showed me the picture at his home. "There was never a bigger fan of Joe Nuxhall than me. All I learned from him, all the laughter, all the tears," he said. In January 2019, when Brennaman announced his retirement at the end of the season, he recounted the story for the media. Marty's voice cracked as he stammered to say: "He was special. He was—He was—I mean—I was thrilled just to call him my friend."

Me too.

⚾ ⚾ ⚾

When you talk about your Cincinnati sports icons, Joe Nuxhall is at the top of my list, certainly, without a doubt. Nuxy was beloved for his 64 years with the Reds as a player, a broadcaster and an unselfish ambassador for the game who never refused an autograph. He was a generous, humble supporter for the developmentally disadvantaged; character education; tax levies to support schools and senior services; and scholarships to attend college, something he didn't do. To this day, Joe the gentle giant of giving continues to inspire and to make a huge impact 14 years after his death.

I miss Joe, in all honesty. Especially his folksy way of speaking, the Old Lefthander's lexicon, that's for dang sure. The fun part of this old lefthander's research has been listening to recordings of Marty and Joe, and being immersed in Nux-stalgia, I'd guess you'd call it. As Joe once told me: "It's been interesting, and it's been fun, when you look back at it." That's for dang sure.

Nuxy was the best. I've never met a finer person. No question about it, in all honesty, without a doubt.

Joe Nuxhall Major & Minor League Pitching Statistics

Source: baseball-reference.com, Cincinnati Reds Yearbooks

Year	Age	Team	League	W-L	ERA	G	GS	CG	SHO	SV	IP	H	R	ER	HR	BB	SO
1944	15	CIN	NL	0-0	67.50	1	0	0	0	0	0.2	2	5	5	0	5	0
1944	15	BIRM	SA	0-0	54.00	1	1	0	0	0	1.0	1	6	6	0	5	1
1945	16	SYRACUS	IL	0-2	7.94	7	4	0	0		17.0	21	19	15		21	12
1945	16	LIMA	OSL	10-5	2.57	16	16	2	2		126.0	88	53	36		90	35
1946			(Did not play professional baseball; voluntarily retired to regain amateur status)														
1947	18	MUNCIE	OSL	7-7	3.78	18		7	1		100.0	55	62	42		145	119
1948	19	TULSA	TX	0-0	2.25	6	1	0	0		12.0	10	6	3		12	9
1948	19	COLMBIA	SAL	2-9	4.81	23		2	0		86.0	79	72	46		101	52
1949	20	CHARLSTN	CL	8-10	3.24	28	14	14	0		186.0	148	91	69		151	139
1950	21	CHARLSTN	CL	10-9	4.83	25		11	1		138.0	136	100	74		98	100
1951	22	TULSA	TX	13-22	3.43	43	33	21	3		257.0	241	114	98		102	105
1952	23	CIN	NL	1-4	.200	37	5	2	0	1	92.1	83	33	33	4	42	52
1953	24	CIN	NL	9-11	.450	30	8	5	1	2	141.2	136	77	68	13	69	52
1954	25	CIN	NL	12-5	3.89	35	14	5	1	0	166.2	188	77	72	11	59	85
1955	26	CIN	NL	17-12	3.47	50	29	14	5	3	257.0	240	108	99	25	78	98
1956	27	CIN	NL	13-11	3.72	44	32	10	2	3	200.2	196	96	83	18	87	120
1957	28	CIN	NL	10-10	4.75	39	28	6	2	1	174.1	192	104	92	24	53	99
1958	29	CIN	NL	12-11	3.79	36	26	5	0	0	175.2	169	78	74	15	63	111
1959	30	CIN	NL	9-9	4.24	28	21	6	1	1	131.2	155	76	62	10	35	75
1960	31	CIN	NL	1-8	4.42	38	6	0	0	0	112.0	130	58	55	8	27	72
1961	32	KCA	AL	5-8	5.34	37	13	1	0	1	128.0	135	81	76	12	65	81
1962	33	TOTAL		5-0	3.03	17	9	1	0	1	71.1	66	26	24	4	30	59
1962	33	LAA	AL	0-0	10.13	5	0	0	0	0	5.1	7	6	6	0	5	2
1962	33	CIN	NL	5-0	2.45	12	9	1	0	1	66.0	59	20	18	4	25	57
1963	34	CIN	NL	15-8	2.61	35	29	14	2	2	217.1	194	73	63	14	39	169
1964	35	CIN	NL	9-8	4.07	32	22	7	4	2	154.2	146	73	70	19	51	111
1965	36	CIN	NL	11-4	3.45	32	16	5	1	2	148.2	142	57	57	18	31	117
1966	37	CIN	NL	6-8	4.50	35	16	2	1	0	130.0	136	71	65	14	42	71
16 Yrs				135-117	3.90	526	274	83	20	19	2302.2	2310	1093	998	209	776	1372
		CIN	(15 yrs)	130-109	3.80	484	261	82	20	18	2169.1	2168	1006	916	197	706	1289
		KCA	(1 yr)	5-8	5.34	37	13	1	0	1	128.0	135	81	76	12	65	81
		LAA	(1 yr)	0-0	10.13	5	0	0	0	0	5.1	7	6	6	0	5	2

Joe Nuxhall Major League Batting Statistics

Source: baseball-reference.com

Year	Age	Tm	Lg	G	AB	R	H	2B	3B	HR	RBI	SB	CS	BB	SO	BA	OPS
1952	23	CIN	NL	37	23	0	2	0	0	0	0	0	0	0	8	.087	.174
1953	24	CIN	NL	30	49	6	16	2	0	3	8	0	0	4	13	.327	.928
1954	25	CIN	NL	36	52	13	9	0	0	3	7	0	0	8	12	.173	.620
1955	26	CIN	NL	53	86	10	17	4	1	3	14	0	0	8	24	.198	.617
1956	27	CIN	NL	44	59	6	11	2	1	2	7	0	0	4	15	.186	.590
1957	28	CIN	NL	42	59	6	14	1	0	0	7	0	0	5	15	.237	.580
1958	29	CIN	NL	36	62	4	13	1	0	0	5	1	2	1	13	.210	.445
1959	30	CIN	NL	28	44	5	11	3	0	0	2	0	0	1	4	.250	.601
1960	31	CIN	NL	39	26	3	2	1	0	0	1	0	0	1	6	.077	.223
1961	32	KCA	AL	56	65	5	19	2	1	2	13	0	0	6	18	.292	.798
1962	33	TOTAL		17	26	3	7	1	0	1	5	0	0	0	3	.269	.719
1962	33	LAA	AL	5	0	0	0	0	0	0	0	0	0	0	0	0	
1962	33	CIN	NL	12	26	3	7	1	0	1	5	0	0	0	3	.269	.719
1963	34	CIN	NL	35	76	6	12	2	0	0	3	0	0	0	25	.158	.353
1964	35	CIN	NL	34	54	2	7	0	0	1	1	1	0	0	20	.130	.315
1965	36	CIN	NL	32	45	5	8	1	0	0	3	0	0	2	9	.178	.413
1966	37	CIN	NL	35	40	2	4	1	0	0	2	0	0	0	14	.100	.225
16 Yrs				555	766	76	152	21	3	15	78	2	2	40	199	.198	.532
		CIN	(15 yrs)	494	701	71	133	19	2	13	65	2	2	34	181	.190	.507
		KCA	(1 yr)	56	65	5	19	2	1	2	13	0	0	6	18	.292	.798
		LAA	(1 yr)	5	0	0	0	0	0	0	0	0	0	0	0	0	

Sources and Credits

Books

Anderson, Sparky and Burick, Si. *The Main Spark: Sparky Anderson and the Cincinnati Reds,* Doubleday, 1978.

Bass, Mike. *Marge Schott Unleashed,* Sagamore Publishing, 1993.

Brosnan, Jim. *The Long Season,* Harper & Brothers, 1960.

Brosnan, Jim. *Pennant Race,* Harper & Brothers, 1962.

Nuxhall, Joe and Hoard, Greg. *Joe: Rounding Third and Heading For Home,* Orange Frazer Press, 2004.

Rose, Pete and Hertzel, Bob. *Charlie Hustle,* Prentice-Hall, 1975.

Smith, Curt. *Voices Of The Game,* Diamond Communications, 1987.

Sullivan, Alan and Cox, Jim. *Voice Of The Wildcats,* University of Kentucky Press, 2014.

Michaels, Al and Wertheim, L. Jon. *Al Michaels: You Can't Make This Stuff Up: Miracles, Memories and the Perfect Marriage of Sports and Television,* HarperCollins, 2014.

Cincinnati Enquirer

1956 "Nuxhall Pops Cork!" May 28, 1956.

1986 "The Old Lefthander," Enquirer magazine, July 13, 1986.

1986 "Letterman Spares Schott Famed Barbs," May 13, 1986.

1987 "This One Belongs To UK," July 28, 1987.

1987 "Marty and Joe Won't Be On TV Any More," Oct. 18, 1987.

1988 "He's A Rotten Umpire," May 4, 1988.

1988 "Sports Legeend Red Barber Recalls Days In Cincinnati," Feb. 18, 1988.

1988 "Tales From The Catbird Seat," Feb. 28, 1988.

1989 "Reds On Radio 60 Years," April 3, 1989.

1991 "Pro-Marriage Marge Scolds Longtime Live-Ins," March 18, 1991.

1991 "For 'Pete Rose Story,' Happy Ending Means Hall Of Fame," July 3, 1991.

1991 "Up To Bat: 'Charlie Hustle' Meets 'The Babe' In NBC's Movie," Oct. 6, 1991.

1992 "Barber Gets Place In Broadcasting Hall," June 5, 1992.

1992 "The Marty & Joe Show," August 23, 1992.

1992 "WLW Workers Watch Their Words: Station's Reds Contract Prohibits Criticism Of Schott," Dec. 12, 1992.

1993 "Brennaman Marks 20 Years In Booth," March 10, 1993.

1996 "The Real Mr. Red," May 16, 1996.

1999 "USA Cable Plans Unauthorized Schott Bio," Dec. 3, 1999.

1999 "Who Gets The Lead In Marge, The Movie?" Dec. 8, 1999.

2000 "Readers Call The Schotts," Jan.3, 2000.

2000 "USA Cable Might Bench Schott Bio," April 3, 2000.

2002 "Letterman An Old Lefthander Fan," April 6, 2002.

2006 "Lymphoma Returns For Nuxhall," June 1, 2006.

2007 "It's For The Kids," April 4, 2007.

2008 "Nuxhall Exhibit Debuts," Sunday, March 23, 2008.

2012: "NBC Icon Began With Reds: Michaels Returns For Bengals On SNF," Oct. 21, 2012.

2013: "MTV Has Snooki. E! Has Kardashians. Now TLC Has Pete Rose," Jan. 13, 2013.

2013 "Pete Rose Show Ended Last Sunday?," Feb. 20, 2013.

2013: "50: Five Decades Ago, Pete Rose Began His Quest For History," March 31, 2013.

2013 "Marty and Joe Almost Got Banned," April 30, 2013.

2014 "True Story Of The Banana Phone," May 4, 2014.

2014: "Top 10 Reasons You'll Love Al Michaels' New Book," Nov.15, 2014.

Other Articles

Associated Press

Cincinnati Post

Cincinnati Reds yearbooks, 1952-1966

Dayton Daily News

Dayton Journal Herald

Hamilton Journal-News

Houston Chronicle

Muncie Star Press

Tampa Tribune

Sports Illustrated

"Special Baseball Issue," April 9, 1956.

"Redleg Musclemen–Klu, Post, Bell," July 15, 1956.

"High, Fast and Forever," June 11, 1979.

Broadcasts & Audio

Baseball Voices: *Marty Brennaman: Voice Of The Reds* CD by Pat Hughes, 2006.

Cincinnati Reds Radio: 1967-2019.

Cincinnati Reds highlights:

The Big Red Machine, 1970.

The New Red Machine, 1972.

… And This One Belongs To The Reds, 1975.

Reds Greatest Hits 1976, 1976.

Best Of The Reds On Radio, audio cassette, Sept. 3, 1993.

A Tribute To Reds Broadcasters, Reds giveaway CD, June 10, 2007.

CBS Television:

> *What's My Line?* June 24, 1956.
>
> *Good Sports*, guest star Marge Schott, March 19, 1991; guest star Pete Rose, May 27, 1991.
>
> *Late Show with David Letterman*, April 6, 2002.

Fox Sports Ohio: David Letterman interview during Cardinals at Reds, Aug. 6, 2017.

Kroger Co.: Marty and Joe commercials, 1984 through 1990s.

Mutual Broadcasting System: 1955 All-Star Game, July 12, 1955.

WCET-TV: *Joe Nuxhall: My Life: Baseball and Beyond*, 2005.

WLW-AM:

> "Riot In the Hyatt" Pete Rose roast broadcast, Sept. 2, 1993.
>
> *Sports Talk*, Lance McAlister with Rollie Fingers, June 18, 2006.

Websites

Baseball-Reference.com

Newspapers.com

Acknowledgments

I couldn't have published this book without the help of many friends: Marty Brennaman; Brian Friedman; Mike Precker; Peter Bronson, Tim VonderBrink; Jim Borgman; Jim Cheng; Chris Eckes; Dick Benson; John Erardi; Greg Gajus; Sam Gingrich; Joe Kay; Hal McCoy; Jeff Suess; Dave "Yiddy" Armbruster; Bill "Seg" Dennison; Jeff Brantley; Chris Welsh; Randy McNutt; Deb Price; Greg Rhodes; Ken Stiens; John Teufel; Fred Valerius; Donzetta, Kim and Phil Nuxhall; and my family, Sue, Joseph, David and Jay Kiesewetter.

Photo Credits

Cincinnati Enquirer: 51, 65, 115, 155, 169, 209, back cover.

Rhodes/Klumpe Reds Hall of Fame Collection: 18, 27, 45, 139, 229.

Cincinnati Reds: 75.

John Kiesewetter archives: 1, 85, 107, 148, 207, 257, 265, 291.

Kim Nuxhall: 9, 199.

Marty Brennaman: 280.

Kroger Co.: 187.

Joseph Kiesewetter: 271.

Marty Pieratt: 239

Bill Renken: 162.

About the Author

Author John Kiesewetter with his favorite item in the Reds Hall of Fame and Museum: Joe's Wiedemann Beer poster. JOHN KIESEWETTER PHOTO

John Kiesewetter has covered broadcasting for 35 years for the *Cincinnati Enquirer* (1985-2014) and Cincinnati Public Radio's WVXU-FM (since 2015). He started his career as a summer intern at the *Middletown Journal* while attending Ohio University, and then worked 40 years at the *Enquirer* as a reporter, suburban news editor and features editor and TV columnist. He lives in Fairfield with his wife, Sue, a freelance reporter for the *Enquirer*. They have three adult sons.